IMAGES
of America

WEATHERFORD
TEXAS

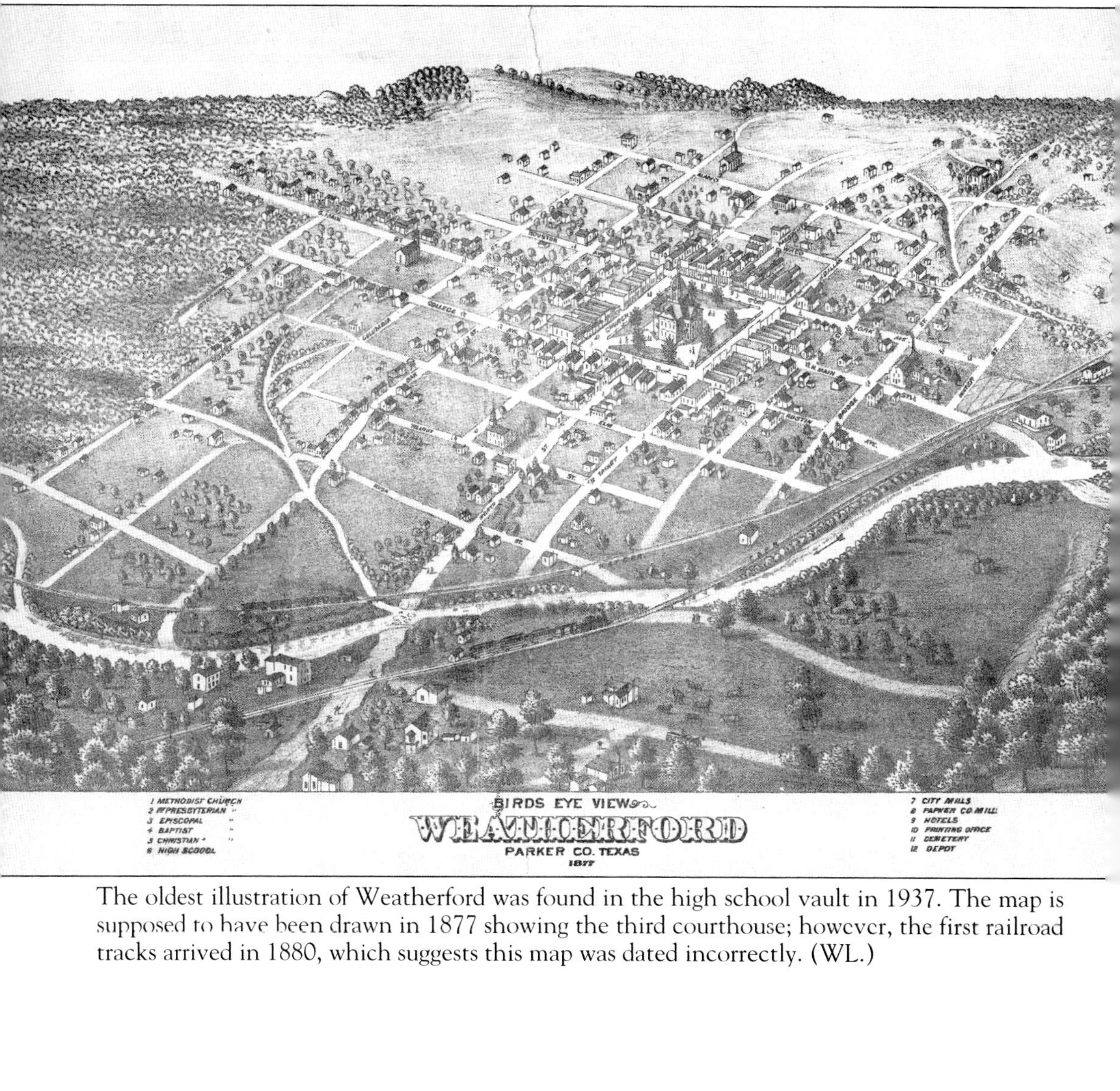

The oldest illustration of Weatherford was found in the high school vault in 1937. The map is supposed to have been drawn in 1877 showing the third courthouse; however, the first railroad tracks arrived in 1880, which suggests this map was dated incorrectly. (WL.)

IMAGES
of America

WEATHERFORD
TEXAS

Barbara Y. Newberry and David W. Aiken

ARCADIA
PUBLISHING

ISBN 978-0-7385-0110-9

Published by Arcadia Publishing
Charleston, South Carolina

Printed in the United States of America

Library of Congress Catalog Card Number: 99-63071

For all general information contact Arcadia Publishing at:
Telephone 843-853-2070
Fax 843-853-0044
E-Mail sales@arcadiapublishing.com
For customer service and orders:
Toll-Free 1-888-313-2665

Visit us on the Internet at www.arcadiapublishing.com

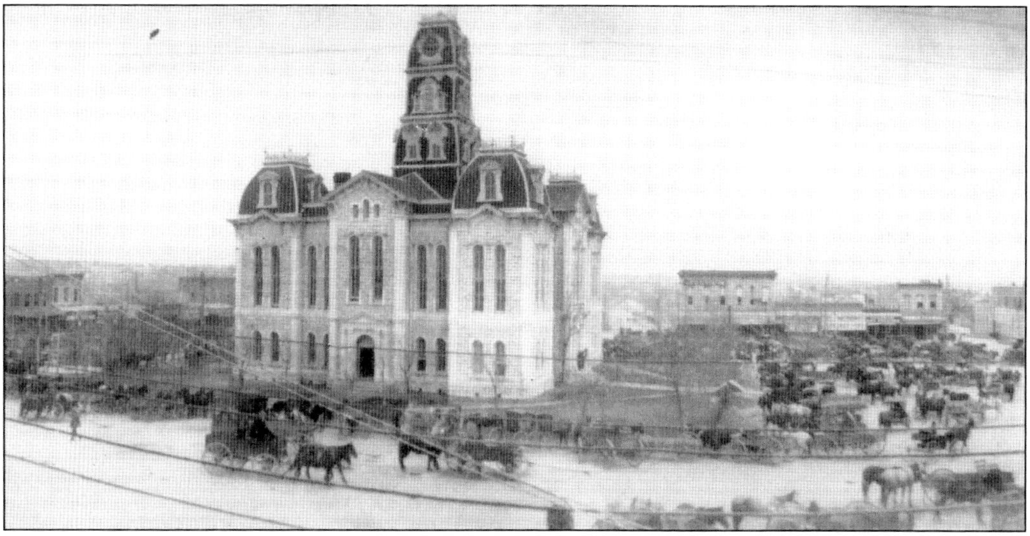

The current courthouse, built in 1885, and the busy square, are shown in this early photograph. Note the "stile" used to cross the fence to the courthouse. On the far left is a bandstand used by the municipal band or by elected officials speaking to the people. Easily mistaken for a stagecoach, a wagon loaded with a large *armoire* wardrobe is visible in the foreground. (Phoenix Masonic Lodge 275 via Dexter Sammons.)

Contents

Acknowledgments		6
Introduction		7
1.	Indians and Pioneers	9
2.	The Square and Businesses	15
3.	City Services	31
4.	Homes and Gardens	45
5.	Dress Up	59
6.	Worship	67
7.	Education and Child Care	75
8.	Transportation	85
9.	Agriculture and Ranching	97
10.	Fun and Entertainment	109
11.	Duty, Honor, Country	119

Acknowledgments

There is no single source archive from which the multifaceted Weatherford history could be highlighted for this brief volume. To locate the photographs took the skills of a detective and genealogist to locate relatives who might now have photographs published years ago. The historical search added the spectrum of a good listener, reader, and researcher.

Weatherford's master of genealogy and history, Evlyn Broumley, was the great guide to sources. Others that searched for sources, memories, or peered at faces in photographs to grasp for names were the following: Jeff Barnett, Jean Baker, Jean Bennett, Kelli Bray, Charles and Martha Cope, David Cowley, Janet Davee, Helen Davidson, Martha Dodson, David Dommert, Donnelle Doss, John Doss, Helen Eldridge, Ken and Pat Galbreaith, Ladonna Gibson, Royce Gilbert, Lawson Gratts, John L. Heartsill, John and Shirley Hall, Carolyn Hamilton, Rector L. Owen Henderson, Mark Littleton, Tommy and Evelyn Loudres, Betty Martin, Kay Carr, Pat Holt, Debbie James, Wynelle James, Winona Jones, Ben Long, Wanda Lovelace, Beth Llewellyn, Mary Kemp, John Kirkpatrick, Kay Martino, Brenda McClurkin, Debbie Means, Tom Park, Bennett Piester, Mary Francis Ratts, Eva Earl Rutledge, Bonnie Sammons, Randy C. Sanders, Virginia Scott, Catherine Smith, Charles Simmons, Dover Simmons, Tom Saunders, Sue Trimble, and Elaine Vandagriff.

We truly appreciate the use of the following photograph archives: Couts Methodist Church archive via Reverend Larry Zellers; Dwight D. Eisenhower Presidential Library; *Fort Worth Star-Telegram*; Grace-First Presbyterian Church archive via Phyllis Vaughn, administrative assistant; Parker County Sheriff's Office via Sheriff Jay Brown; Parker County Sheriff Posse via Wayne Bryant; Phoenix Masonic Lodge 275 via Dexter Sammons; Pythian home, Peggy Hutton, administrator; Smithsonian Institution, Bureau of American Ethnology; Weatherford Chamber of Commerce via Sue Rogers, Tourism Director; Weatherford College Library via Martha Tandy, librarian (credited as WC); *Weatherford Democrat* via American Legion Post 163; Weatherford Fire Department via Fire Captain Craig Swancy; Weatherford Heritage Gallery via Jena Mae Thedford, curator; Weatherford Public Library via Sandra Tanner, librarian (credited as WL); and Michael's Studio.

We owe a debt of gratitude to the following family photograph archivists of Weatherford's history: Glenn Anderson, Bill Bennett, Ed Brown, Pat Bass, Melody Bradford, Randy Carter, Grace Cartwright, Helen Dill, James H. Doss, Sylvia Eidson, Bill Fant, Charles Frost, the late Melvin George, Donald George, Mary Ellen Guay, Jess Hall Jr., Gary and Linda Hagman, Lynn Harris, Ted Hartness, Robert P. and Alice Henry, Carla Hollingsworth, Don Huddleston, Vernell Hutcheson, Lafrieta Hutton, Phil Jordan, Beth Lewellyn, V.A. Littleton, Kirk Martin, James Mathison, Maurine McCoy, Martha McClung, Louise McFarland, Cleo McQueen, Charles Milliken, Richard Pina, late Eugene Polser, Bernice Roberts, Eloise Smyth, Marie Grigsby Schaub, Zan Statham, Jon Vandagriff, and Bill Witherspoon.

We invite interested readers to donate photographs, film, videos, documents, memorabilia, and funds to the Weatherford Heritage Gallery for their museum project.

We appreciate the fantastic effort of Hartness Printing Company. Lori Bennett, manager and specialist on laser scans, and her assistant, Linda Holder, have truly benefited this project. Our best accolades are too small for the quality of the Hartness team.

To our acquisitions editor, Allison Carpenter, daughter of Jim and Molly Carpenter, who once owned Mary Martin's birth home, for her love and knowledge of the city's history, and for giving us the opportunity to bring this project to you.

We dedicate this book in memory of Melvin George, Eugene Polser, and Doss Yardley, who never saw the finished work.

—Barbara Y. Newberry and David W. Aiken
June 1999

INTRODUCTION

In 1854, 15 pioneer families, led by Methodist Reverend Pleasant Tackett, moved into the area they called Goshen, which became part of Parker County. An abandoned cabin, built about 1852–3, found about 6 miles south of Weatherford on the J.H. Voorhies farm, suggests that an earlier attempt to colonize the area was not met with success.

In 1855, State Representative Isaac Parker of Birdville and State Senator Jefferson Weatherford of Dallas pushed a bill through the state capitol to establish the county. In 1856, Major Robert S. Neighbors, commander of Fort Belknap, moved many American Indian tribes to the Brazos River Reservation, west of the present city of Graham; thus more land opened for settlement. Conflict with remaining Kiowa and Comanche tribes began. Chief Justice James T. Morehead from Fort Worth held court with 40 men under a post-oak tree near the road to Fort Belknap to elect county officials and locate the county seat, named Weatherford, about 5 miles south of the oak tree.

Captain John R. Baylor, from Fort Belknap, was appointed agent of the Brazos River Reservation, but was quickly discharged from duty by Major Neighbors. This brought a feud between the two. Baylor moved to a ranch near Weatherford and began to incite the city's settlers to defend themselves against imminent attacks from the reservation. Indian attacks happened, but not from the reservation.

Baylor's revenge on Neighbors finally took shape in May 1859, when Baylor raised an "army" of 500 Weatherford-area settlers to march against the reservation. A silk flag marked with "Necessity Knows No Law" was presented to Baylor by "patriotic women of Weatherford."

The reservation Indians, under Anadarko Chief Jose Maria, were joined by Major Neighbors's federal troops in defense. The "army" arrived at the reservation and Baylor retreated, but the grudge continued. Neighbors moved the reservation to Oklahoma in August, but was assassinated by a person thought to be a friend of Baylor.

The real threat from Kiowa and Comanche kept paranoia at its peak. The Reverend Tackett, now pastor of the First Methodist Church in Weatherford, once had someone burst in the church to yell, "Indians are on the square." Tackett grabbed his pistol and rifle, which were always at the pulpit, and assisted in the defense.

By 1860, buffalo hunters had the slaughter to a system. Only the prime cuts of buffalo humps and tongues were saved. One Parker County citizen wrote of 1,000 buffalo tongues in her smokehouse. The remaining Kiowa and Comanche saw their food supply disappear.

The Parker County Agricultural and Mechanical Association sponsored the first county fair in 1860 on "five acres enclosed by a plank fence ten feet high." Among the items sold were "melons," perhaps the first mention of the watermelon for which Weatherford became famous.

John Baylor began the *White Man*, the city's first newspaper. Its anti-Indian stance continued his extremist views. His secessionist editorials demanded a special session of the Texas legislature, and in February 1861, Texas became part of the Confederacy. Baylor was elected a lieutenant colonel in the Second Cavalry. He was then made Confederate military governor of Arizona in 1862, and exterminated Apaches who were surrendering. He was thus removed from rank and command, but Parker County citizens voted him as representative to the Confederate Congress of 1863 in Richmond, Virginia.

Nine companies of men went to war from Parker County. The Parker County's Company E of the 19th Texas Calvary was undefeated. With a majority of Weatherford's men gone, this left the home territory ripe for Indian raids. The Confederate State of Texas authorized the formation of frontier regiments in December 1861. Weatherford was headquarters for Company D, of the First Frontier District commanded by Major William Quayle. Over 70 men served in Company D to protect Weatherford's citizens from the Kiowa and Comanche. In May 1864, many in the company were ordered to fill gaps in the regular Confederate armies. The war's end added to the settlers' defense with battle-experienced men, yet Parker County has more graves marked, "killed by Indians" than any other county.

In 1866, cattlemen Charles Goodnight and Oliver Loving rode west to New Mexico, Colorado, and Wyoming to deliver herds. Loving died of wounds the next year from an Indian attack. Goodnight made good the promise to have him buried in Weatherford. When one of his cowboys, Bose Ikard, passed away, Goodnight wrote the respected epitaph that speaks of the harsh life of that time, " . . . served with me four years on the Goodnight-Loving Trail, never shirked a duty or disobeyed an order, rode with me in many stampedes, participated in three engagements with Comanches, splendid behavior."

For the first time in America, in July 1871, two Kiowa chiefs were brought to trial for the Henry Warren mule-train massacre out of Weatherford. One of Warren's freighters was roasted alive. The prosecutor, new district attorney Samuel W.T. Lanham, and defense attorneys were all from Weatherford. The hanging sentence for Council Chief Santana and War Chief Big Tree was commuted to life imprisonment. Indian attacks near Weatherford ended in 1874.

Comanche Chief Quanah Parker surrendered in 1875, and in July 1877, the Texas Governor Hubbard proclaimed, "Parker County is no longer a frontier county, and is not now liable to incursions of hostile Indians," and then banned the wearing of guns.

More than 100 wagons a day were passing through Weatherford with buffalo hides. In December 1877, the *Weatherford Times* editorial pushed for a state law to control the buffalo slaughter. In 1877, the colorful history prompted Mr. H. Smythe to write *The Historical Sketch of Parker County* and *Weatherford, Texas*.

Interrupted by one man's feud, Indian attacks, and the Civil War, Weatherford was now ready to grow and the railroads were coming.

One

Indians and Pioneers

"Indian raids every full moon! Life in a tent for seven or eight months! Home building without the conveniences of lumber companies, architects or carpenters!" pioneer Sam Milliken remarked, "Parker County served as a buffer between savages and advancing civilization."

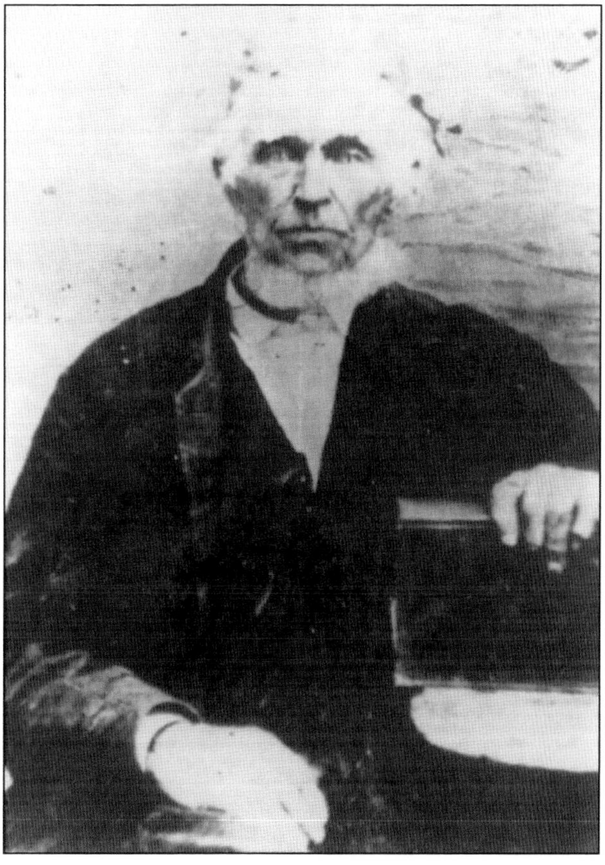

In 1855, State Representative Isaac Parker, seen here, of neighboring Tarrant County, cosponsored the bill to establish the county later named for him. In 1836, Isaac Parker's brother was killed by Comanches, and his niece, Cynthia Ann Parker, was captured and became wife of Comanche Chief Peta Nocona and whose son became Chief Quanah Parker, the last Comanche chief. (WL.)

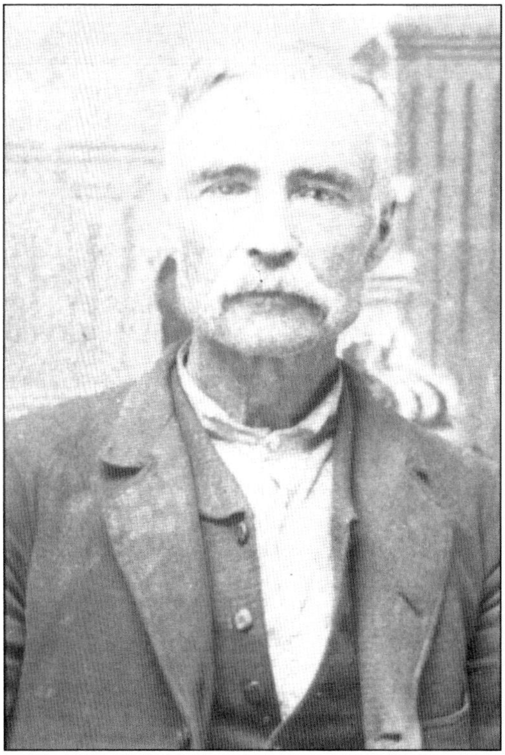

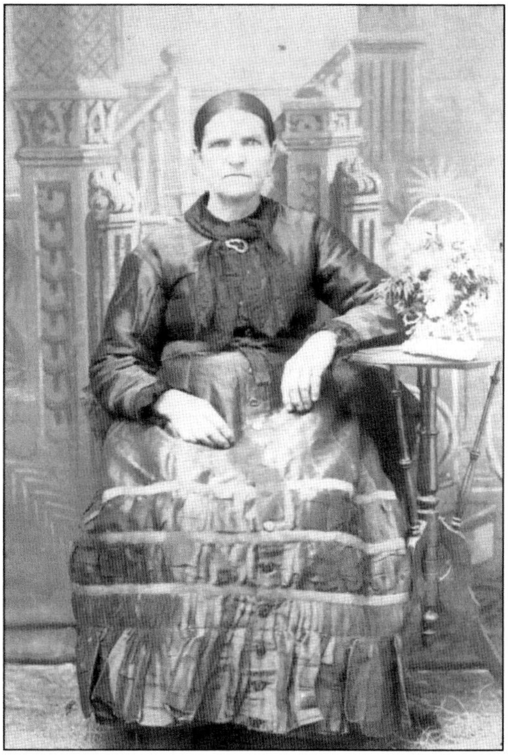

Pioneers Thomas Jefferson Sullivan and his wife, Margaret, are pictured here in 1885. They moved to the Weatherford area in 1855. They fought off an attack by Indians at their home in 1866. (WL.)

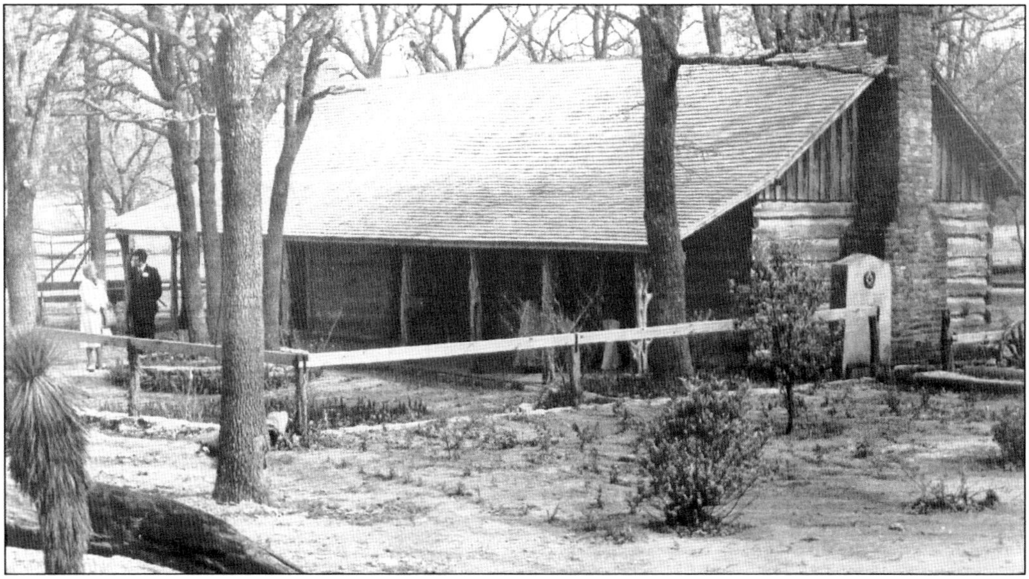

G.A. Holland, mayor from 1930 to 1938, saved two area log cabins and put them together at his lake property to show what was typical of the early paired cabins in the county. The City acquired the property in 1935. Grace Cartwright, at left, guided various volunteer groups to beautify the property in 1971. (Grace Cartwright.)

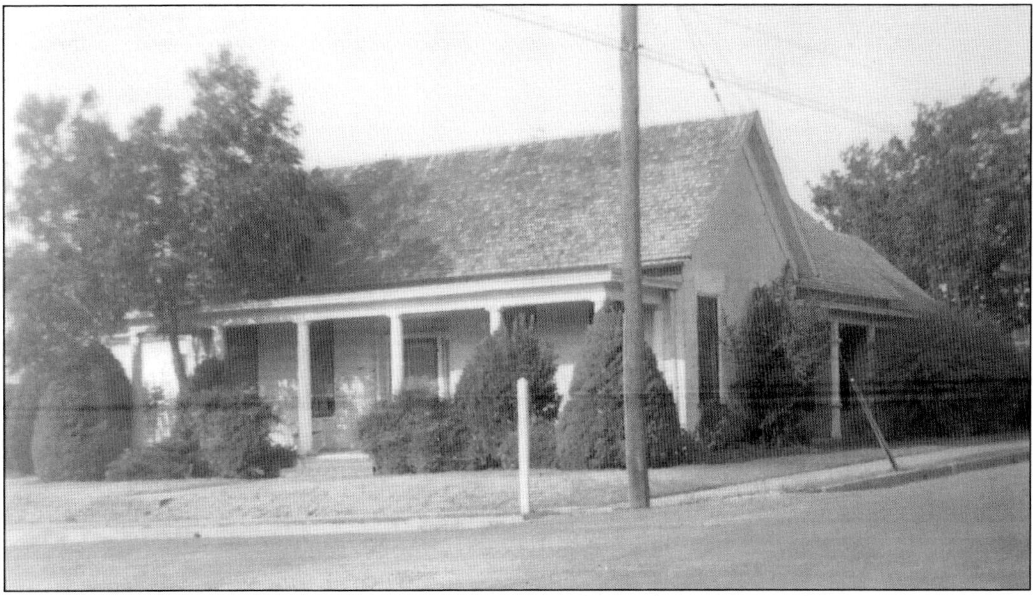

In 1871, the cellar of the Joseph Woolfolk home, located at 202 South Waco, served as a temporary jail for Kiowa Chiefs Santana and Big Tree when brought to trial for a massacre near Weatherford. Mr Woolfolk was a defense lawyer in this "Trial of the Century." (WL.)

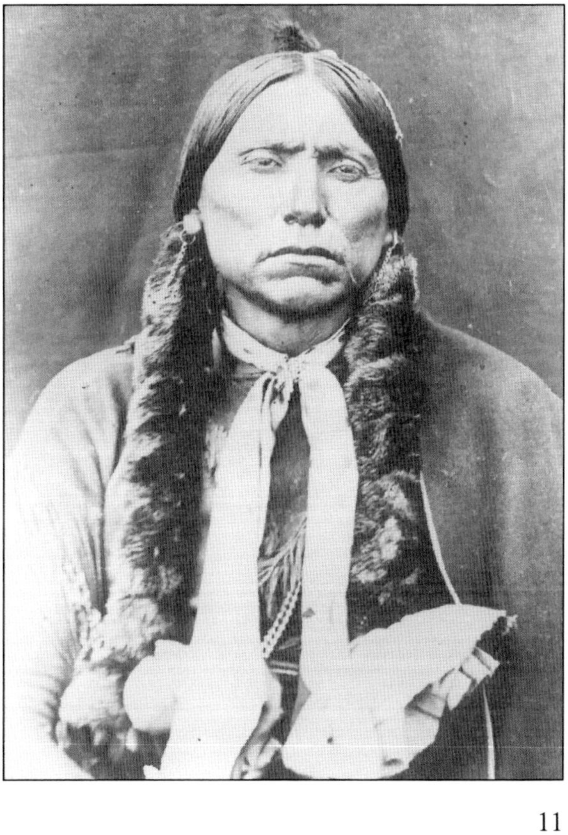

Quanah Parker, Comanche chief, fought the buffalo-hide hunters' continued slaughter of the Indian way of life in 1874, but surrendered the next year. (Smithsonian Institution, Bureau of American Ethnology.)

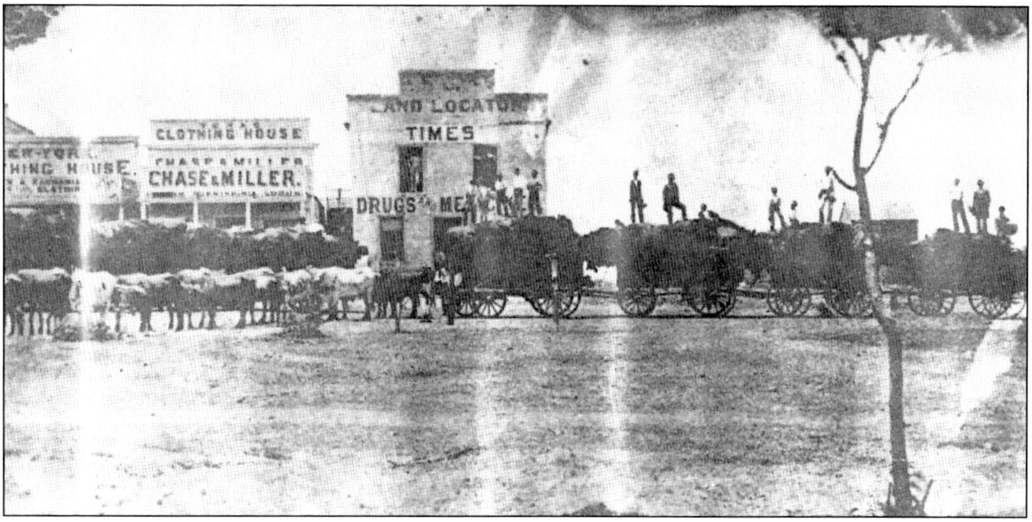

The earliest photograph of Weatherford known was found at the city dump in 1926. A string of buffalo-hunter wagons filled with hides came from Buffalo Gap, near Abilene. The late Oscar Barthold said this photograph was taken in 1868. On the west side of the square, located at about 100 Houston Avenue, the Gant and Atkins Drugs shared their building with the *Times* newspaper in 1877. (*Fort Worth Star-Telegram*, March 18, 1945.)

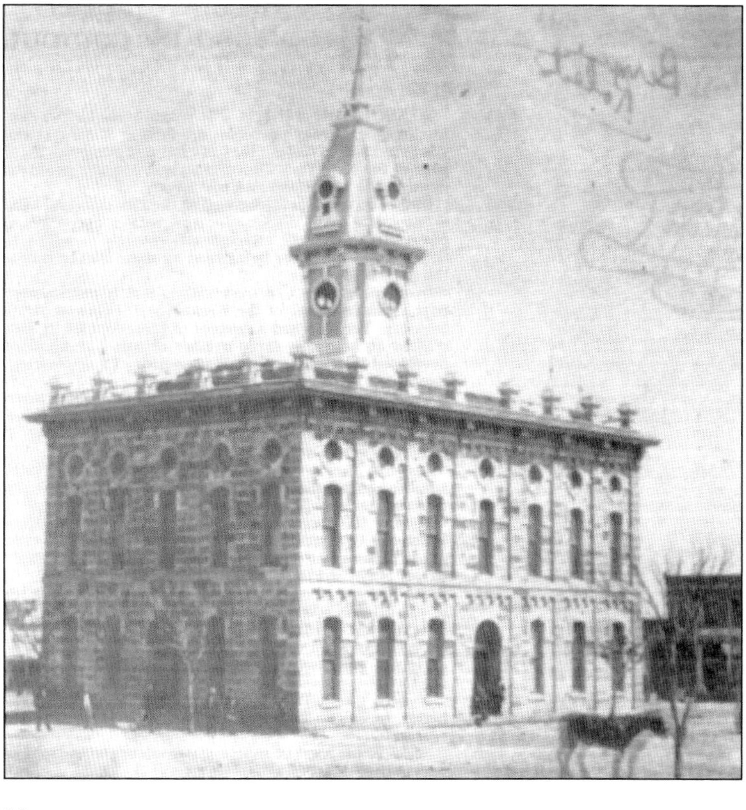

This is the only known photograph of the third Parker County courthouse. It was completed in 1880 from cut stone, but torched by a tax dodger on March 1, 1884. (Carlos Hartnett via Bernice Roberts.)

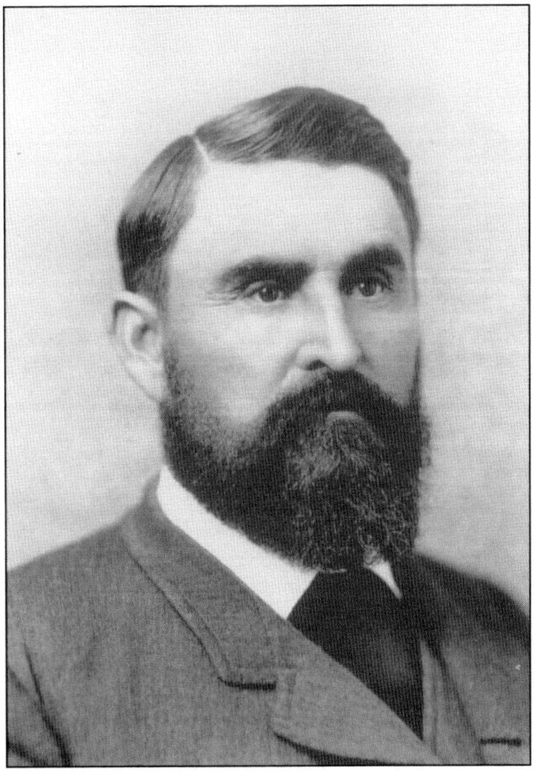

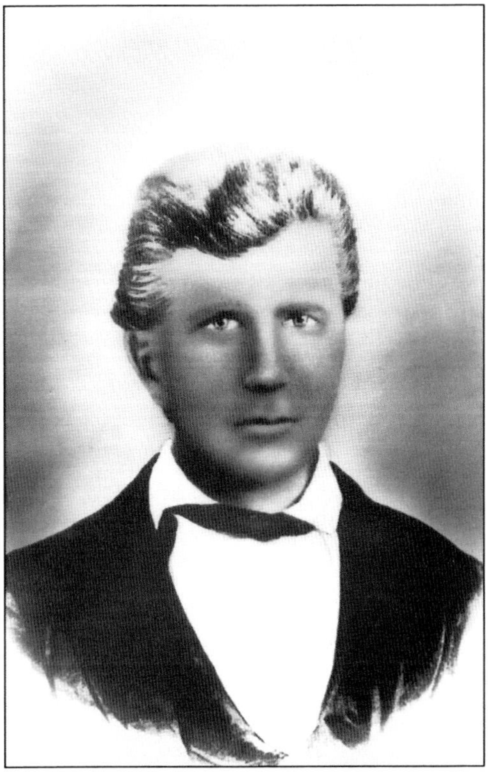

Cattlemen Charles Goodnight (top left), former Texas Ranger, and Oliver Loving (top right), pioneer and former lawman, developed a cattle trail out west in 1866. (Goodnight portrait courtesy of the Weatherford Heritage Gallery; Loving portrait courtesy of Phoenix Masonic Lodge 275 via Dexter Sammons.) A former slave, Bose Ikard (right) was a highly respected cowboy for them. He is buried in Weatherford near Loving. *Lonesome Dove* is a fictionalized history of the three men. (Cleo McQueen via Heritage Gallery.)

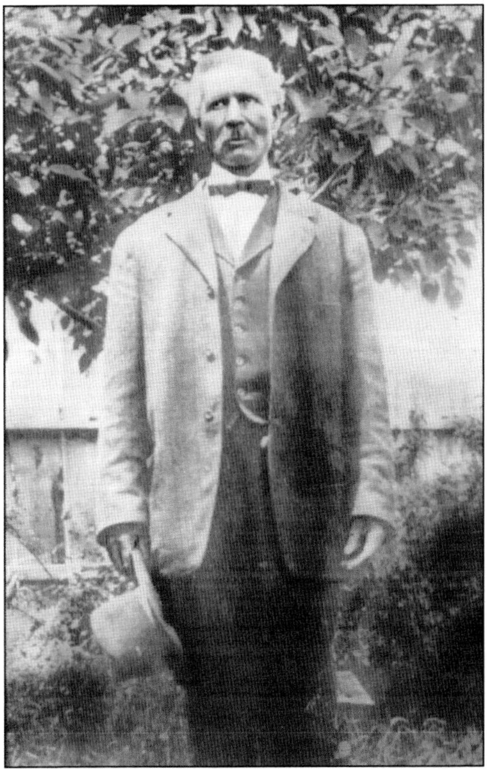

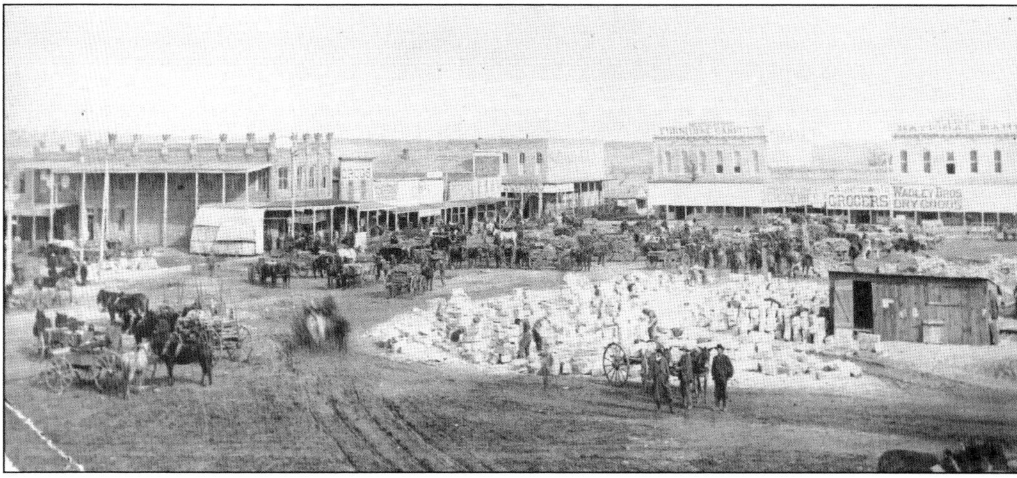

The construction of the current courthouse began in June 1884 from limestone quarried here. The cost of construction was $55,555.55. (James H. Doss.)

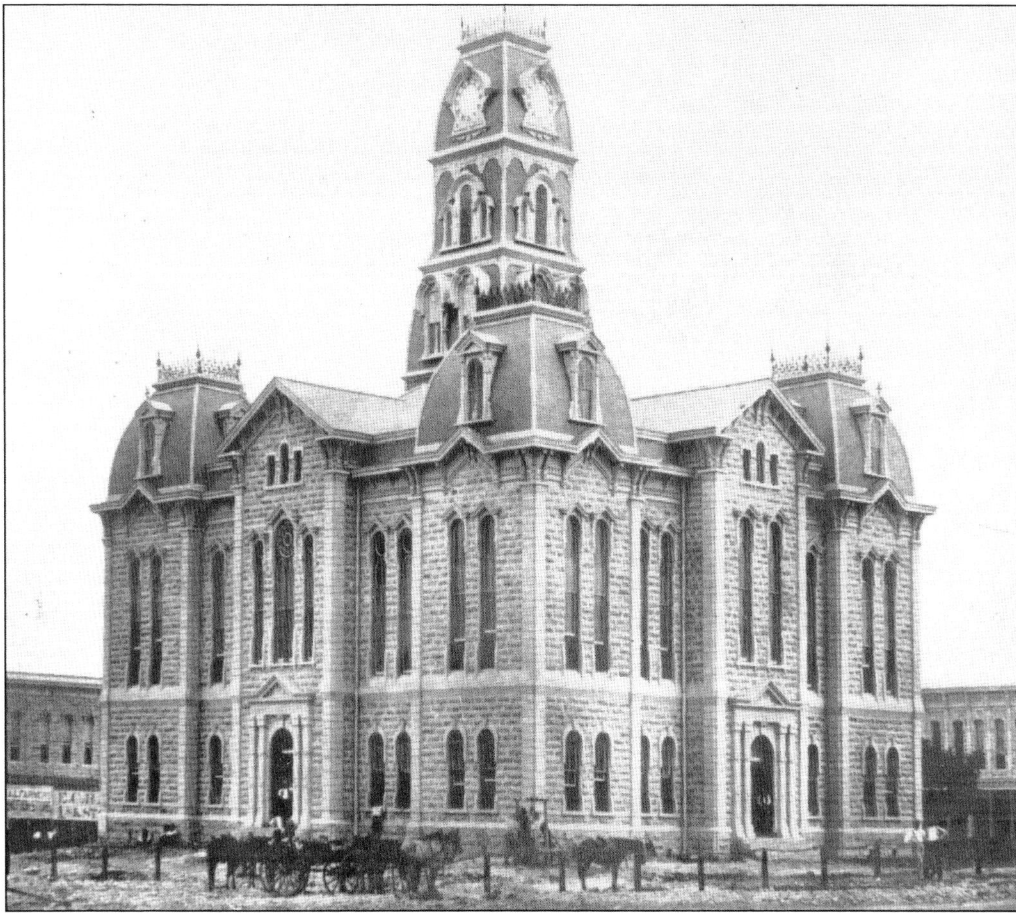

Near completion in June 1886, the courthouse still must receive its first clock, whose face was then painted black with white hands. This French Second Empire style was designed by Wesley C. Dodson of Waco, Texas. (Zan Statham.)

Two

The Square and Businesses

Settlers nestled around the community gathering spot, the square, surrounded by small hills on most sides. For 100 years, Weatherford's businesses were centered on the square. Changes came when the trucking industry developed after 1945. While the city continues to grow beyond the square, history continues to be made on the square.

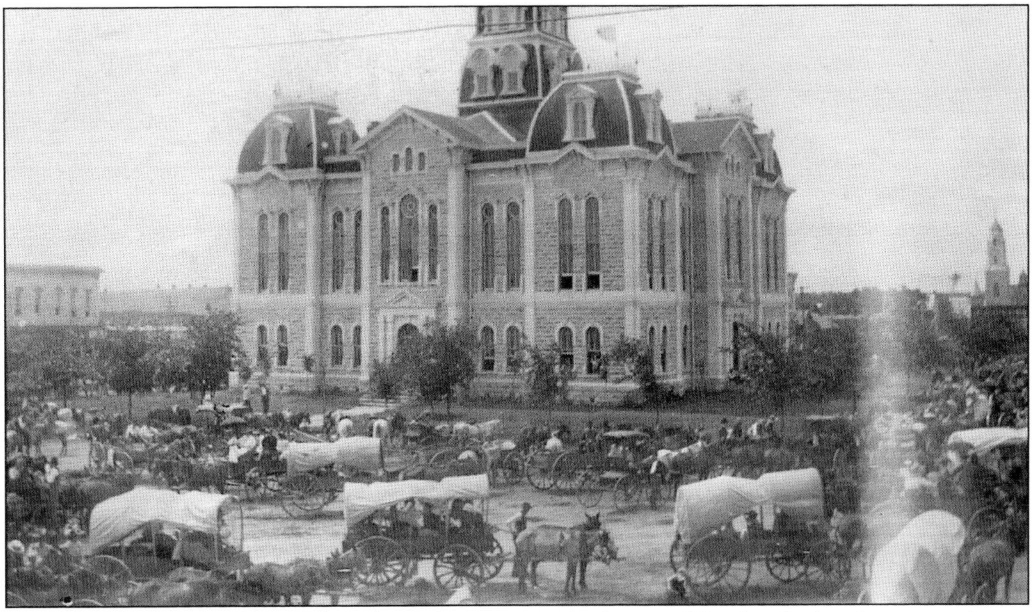

Voting day and election speakers brought county people into Weatherford to listen, as shown by the number of covered wagons and wagons without trade goods. Note the large fenced-in grassy area around the courthouse for listeners to gather. The First Methodist Church in the distance was built in 1892. (Heritage Gallery, Charles Russell Collection.)

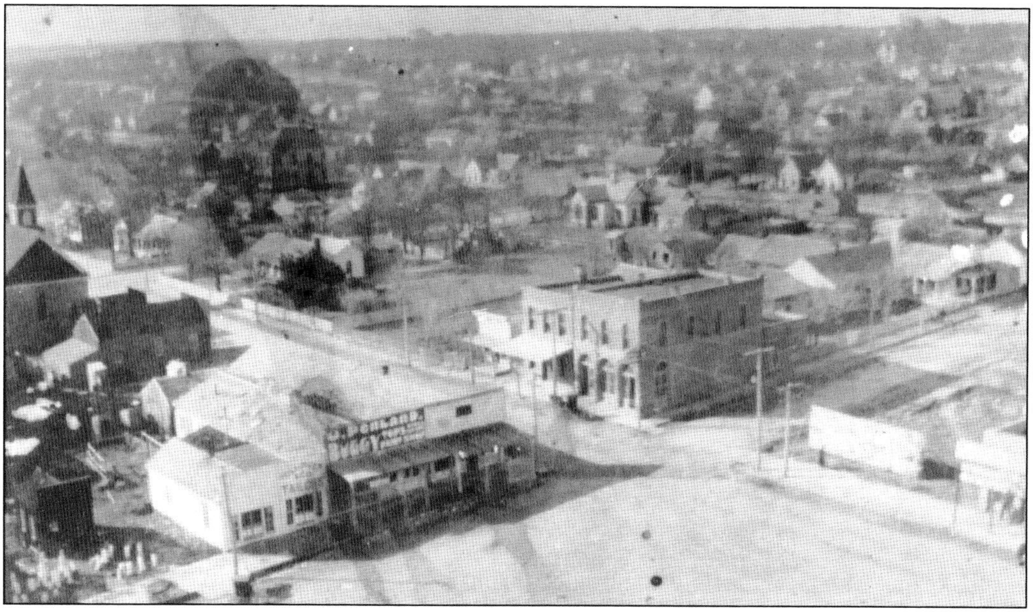

About 1902, the development of the south side of the square reveals the marble yard for Rawlins Monuments, Hollinger Tailors, and Omar Penland's Buggy Parts Shop. Omar became a police chief. Of the two-story buildings, the one at left had W.A. White Undertakers in 1919. The other building once housed the Franco-Texan Land Company, then the short-lived Henry Warren Bank. Behind was the Hotel Montfort, which burned in the 1960s, formerly known as Ma Sikes House, then Thomson House. (V.A. Littleton.)

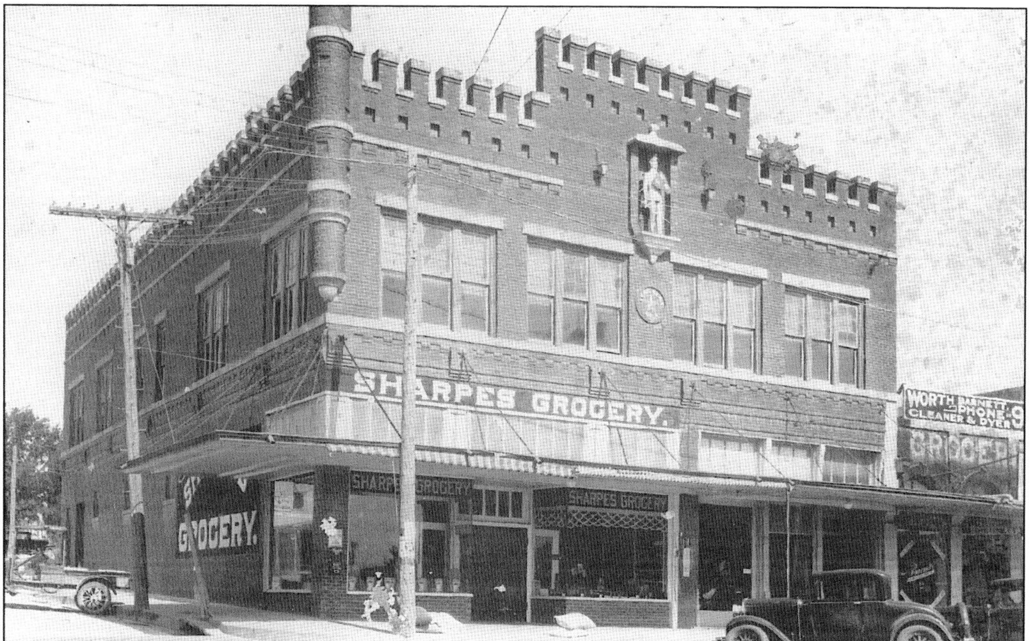

The fraternal Knights of Pythias built their lodge in 1902 at 112 Houston Avenue. The foundation beginnings show in this photograph. Lieper Pianos leased the ground floor in the first years, then Sharpe's Grocery stayed there for many decades. (Bill Bennett.)

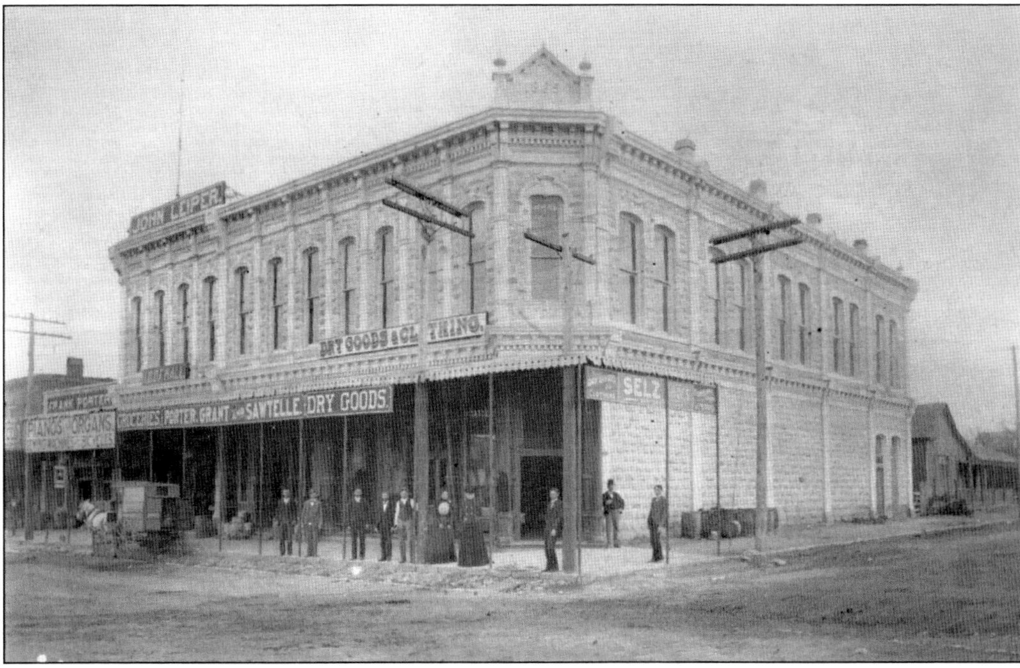

The Porter-Kidwell Building leased space to the International Order of Odd Fellows and the Porter, Grant and Sawtelle Dry Goods in 1885. In 1912, Frank Porter sold the facility to J.L. Hill after a major fire. (WL, Jeff Bledsoe Collection.)

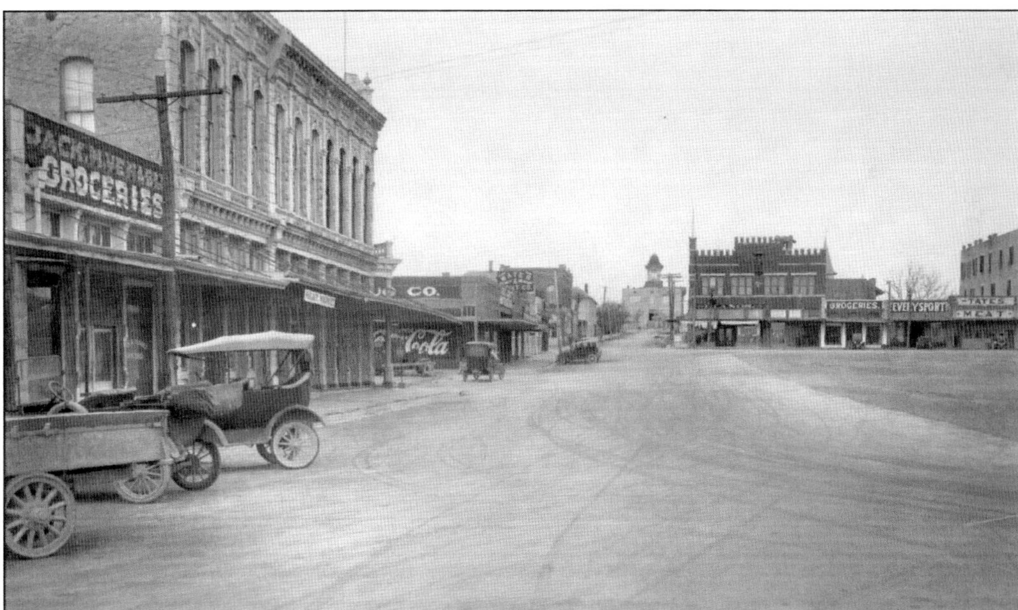

Found in an antique store in Austin, Texas, this photograph shows a steamroller at the corner of South Main while paving in 1919. At right is the unpaved parking area next to the courthouse. Looking west in the distance is the 1909 high school and the bell tower on the old 1885 Central School. (Martha McClung.)

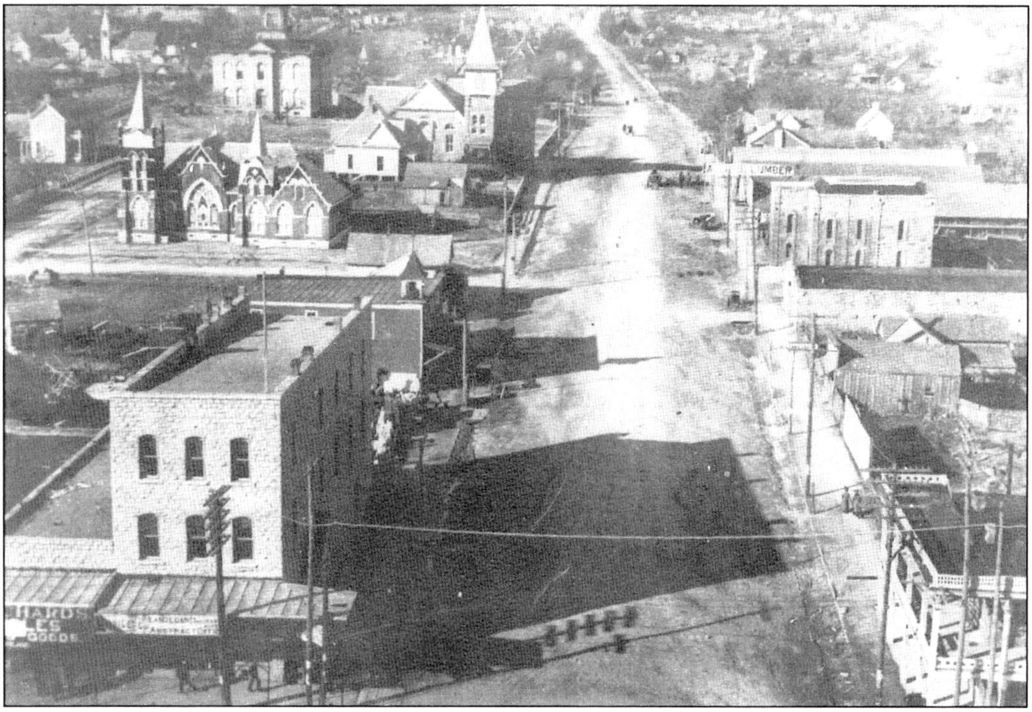

In 1906 behind the Carson-Lewis House, looking west on Palo Pinto Street, are Sam Wing Chinese Laundry, the A.J. Roe Lumber Co., and the new jail in the second block. On the south side of the street, the fire hall is barely visible. In the next blocks are Cumberland Presbyterian Church, First Baptist Church, and the "Central Free School." (WL.)

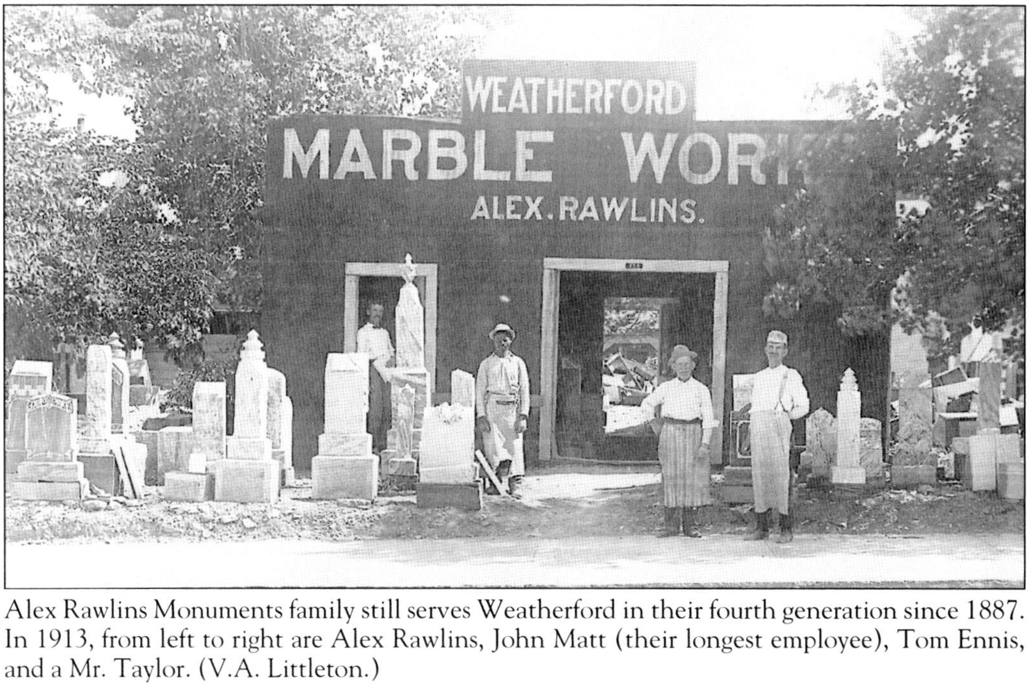

Alex Rawlins Monuments family still serves Weatherford in their fourth generation since 1887. In 1913, from left to right are Alex Rawlins, John Matt (their longest employee), Tom Ennis, and a Mr. Taylor. (V.A. Littleton.)

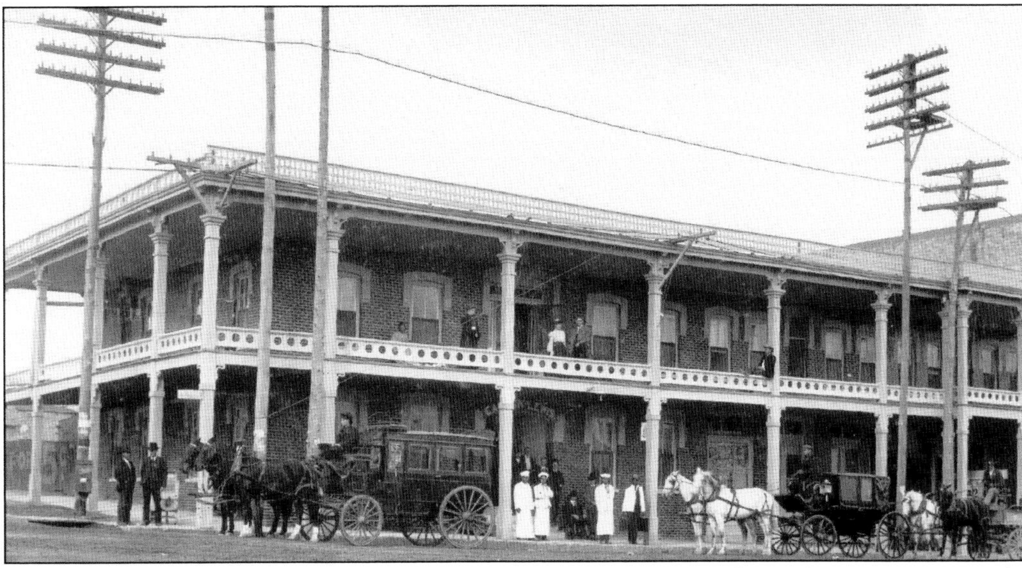

In 1860, Carson and Lewis House was the pristine luxury for those that came west. The restaurant waiters even wore slippers in the 1880s to prevent interference to conversation. After the building was destroyed by fire, it was replaced in 1910 with the Kuteman Building. (James H. Doss.)

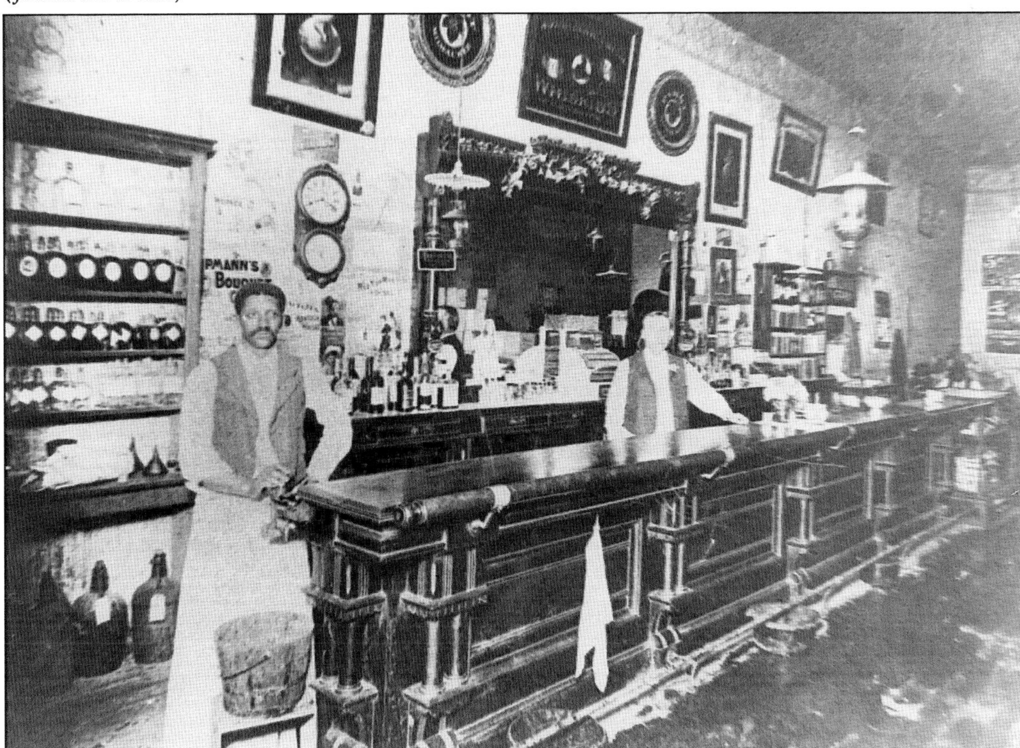

As with many frontier towns, Weatherford hosted many saloons. Ben Hartgraves, right, was saloonkeeper at the Tillman Saloon, which moved to 614 North Main in 1894. (Jon Vandagriff.)

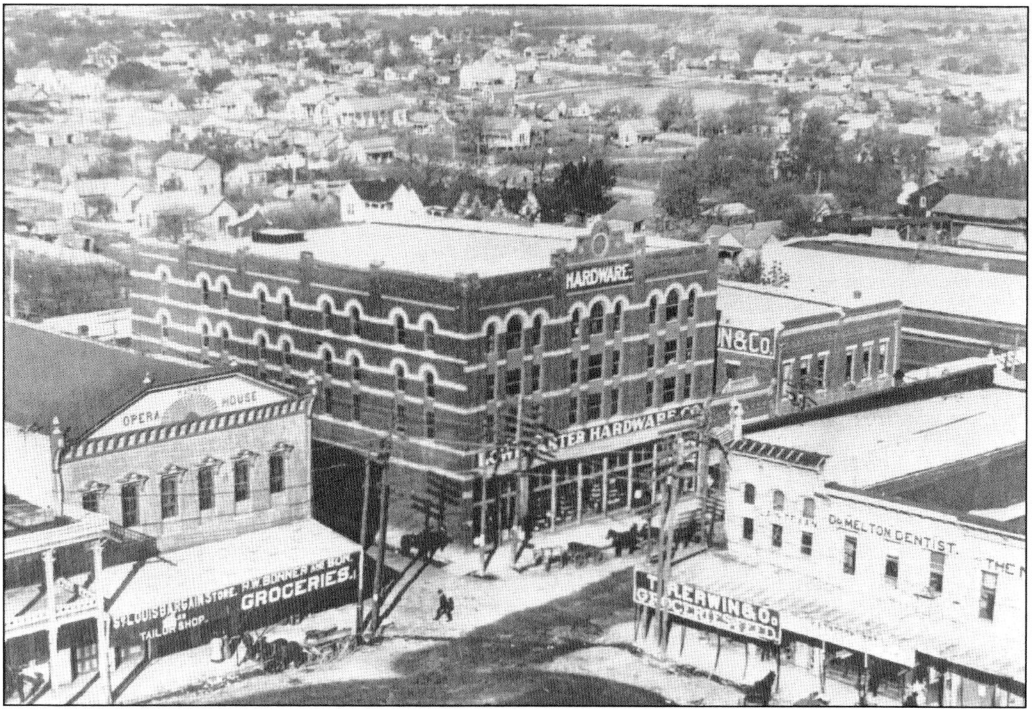

Lowe bought the property on the northwest corner of the square in 1902. The four-story Lowe-Carter Hardware became the largest building in town. The famous Haynes Opera House is on the left with the Carson-Lewis Hotel. In the fall of 1909, the *Plain Texan* newspaper was above Erwin Groceries at 112 Dallas Avenue. (Zan Statham.)

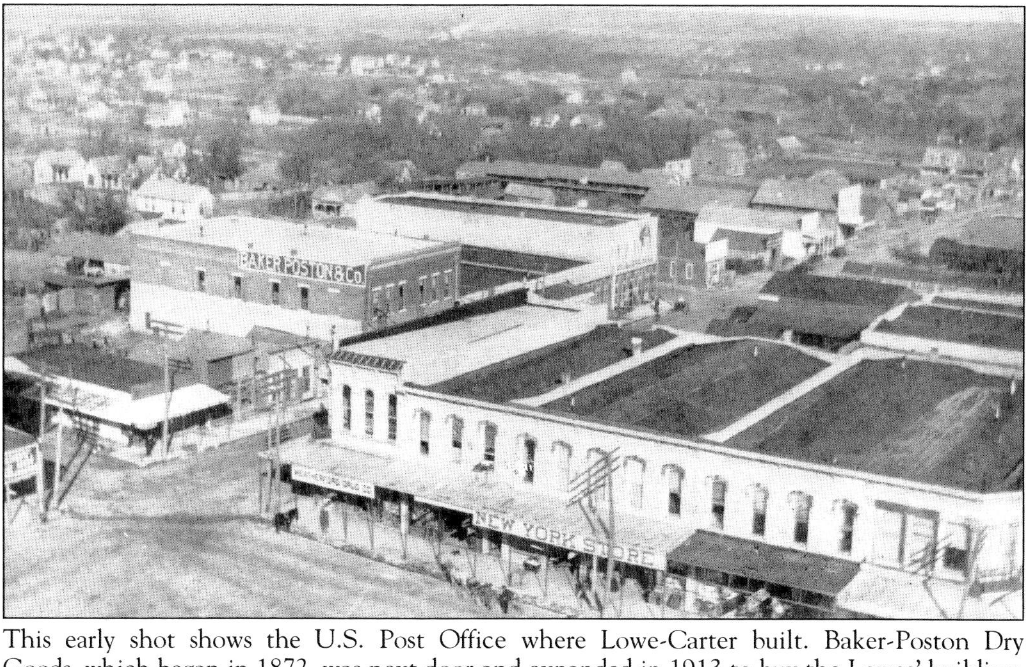

This early shot shows the U.S. Post Office where Lowe-Carter built. Baker-Poston Dry Goods, which began in 1872, was next door and expanded in 1913 to buy the Lowes' building. (Helen Dill.)

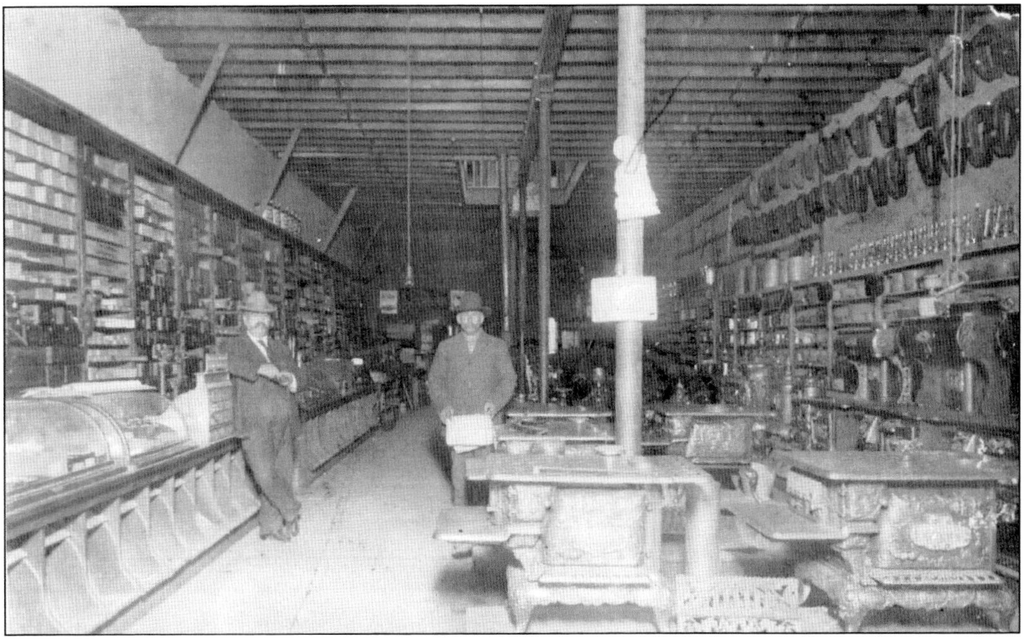

John R. Lewis sold his hardware store to Thomas S. Carter, left, in 1902. Enter the store today is to step back in time. Studebaker Wagons were assembled upstairs and brought down by the elevator, which still exists. (Randy Carter.)

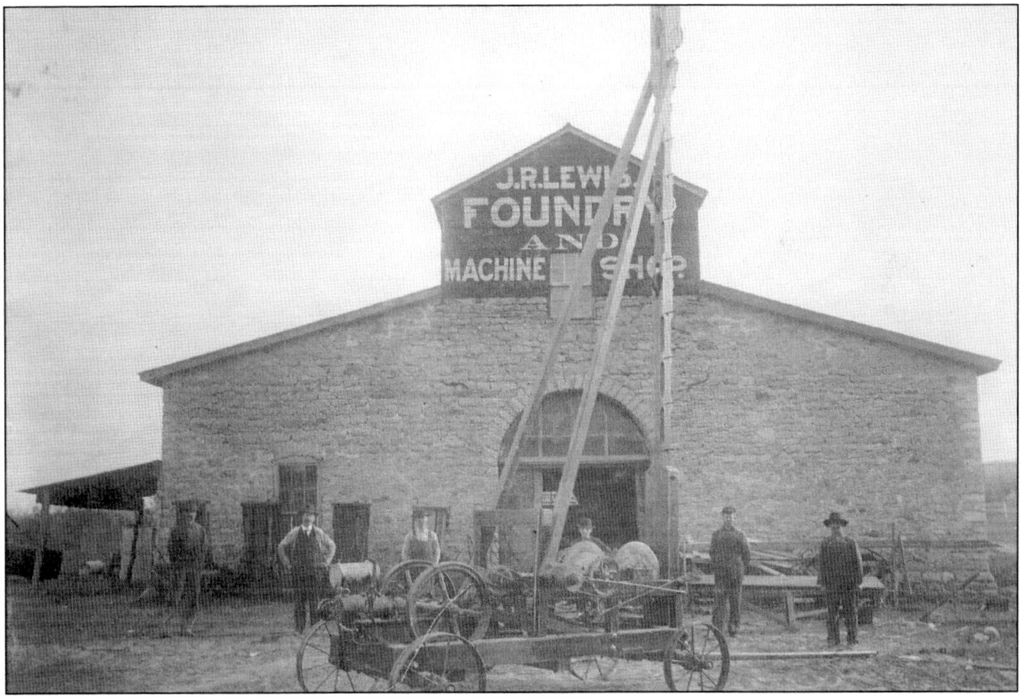

In 1908, at 200 Front Street, was the J.R. Lewis Foundry and Machine Shop. The business closed shortly after this photograph was taken and became the meeting place for many fraternal and business organizations, from the American Legion to the Rotary Club. The structure burned down in the 1980s. (WL.)

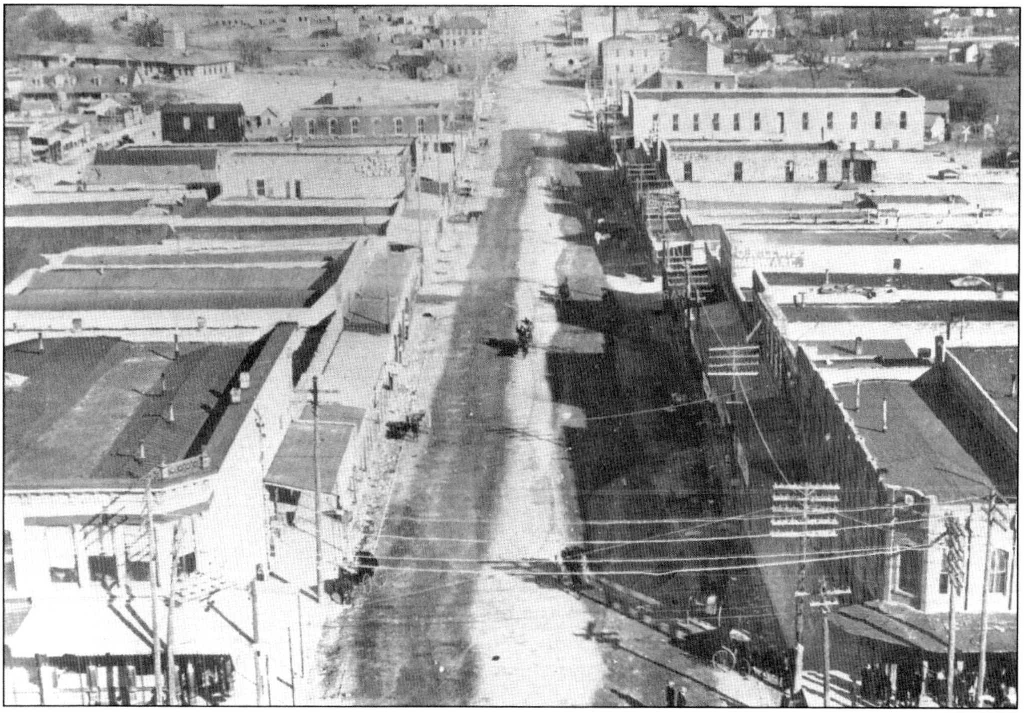

In September 1909, oil was laid down on parts of downtown streets in attempt to keep the dust down from those newfangled contraptions, horseless carriages, which showed up in 1901. At the north end of York Avenue is the McFall Hotel near the T & P Station. Seen in the distance on North Main is the metal bridge built that year crossing "town creek." (Zan Statham.)

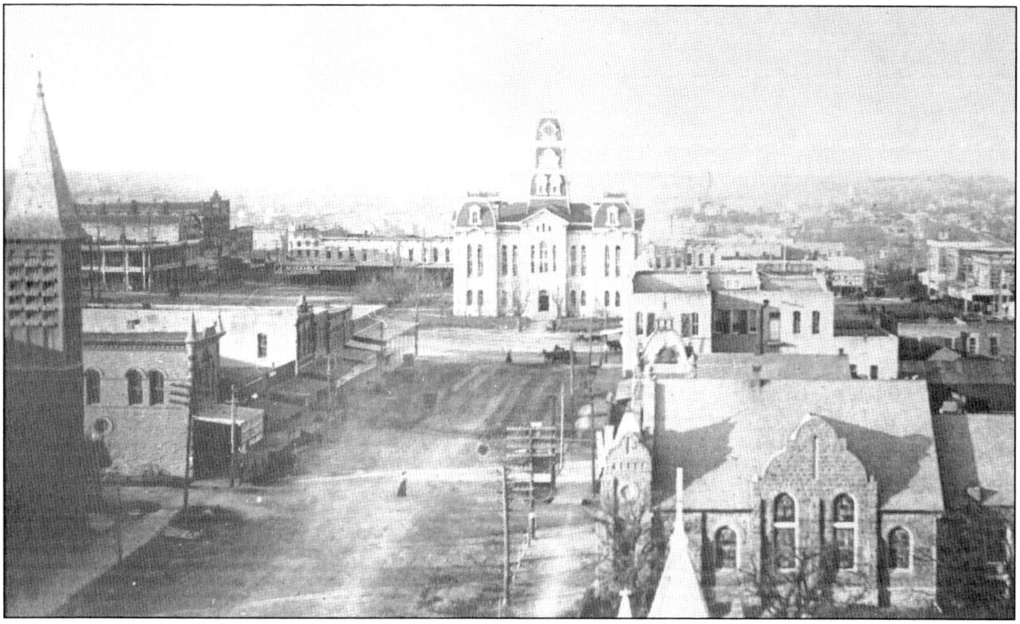

This is a view in 1905 from atop the First Methodist Church. At left is Grace First Presbyterian, then the Masonic Lodge. Seen in the right foreground is the South Main Church of Christ. (Zan Statham.)

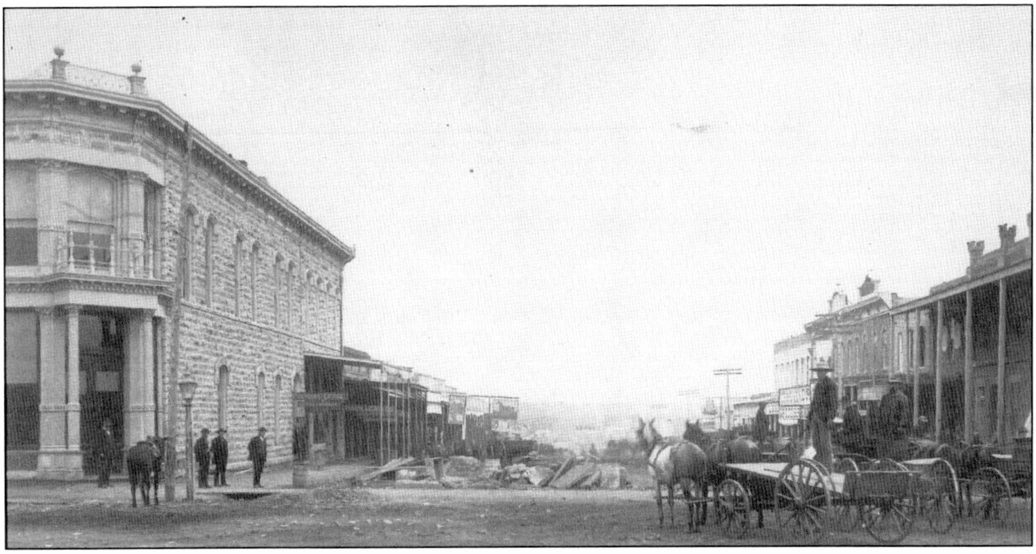

Rock for courthouse construction was dropped near the gas streetlight in front of the Couts and Fain Bank in the summer of 1884. The bank became Citizen's National, and then Weatherford National. It is the oldest bank west of Fort Worth. (Zan Statham.)

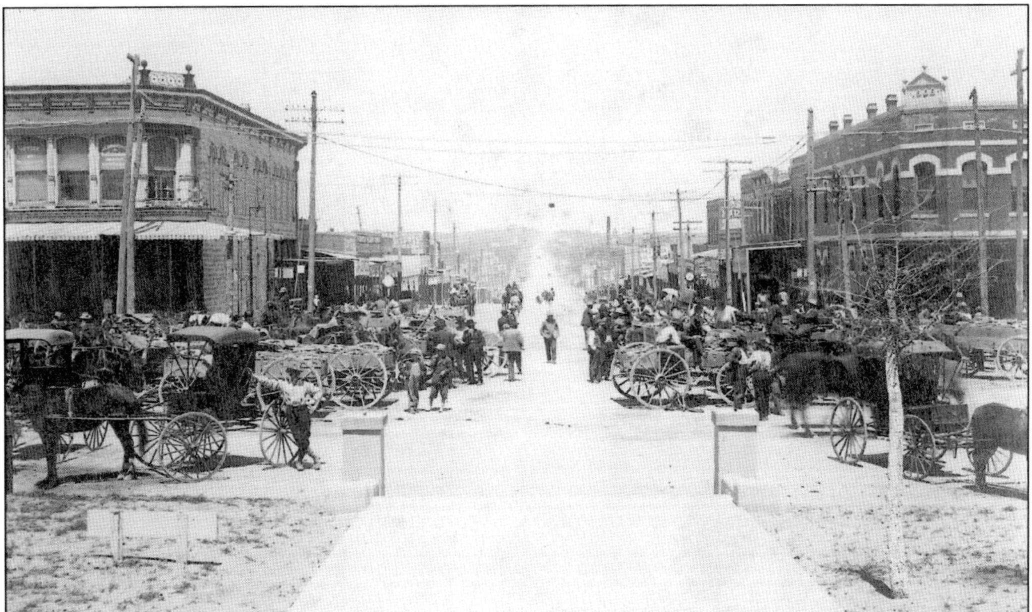

This view of North Main is from the courthouse steps. Gone are the "stile" steps over the fence that bordered the courthouse. Gone is the fence! (Maurine McCoy.)

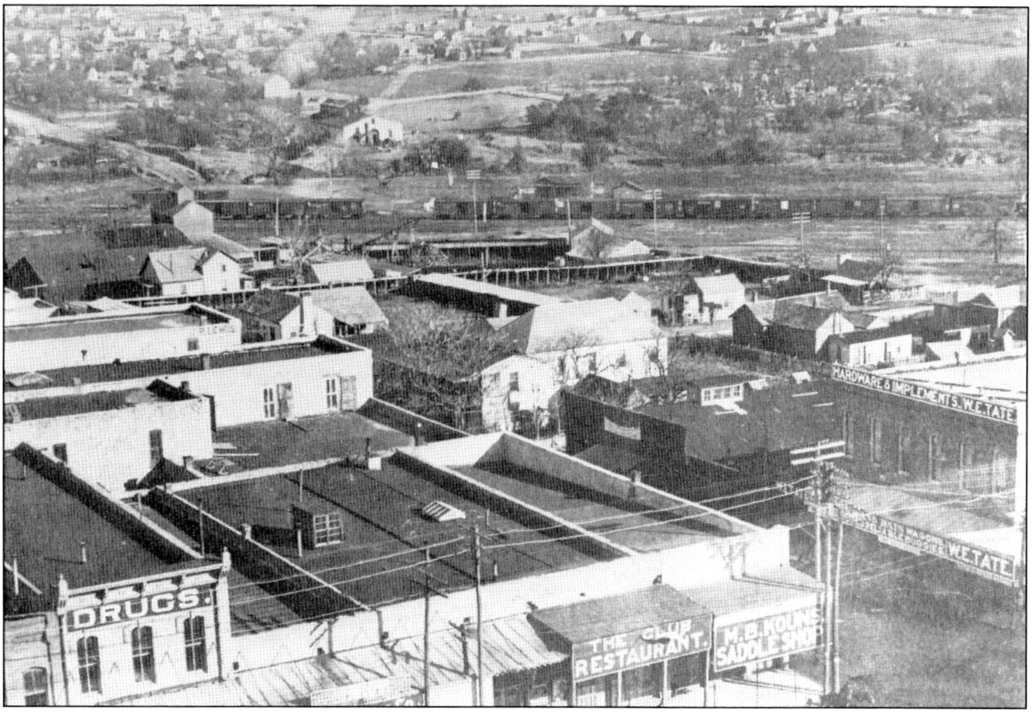

In this view looking across the northeast side of the square in 1909, the unchanged J.R. Lewis sign labels the rear of Carter-Ivy Hardware. The corral/wagon yard has roofed parking. In the distance, Elm Street fords "town creek" near J.R. Lewis Foundry. (Zan Statham.)

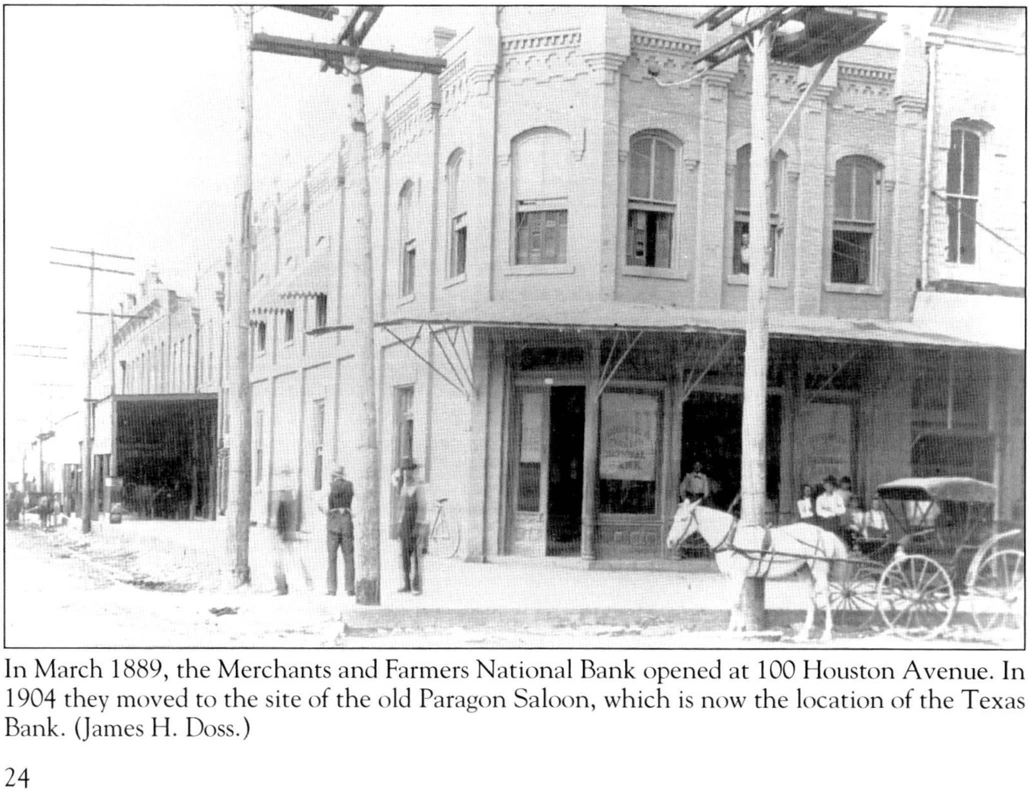

In March 1889, the Merchants and Farmers National Bank opened at 100 Houston Avenue. In 1904 they moved to the site of the old Paragon Saloon, which is now the location of the Texas Bank. (James H. Doss.)

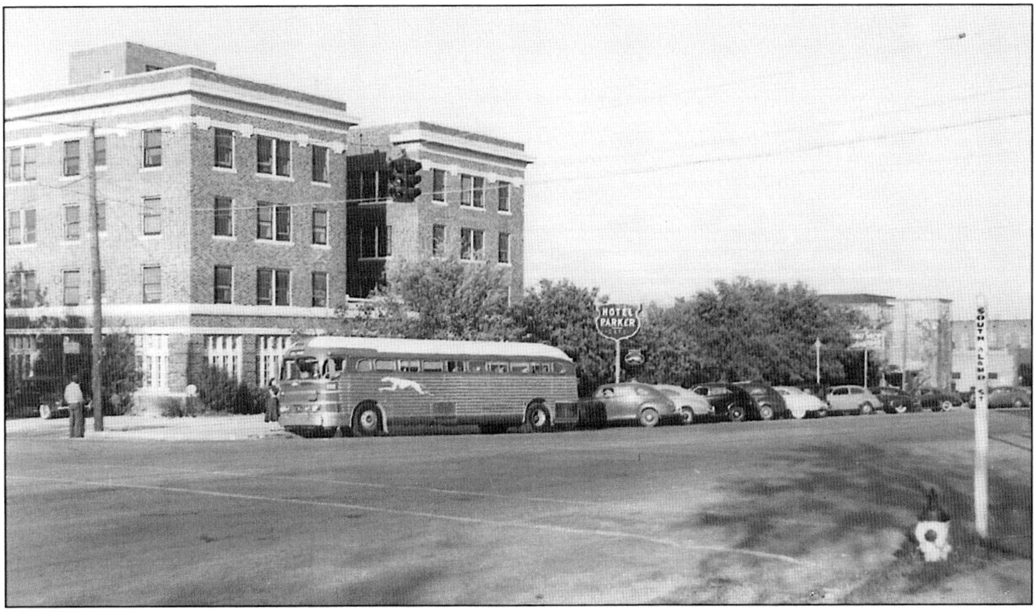

Without the Carson-Lewis Hotel, frequent visitors to Weatherford demanded an excellent place to stay. Hotel Parker was finally built in 1921, with a first-rate restaurant. In 1948, it served as the Greyhound bus station. The jail is on the far right. (Ed Brown.)

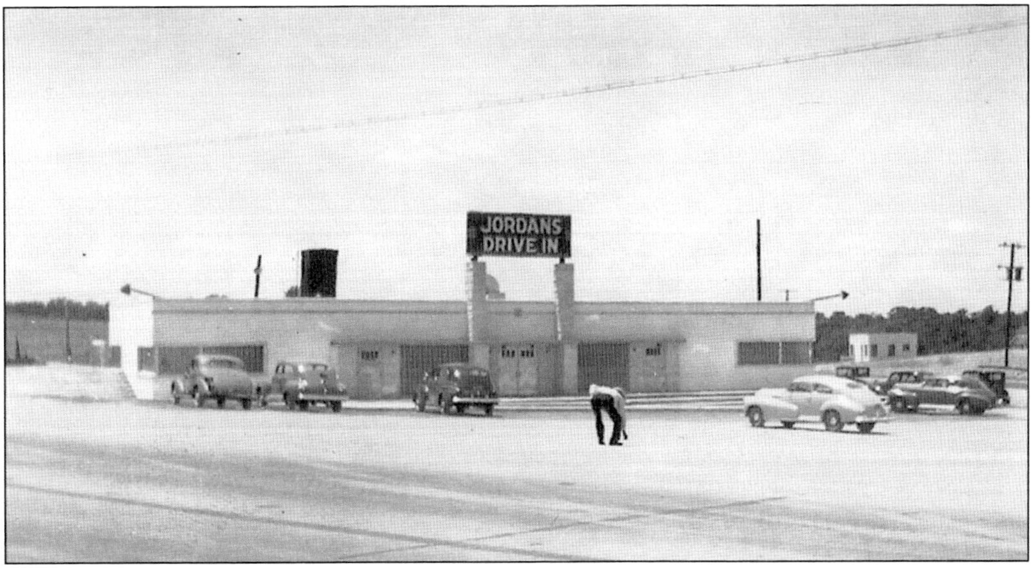

In 1945, the western city limit was at a "Y" in the state highway. Jordan Drive-In, later Restaurant, became the place to feast until the 1970s, when the city was by-passed by Interstate Highway 20. (Phil Jordan.)

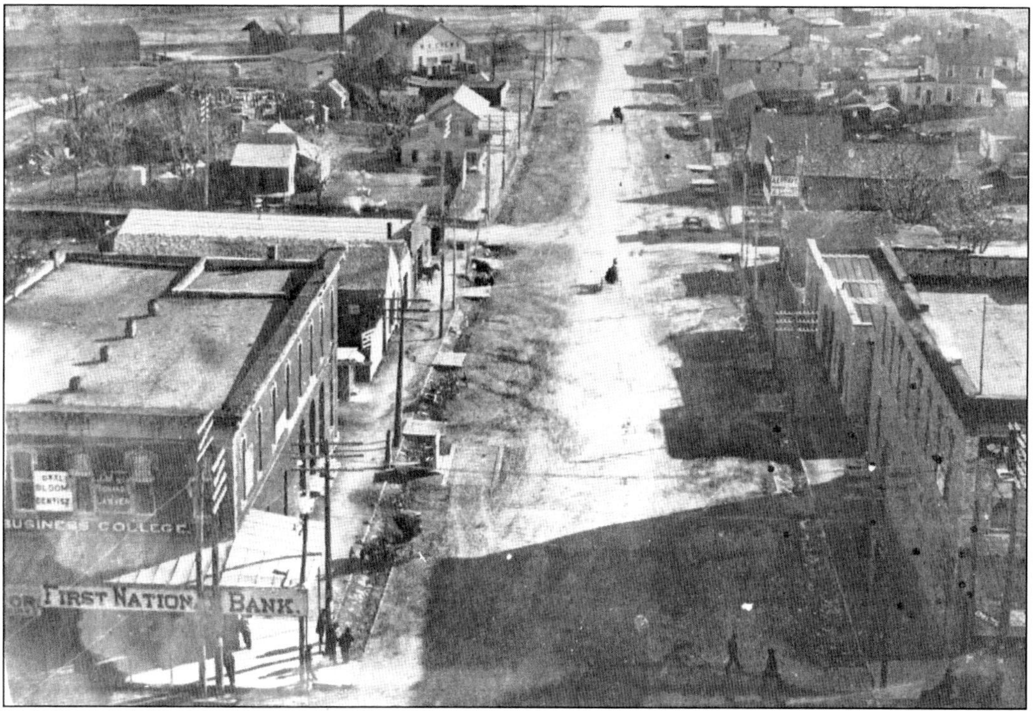

This photograph captures a 1909 view of Fort Worth Street. At the second electric pole is a scale to weigh wagons headed for the cotton compress. At the next corner, horses are led into the Arkansas Wagon Yard. In the distance are the Santa Fe tracks, now Santa Fe Drive. (Zan Statham.)

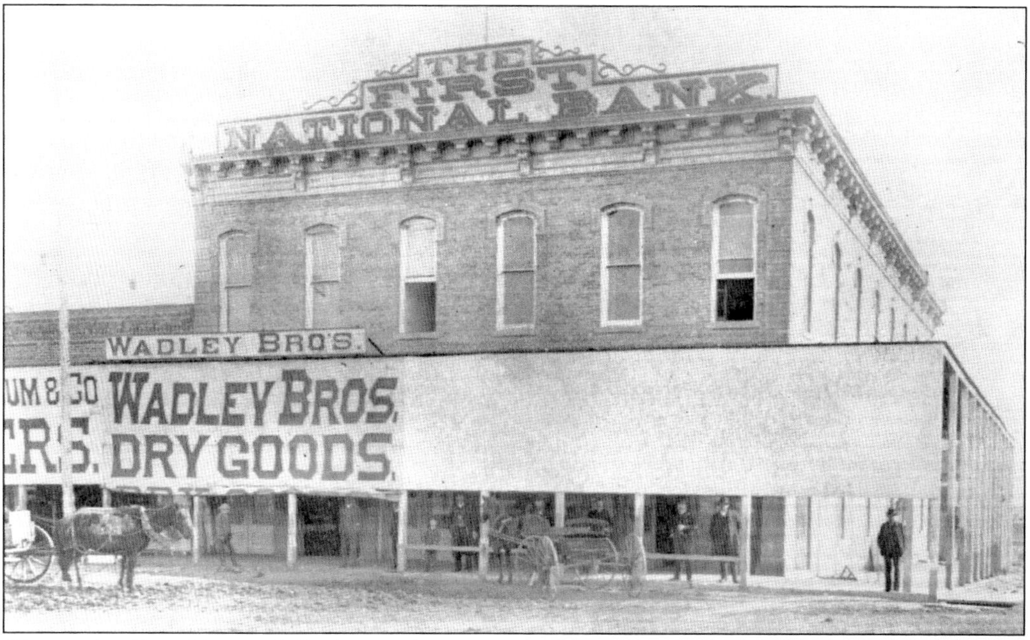

This is the First National Bank, on the square at Fort Worth Street, during the courthouse construction in 1884–5. (Zan Statham.)

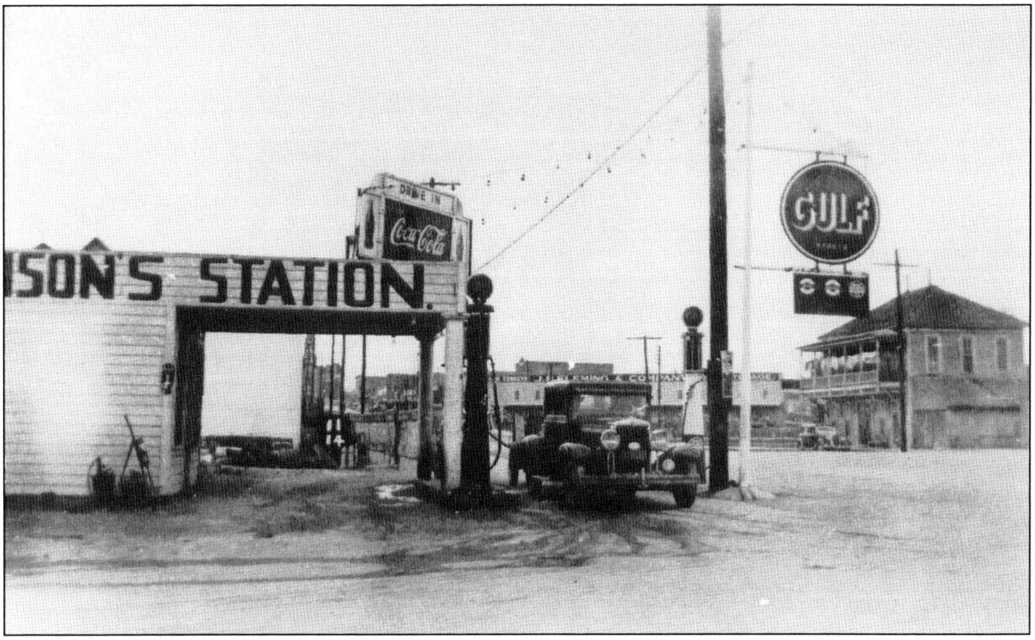

In 1938, Clovis Mathison's Gulf Station was on North Main at Front Street. In the distance is the courthouse. Across the street near "town creek" was the Raper Boarding House, 409 North Main. The upper floor was removed to become a home east of town with the lower floor still serving as a business. (James Mathison.)

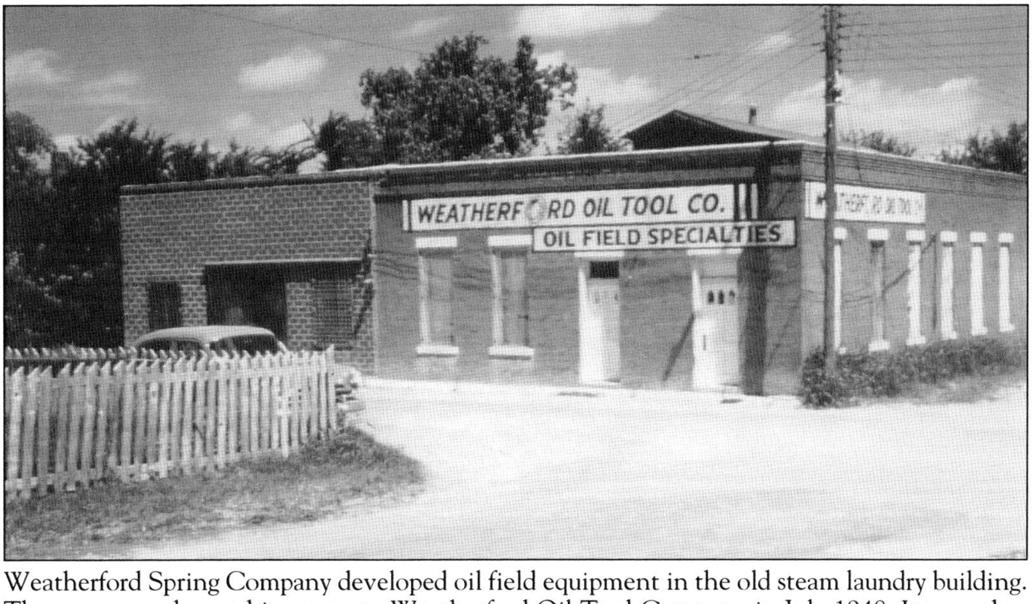

Weatherford Spring Company developed oil field equipment in the old steam laundry building. The company changed its name to Weatherford Oil Tool Company in July 1948. It moved to the site of the old Weatherford Cotton Compress and became a multi-million dollar industry. (Jess Hall Jr.)

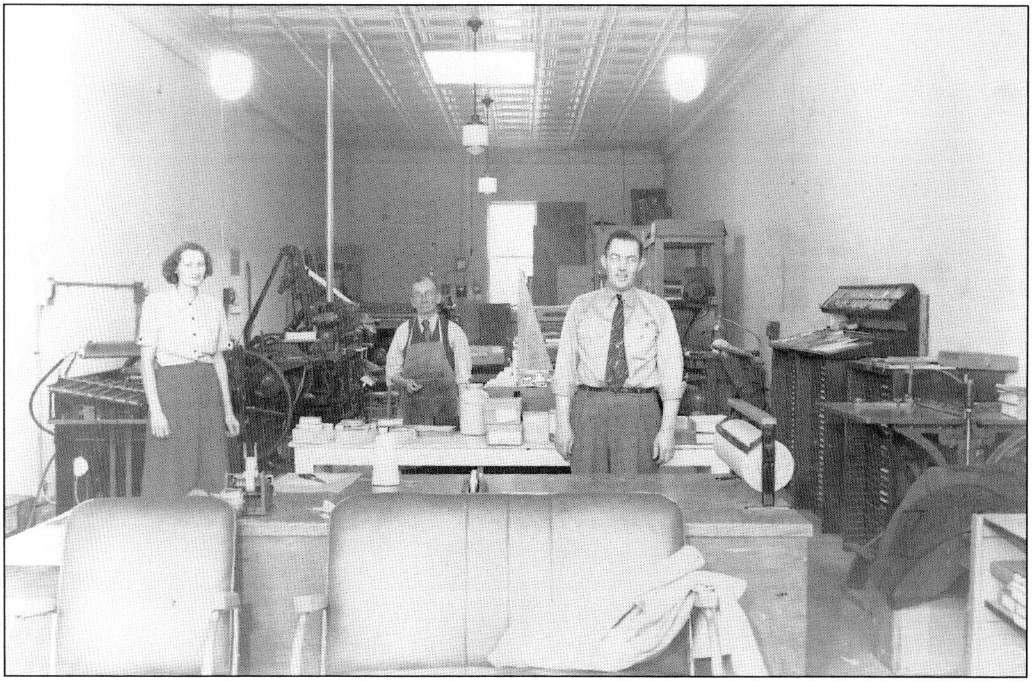

Carl Hartness owned the *Weatherford Democrat* newspaper from December 7, 1941, to June 1946. He began a printing business in 1948 at 127 York Avenue, where this photograph was made with, from left to right, Ruth Potter, Mr. Haddick, and Carl. The family is in its third generation of trusted publication production at 128 Dallas Avenue. (Ted Hartness.)

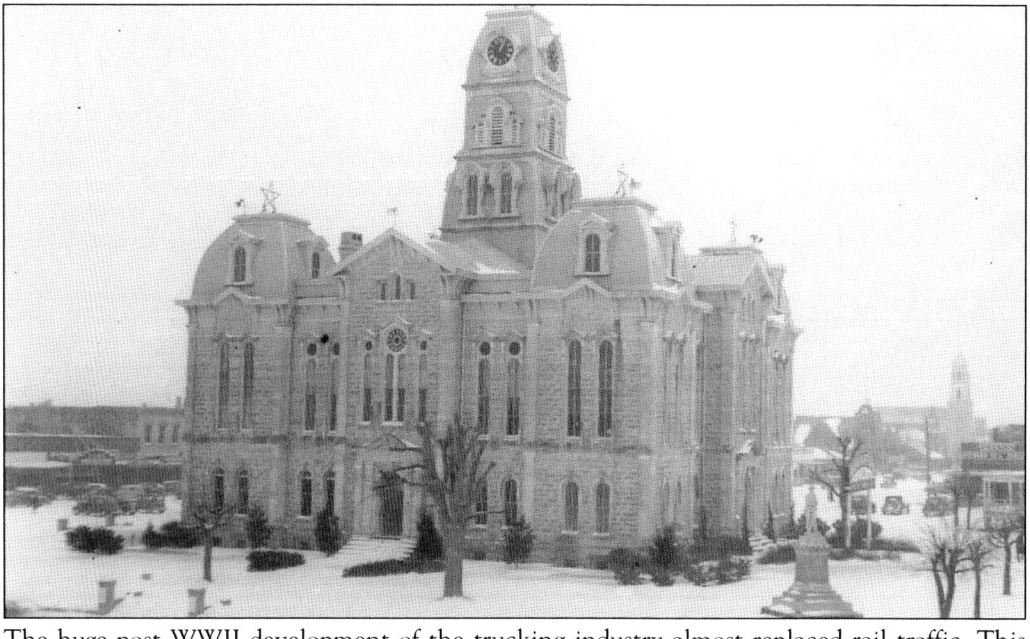

The huge post-WWII development of the trucking industry almost replaced rail traffic. This early February 1947 shot reveals a last view of the square before the state mandated changes for easier truck traffic through the city. Note the old Confederate statue was on the northwest side of the courthouse. Compare this scene with that on page 4 and 15. (Ed Brown.)

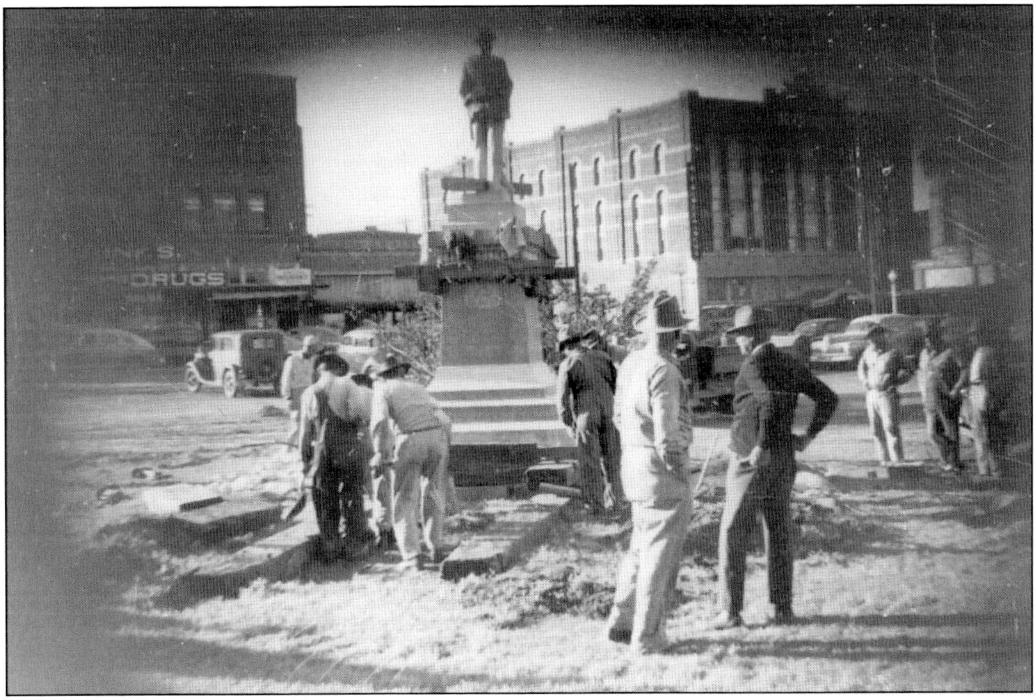

Still active, the Sam Lanham Chapter of the United Daughters of the Confederacy erected the Civil War Memorial between 1915, with the base, and 1925 when the statue was added. It was moved in the fall of 1947 to the southeast side of the courthouse to face south, during the destruction of the grassy area around the courthouse shown below. (Ed Brown.)

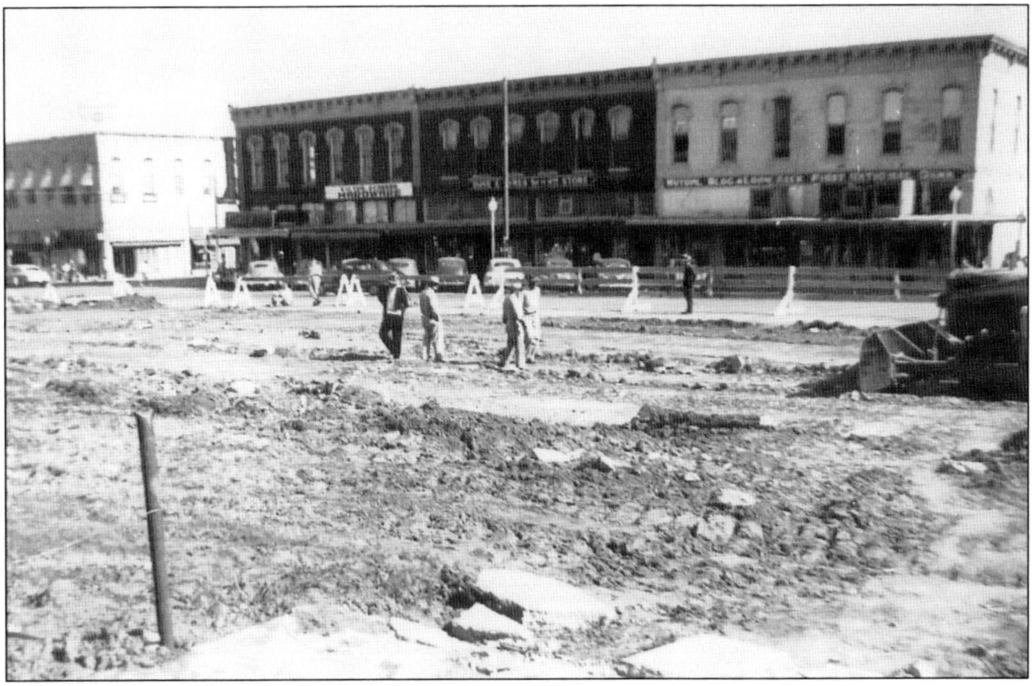

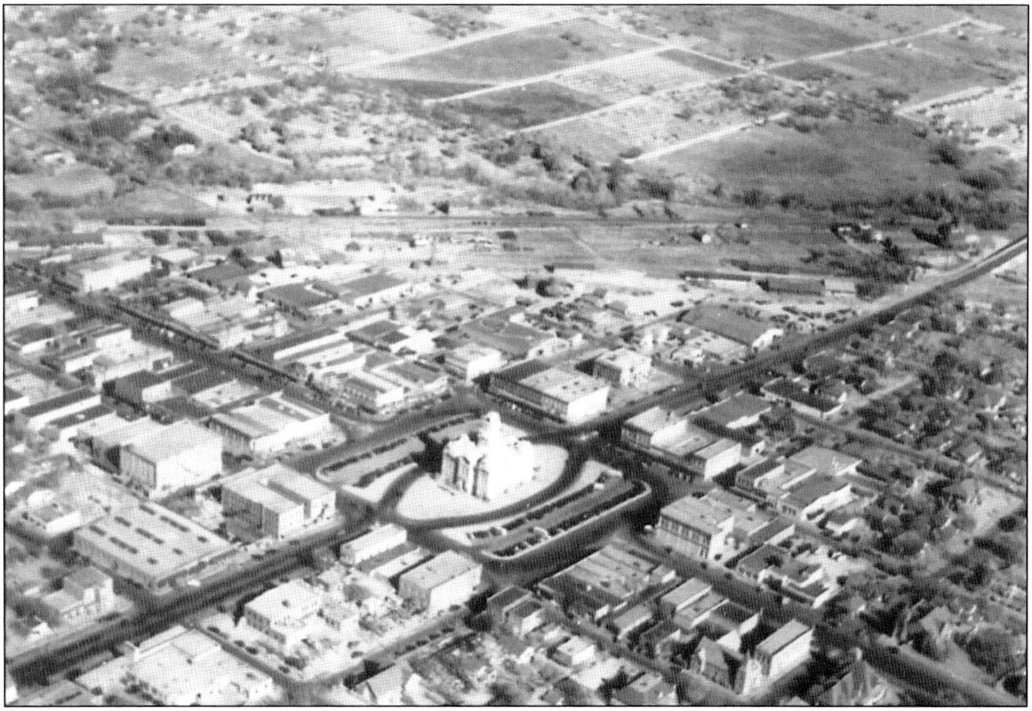

The December 1948 view of the state-mandated changes in the square reveal the traffic pattern between the parking area and the businesses in the square, which still caused death or injury to customers. (Ed Brown)

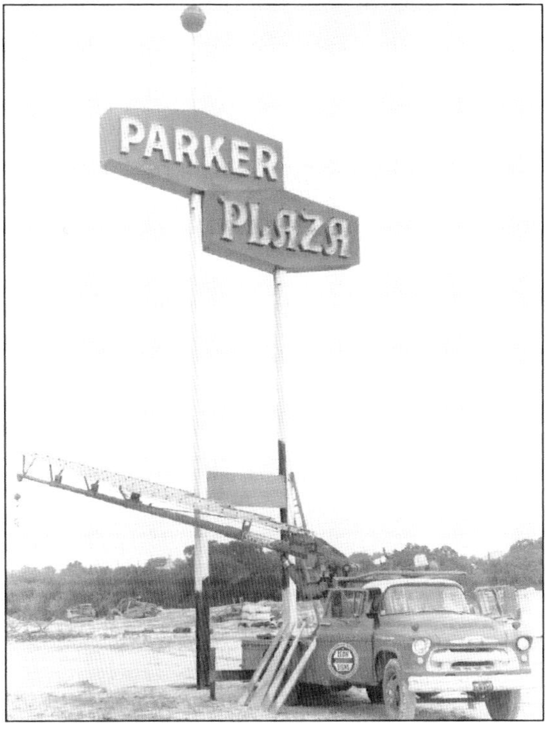

In 1964, the First National Bank moved to 220 Palo Pinto, and J.C. Penny moved to 601 Palo Pinto in Weatherford's first major strip mall, Parker Plaza. Citizen's National Bank cleared the property at 120 Palo Pinto, intending to move, until news came of a further state-mandated change to the square, made in 1967. (Chamber of Commerce.)

Three

City Services

Busy communities sometimes forget that the city serves to build streets, keep the peace, and provide water and electricity, hospitals, and parks. One voice, a Bowie or Cartwright, can even make a difference in the quality of our lives. But Weatherford learned early that fire continues to challenge. The number of highly regarded businesses lost to fire recorded in this volume saddens even the hardened fireman.

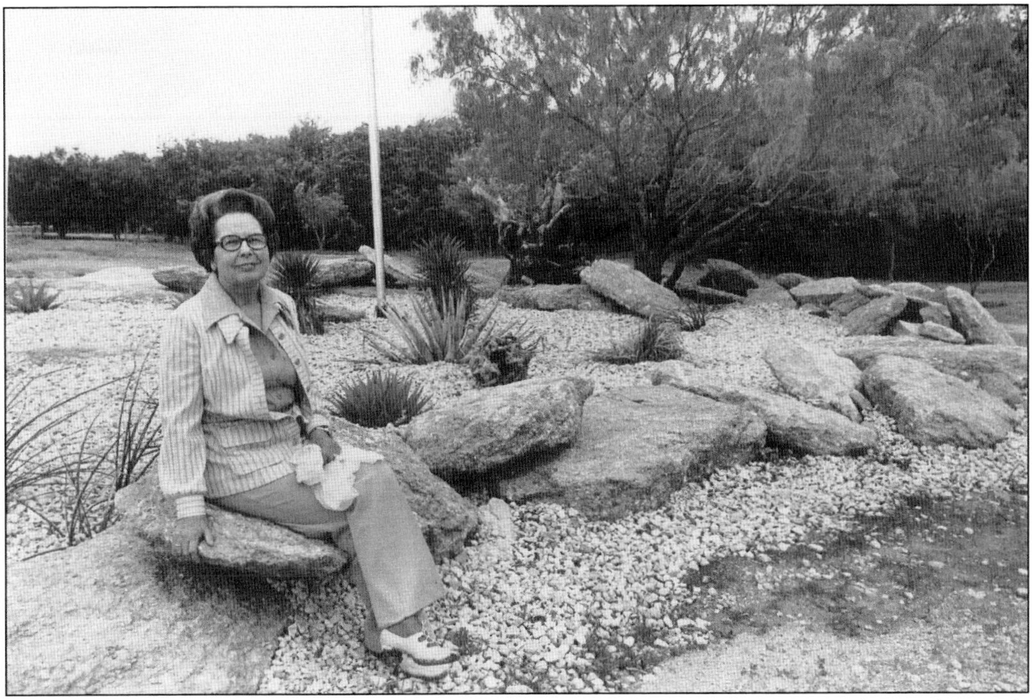

In 1978, Grace Cartwright, inductee into the Texas Women's Hall of Fame, admires the result of her leadership of the Soldier Park beautification project. The park had deteriorated until her guidance to facelift the various city parks. In 1859, it was used as an encampment before marching against the Indians. Later it was a Confederate reunion site, and, in 1908, it was the location of the last legal hanging. (Grace Cartwright.)

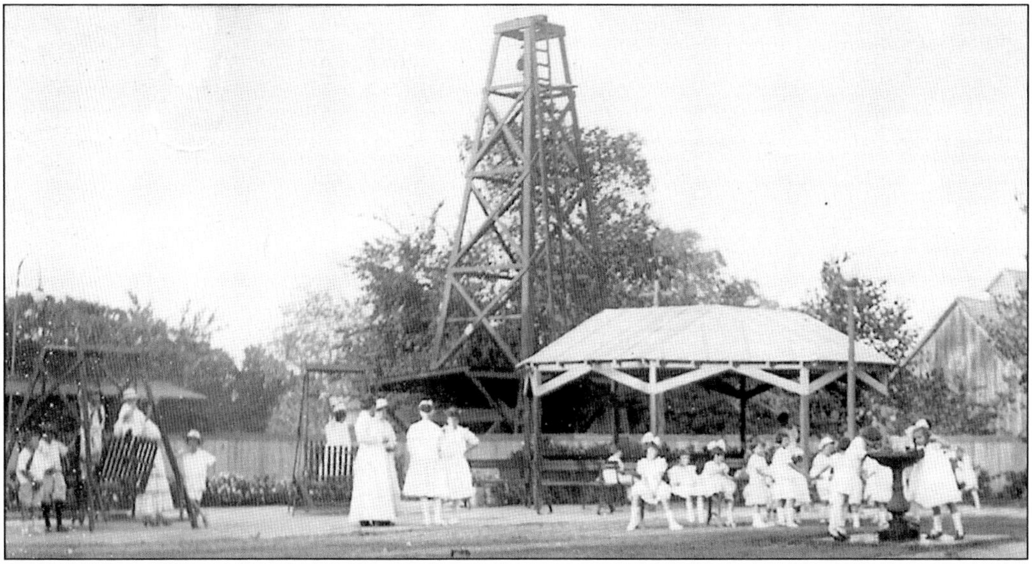

The first "Park Lady" was Mrs. Margaret Armstrong Bowie, wife of civic leader Colonel George M. Bowie. She developed Aberdeen Park in 1911, the first park for the city, at the southeast corner of Soward and North Main. It is now gone, but McGratten Park was made across the street. This view is her small park at the corner of Lee and Davis Streets, which was enlarged into Cherry Park. (Heritage Gallery.)

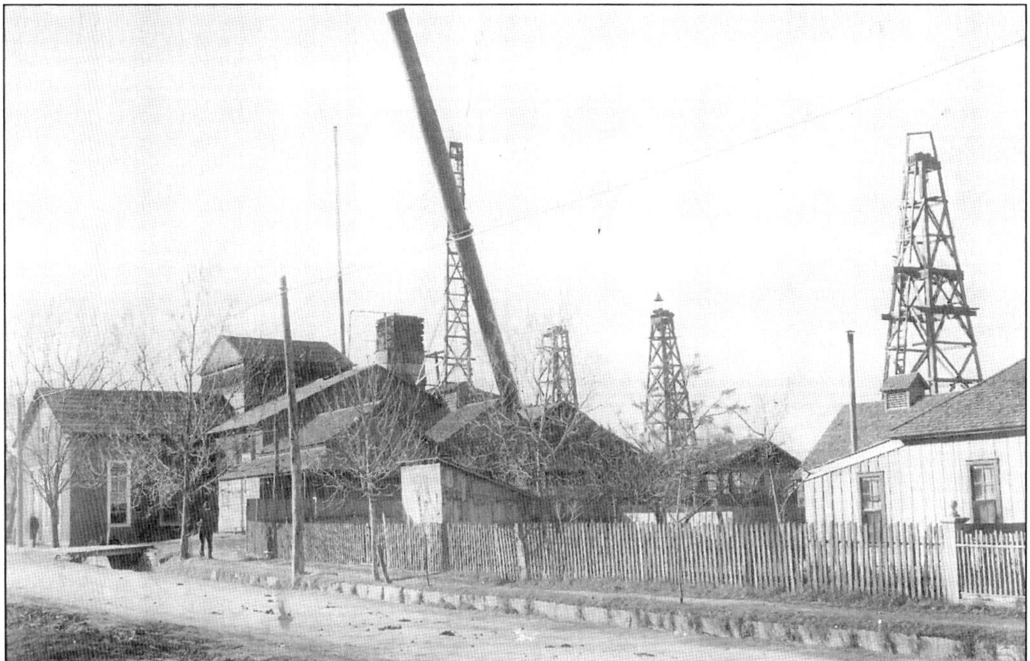

Frank Cherry ran the Weatherford water and electric utility from 1911 to 1928. The three water wells were capped and the electric plant stack was removed when the facility was moved to Fort Worth Street. This sector of Lee Street now has the public swimming pool. (Heritage Gallery via Robert P. Henry.)

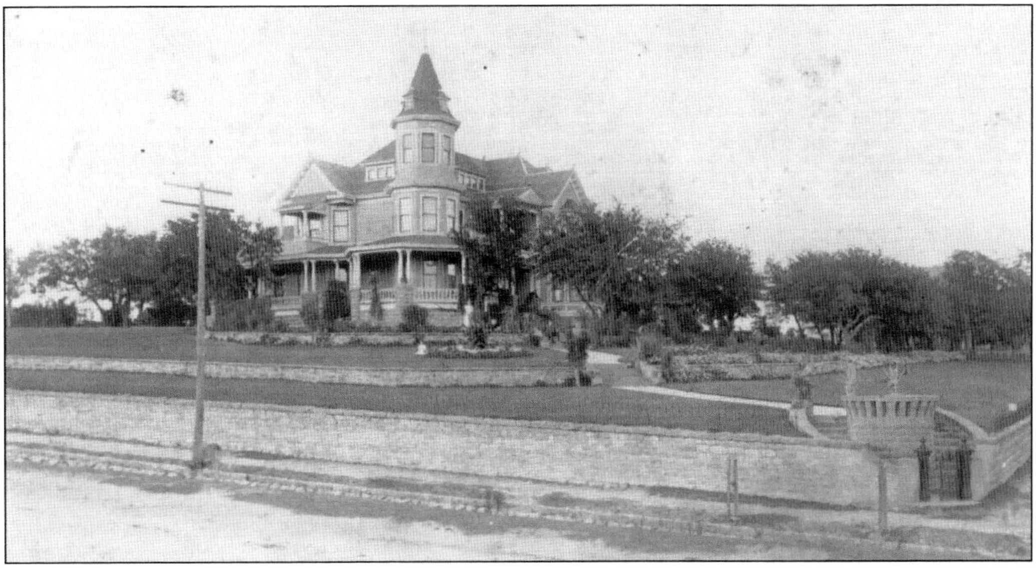

The Colonel George Moreland Bowie home was located on 100 Throckmorton at North Main. Mrs. Bowie hosted a yearly May Fest on the lawn. The home became the Bowie Memorial Hospital, which burned in 1938. Dr. E.D. Fyke bought the property, built Fyke Hospital on the remains, and, in 1945, sold it to the county. (Martha McClung.)

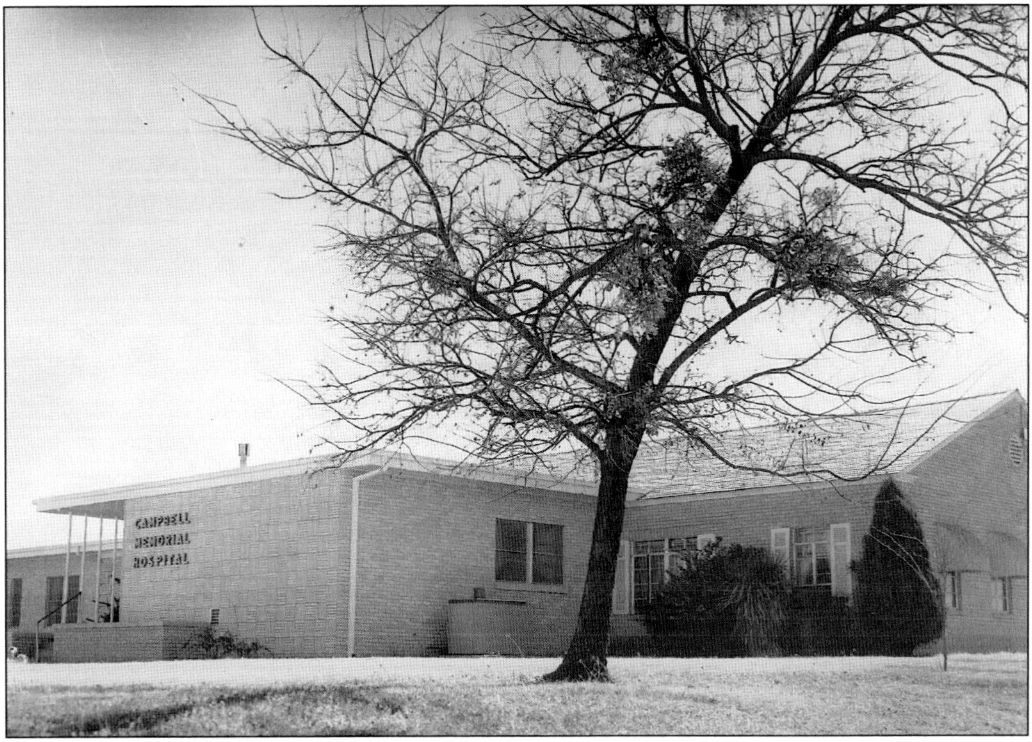

In 1958, Dr. W.M. Campbell died, and the Parker County Hospital was named in his memory. The hospital moved to 713 Anderson Drive in 1972. The old unoccupied facility burned in the mid-1980s. The stone wall is all that is left—even the ornate staircase in the rock wall was later damaged in street work and removed. (Chamber of Commerce.)

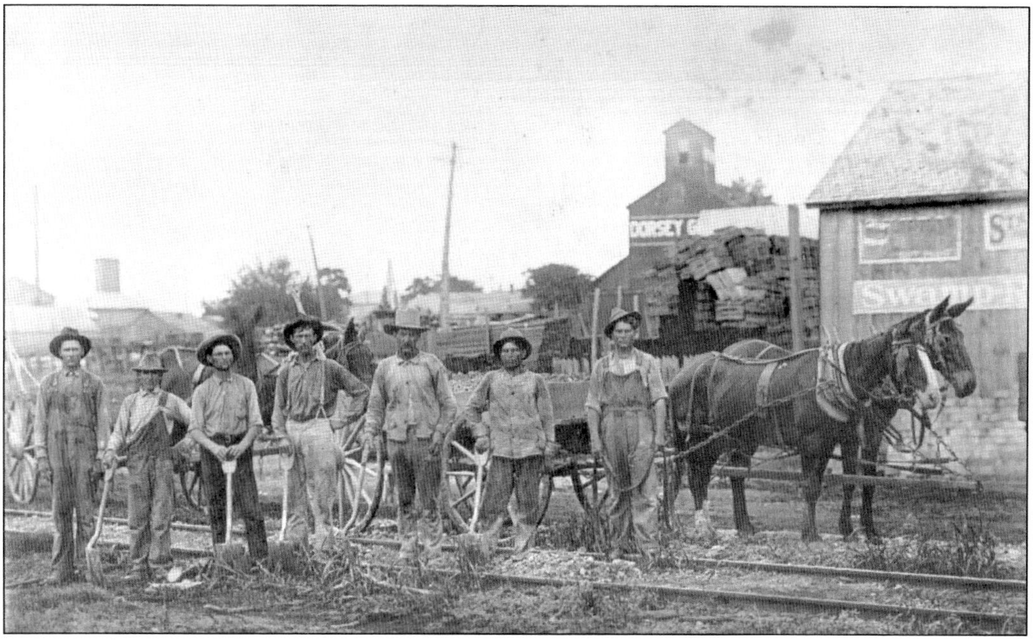

A city ordinance had workdays for citizens to perform road building and maintenance. Fines were levied for absence. In 1910, city alderman Jim Burrows, later police chief, took this photograph of a work group. (Jon Vandagriff.)

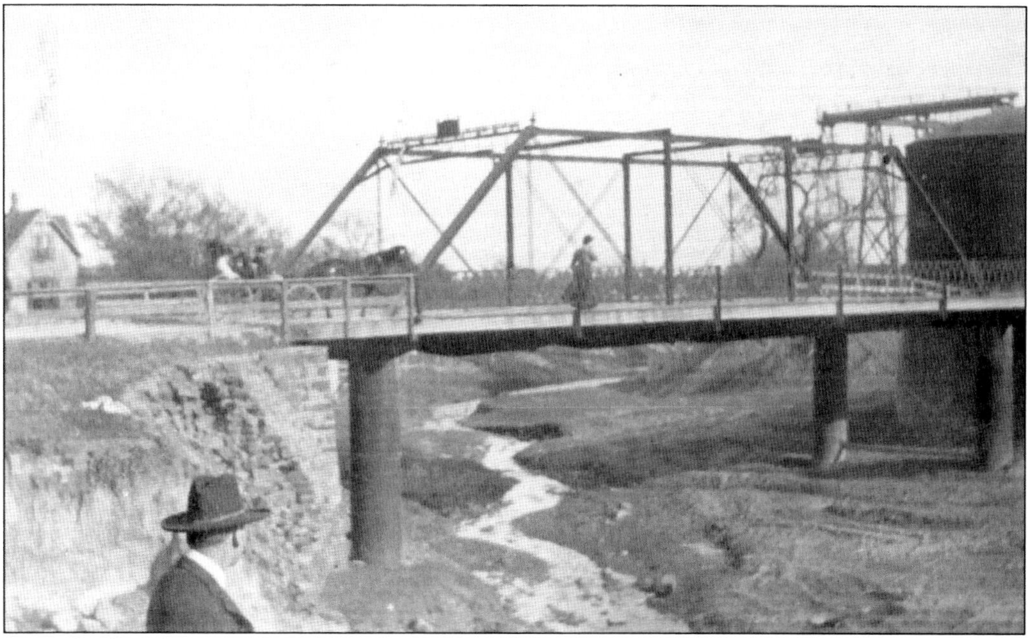

From the founding of Weatherford, the north part of the city was almost cut off by "town creek" in the rainy season. The 200-foot wooden bridge on North Main designed in 1887 was not wide enough for two wagons to pass. In this photograph, people head to town across the metal bridge, built in the fall of 1902. It failed from the weight of a cattle herd in 1912 or 1914. The current, wider concrete bridge, despite rumor, was not honored by "Ripley's Believe It or Not" as the "widest bridge in the world." (Zan Statham.)

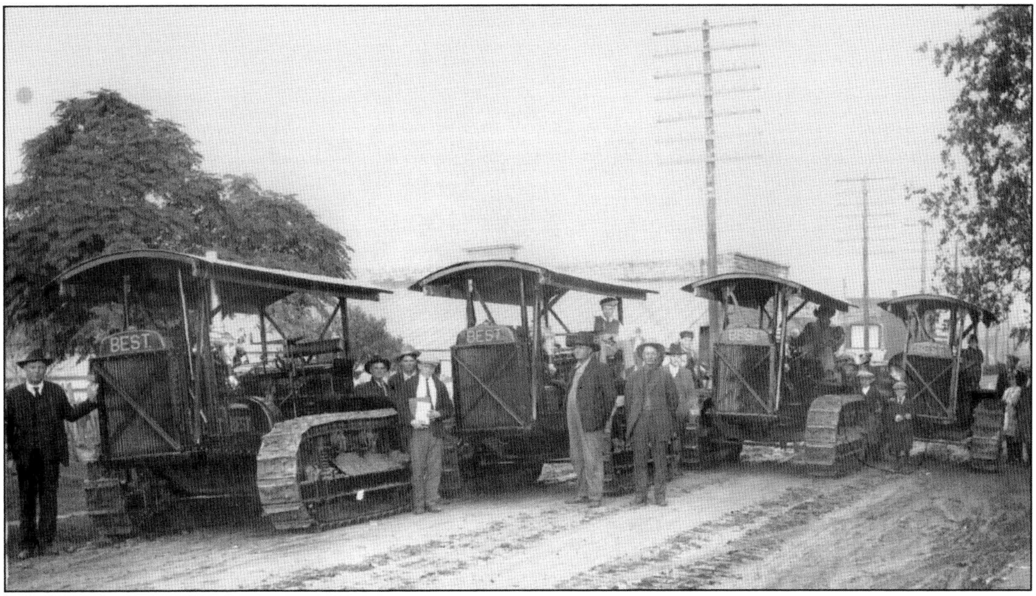

This photograph proudly displays the first tractors for road building bought by Parker County. Sidewalk paving began in 1890 on North Main and York Avenue, and street paving began in 1919. (WL.)

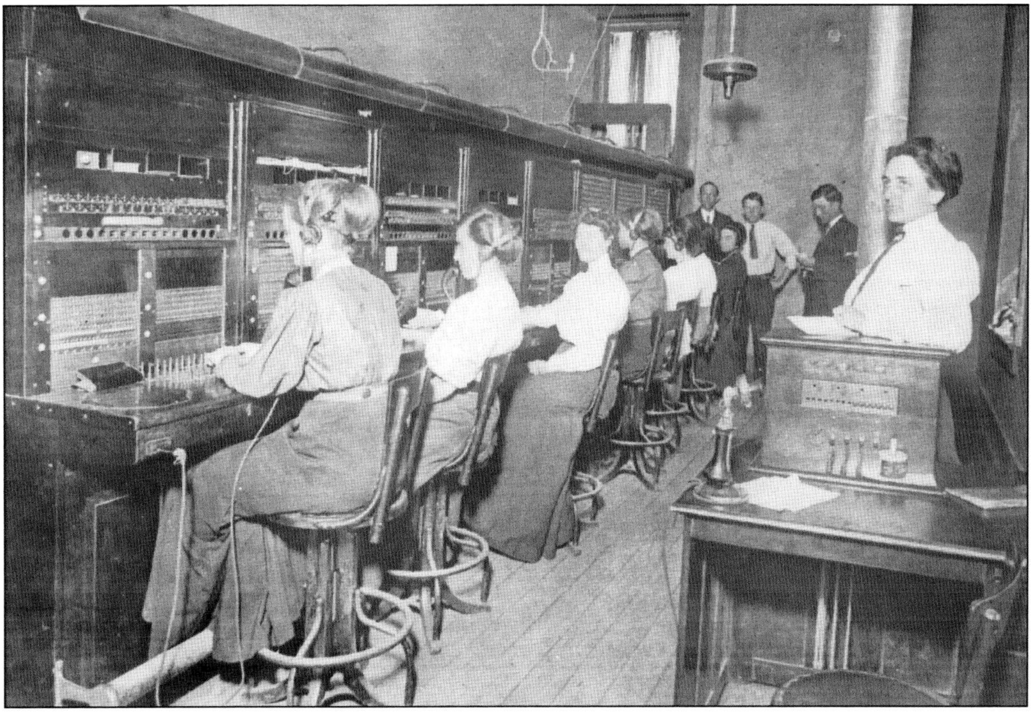

The telephone company local exchange in March 1910 was on the second floor of 103 College Avenue in a building once used by the post office. The switchboard operators and supervisors are, from left to right, "Jodie" Huddleston; Winnie McCarty; Sally Baggett; Pearl Walker; three unidentified; Mr. Laney, the manager; Horner Story; Sam Turrentine, a volunteer fireman; and Mary Park, chief operator. (Martha McClung.)

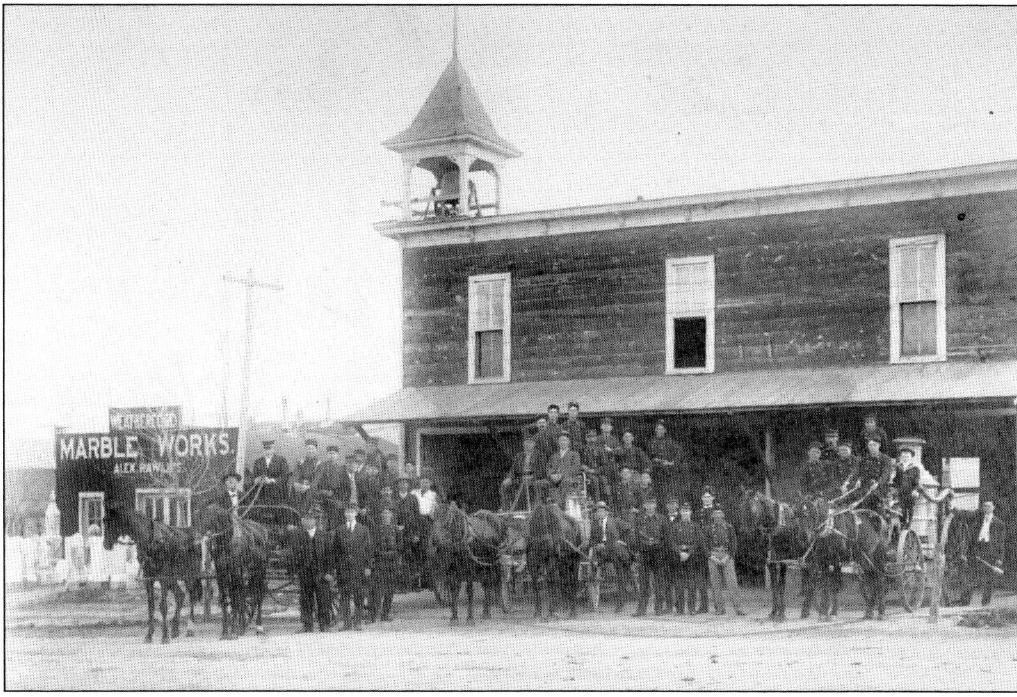

The three companies in the Weatherford Volunteer Fire Department are pictured here on January 24, 1909. Fire equipment was drawn by man until the first horse-drawn teams were used. (WL.)

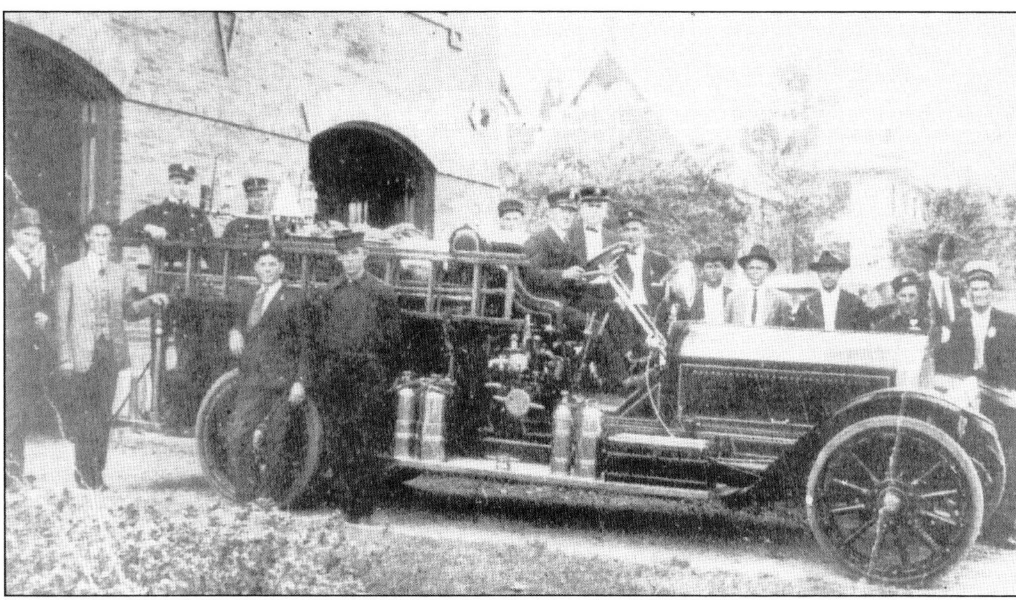

When chemicals ran out and the fires continued, the 1913 LaFrance chemical pumper was quickly sold. In the early 1920s, Veal Carroll (right) was chief with the new 1917 LaFrance water pumper. (WL.)

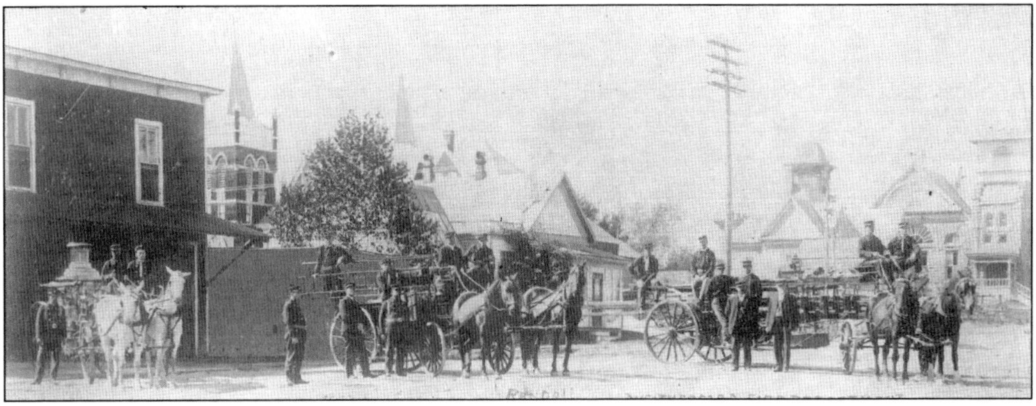

The volunteer Fire Chief William Waldock, shown here fourth from left in this January 24, 1909 photograph, was a local butcher. Randall Photo Studio is in the house to the right of the station. In the far background, to the right of the telephone pole, is the earliest frame building of First Baptist Church, which was sold in 1897. At right is that church's second sanctuary. (WL.)

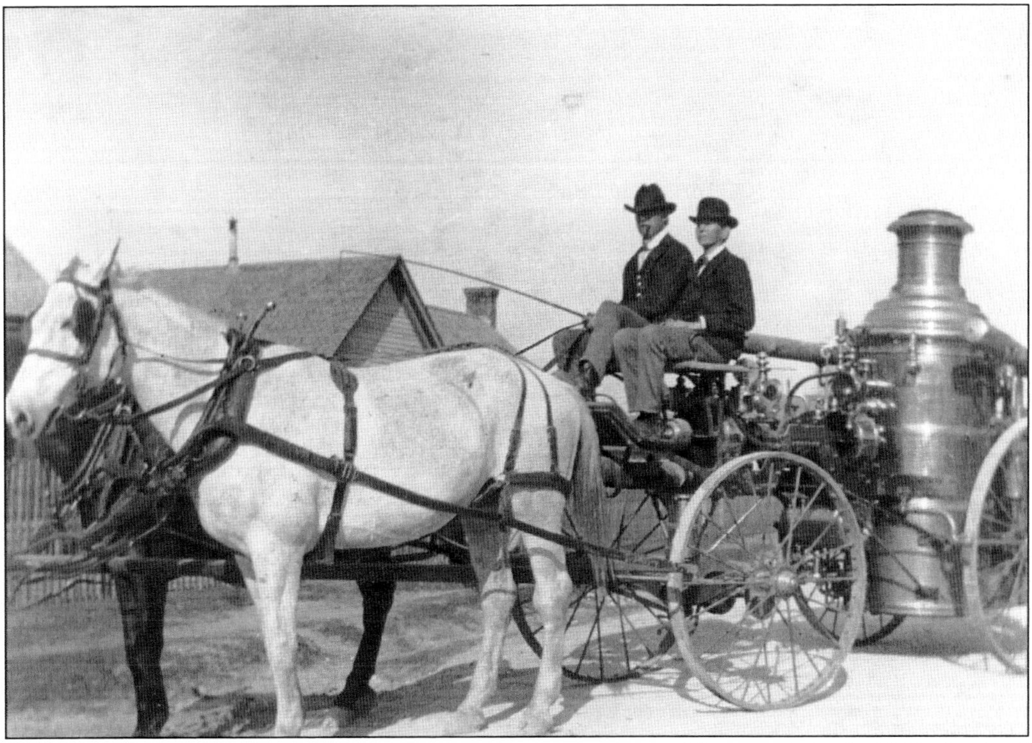

The Silsby Steam Pumper "Engine Company #1" is pictured here in March 1902. Its final fire call was the Haynes Opera House in March 1914. It stood as a memorial at the firehouse until scrapped. The highly trained horses were named "Bob" and "John" for two respected firemen, Bob Norton and John R. Brown. (Weatherford Fire Department via Fire Captain Craig Swancy.)

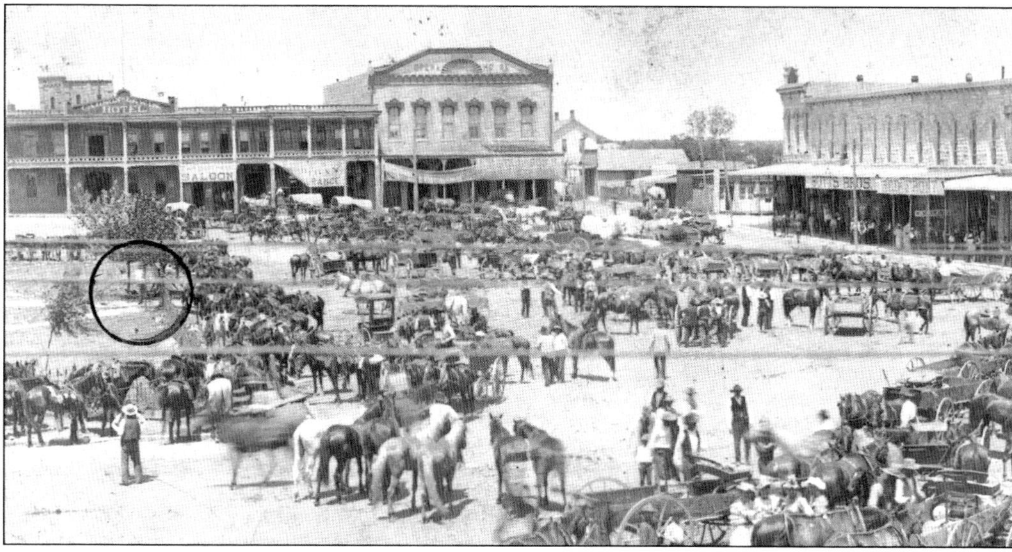

This was not the usual trade's day. The wagons are empty. The circled area reveals the reason for the gathering. Justice was meted sometime between 1888 and 1900. (Zan Statham.)

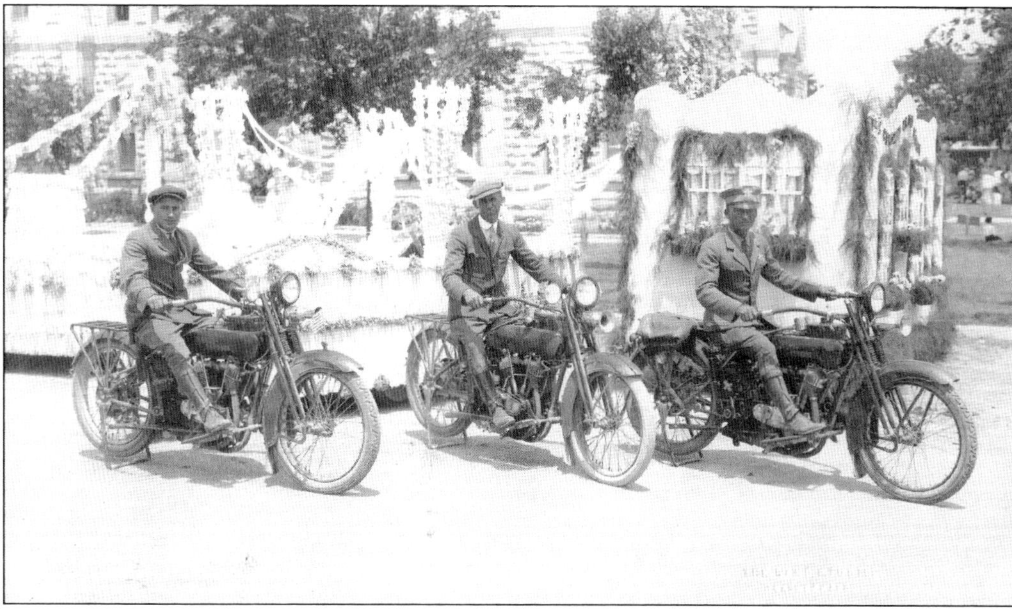

In 1925, two parade escorts new to the police force, Arthur Boyton (left) and Tom Gray (center), join the first uniformed motorcycle policeman, Mr. Gentry, all on 1916 Harley-Davidson motorcycles. Gentry's motorcycle was painted differently from the others. (Richard Pina.)

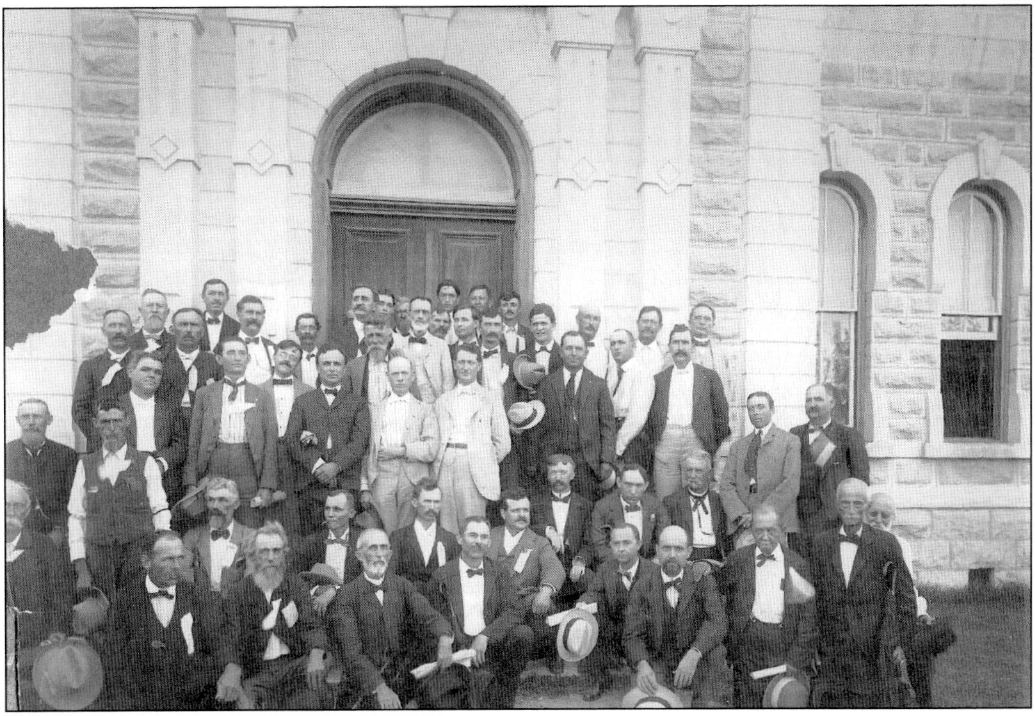

Court is not in session. Judges, lawyers, and bailiffs pose in this damaged photograph from the 1890s. (WL.)

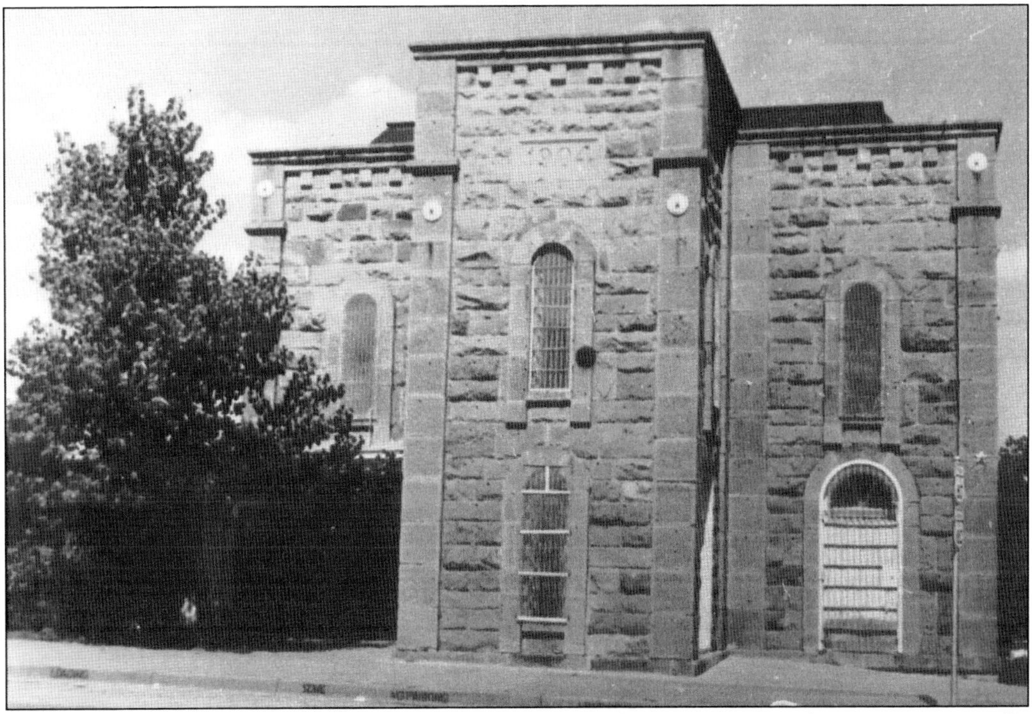

The city jail, 200 Palo Pinto Street, was built from sandstone in 1904. The structure initially had a third floor. The jail was torn down in 1962. (Jon Vandagriff.)

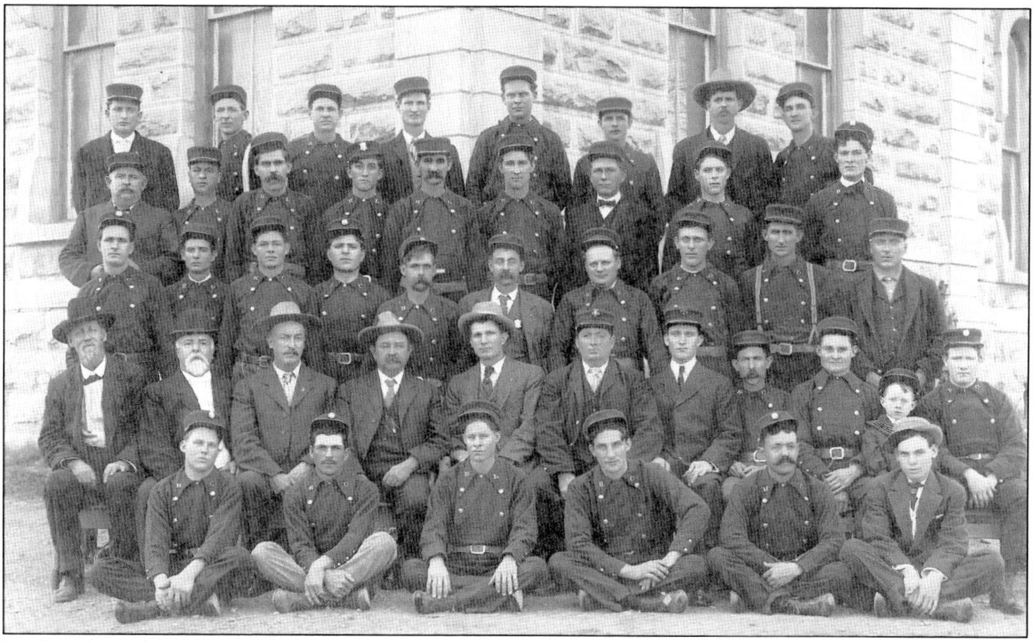

In this formal portrait in 1909 of the police, sheriffs, marshalls, and volunteer fire department, the following men are identified: (second row) Colonel George Bowie, second from left; John R. Brown, fourth from left; and William Waldock, fire chief, sixth from left; (fifth row) Deputy Sheriff "Sang" Gilbert, in the stetson. (WL.)

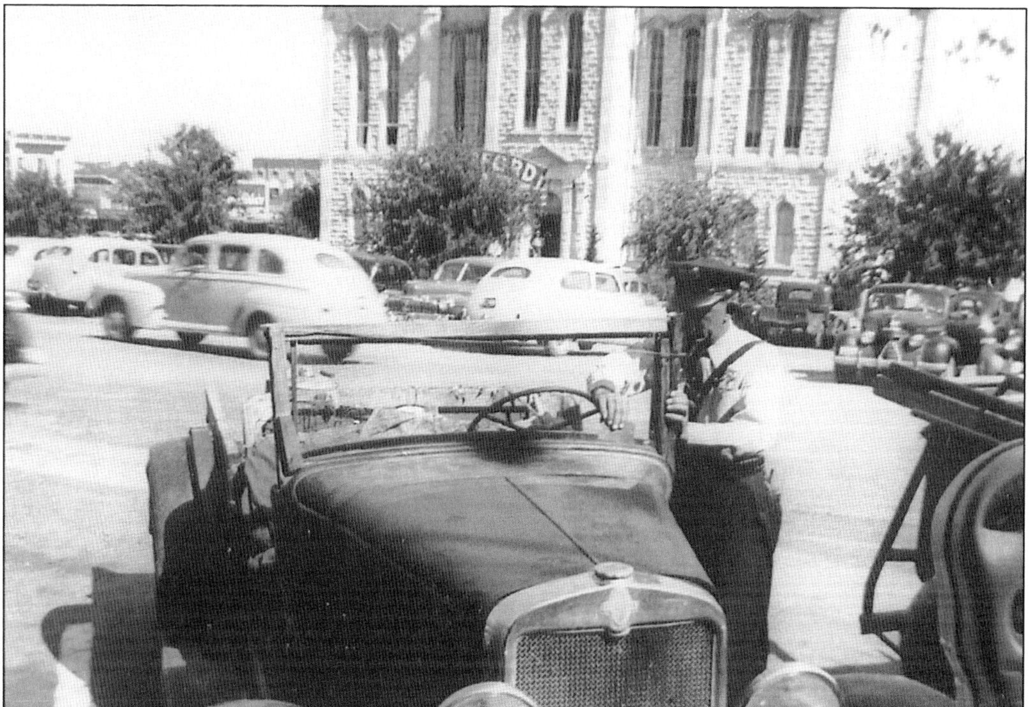

From the 1940s, Patrolman Raymond Anderson gave parking tickets for many decades from his three-wheel motorcycle. (Ed Brown.)

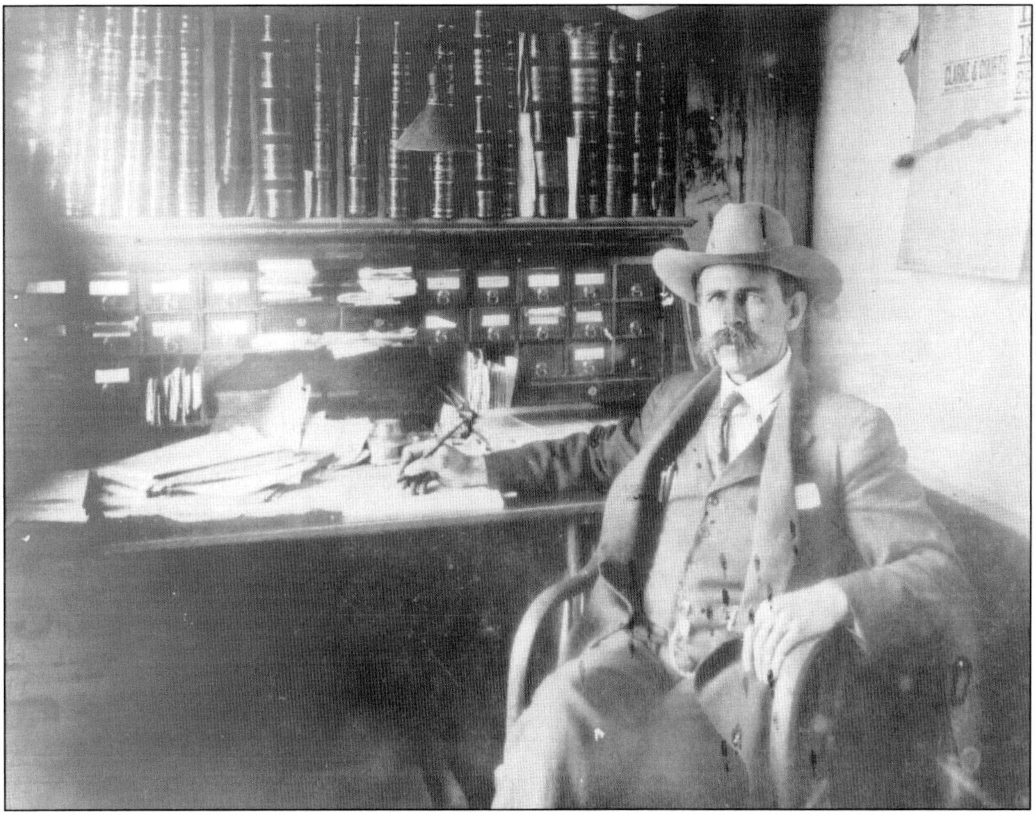

Henry Nelson was the deputy sheriff from 1906 to 1910. (Sheriff's Office via Jay Brown.)

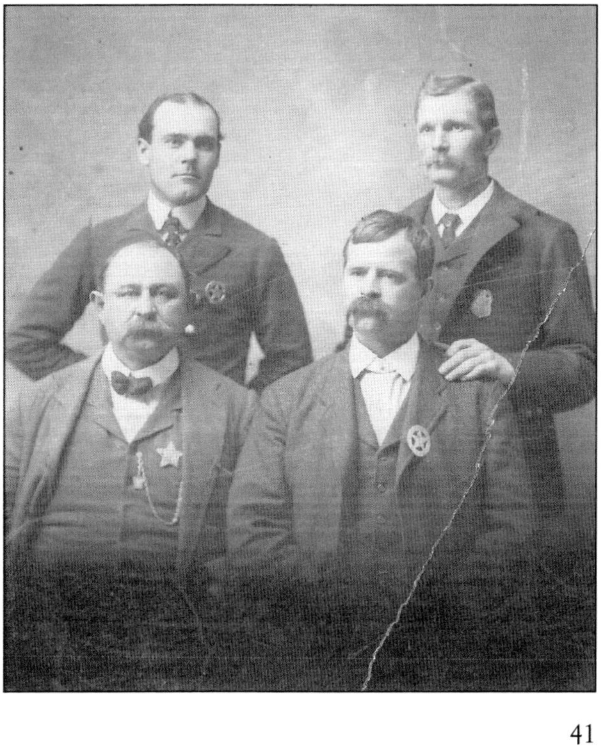

John R. Brown (left front) was marshall until he ran for sheriff in 1918. He was never shot at, shot anyone, or had any escape. Jim Burrows (right front), former city alderman, was police chief with badge number one. At rear are Omar Penland (left), deputy police chief, and Gus Boswell (right), fireman. (Weatherford Fire Department via Fire Captain Craig Swancy.)

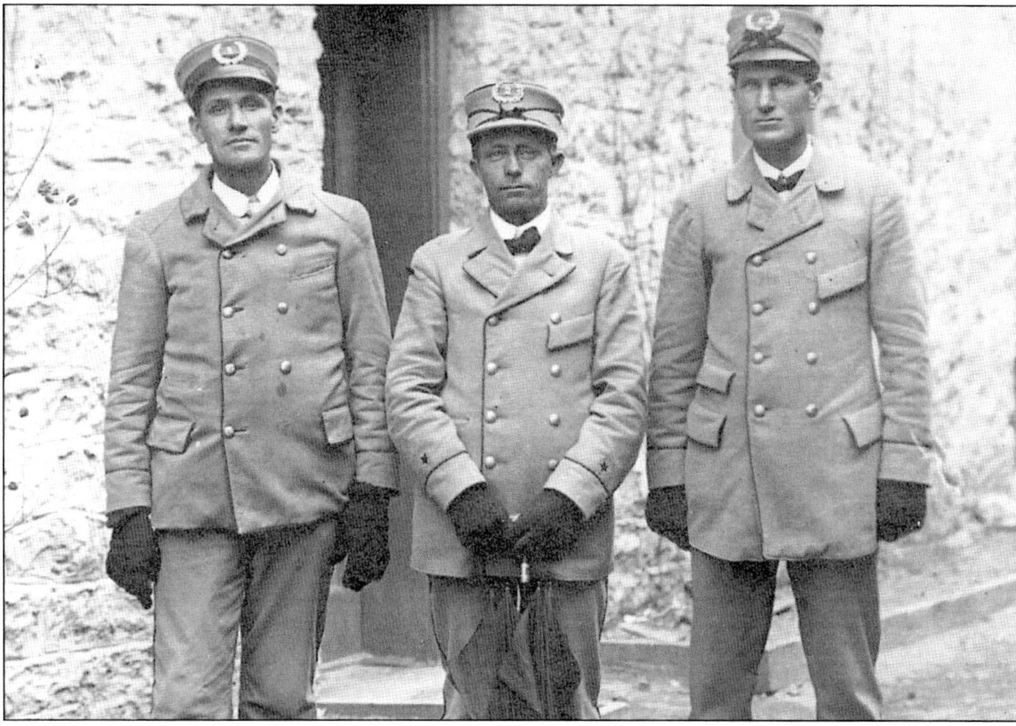

The U.S. Post Office was at 132 York Avenue between 1908 and 1914. The alley behind the post office made a unique setting to pose postal workers W.C. Jones, W.R. Witherspoon, and J.N. Ward. The alley looks the same. (Bill Witherspoon.)

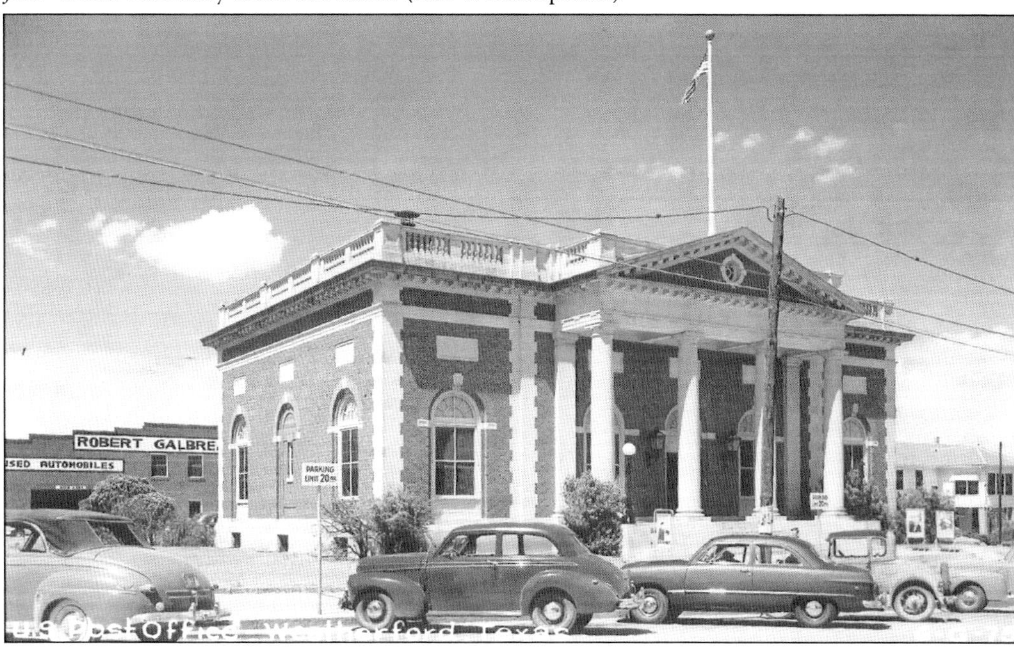

The U.S. Post Office, 109 Fort Worth Street, was built in the Greek Revival style. It is seen here about 1949–50; it opened on December 26, 1914, and closed in October 1996. The building was then purchased by the county for courtrooms. (Bill Witherspoon.)

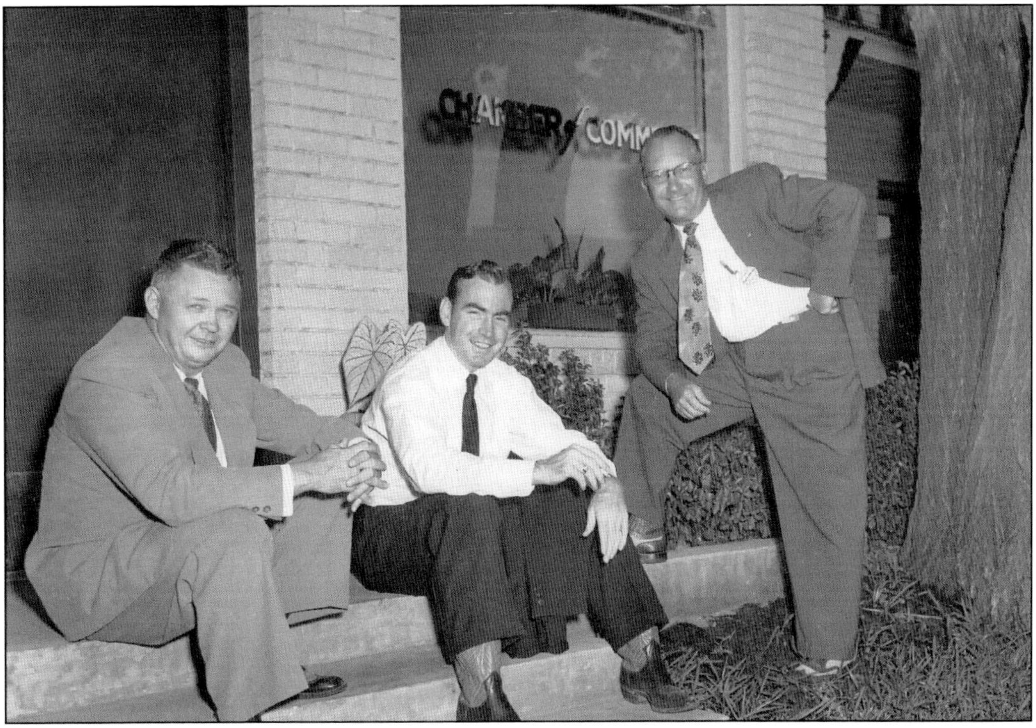

The Weatherford Chamber of Commerce has moved many times. In the early 1950s it was in the tiny building at 109 Palo Pinto. Civic leaders Ben McAdams (left) and Harold Coney (right) flank Mayor Jim Wright, who became U.S. congressman, then Speaker of the House of Representatives. (Chamber of Commerce.)

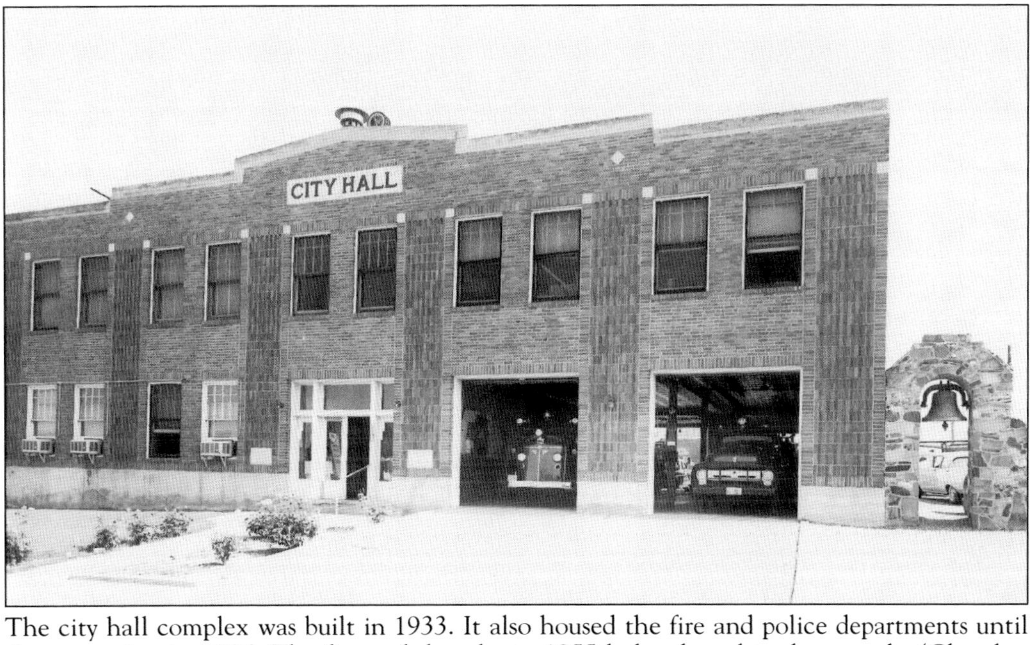

The city hall complex was built in 1933. It also housed the fire and police departments until the expansion in 1986. The firetruck bought in 1955 helps date this photograph. (Chamber of Commerce.)

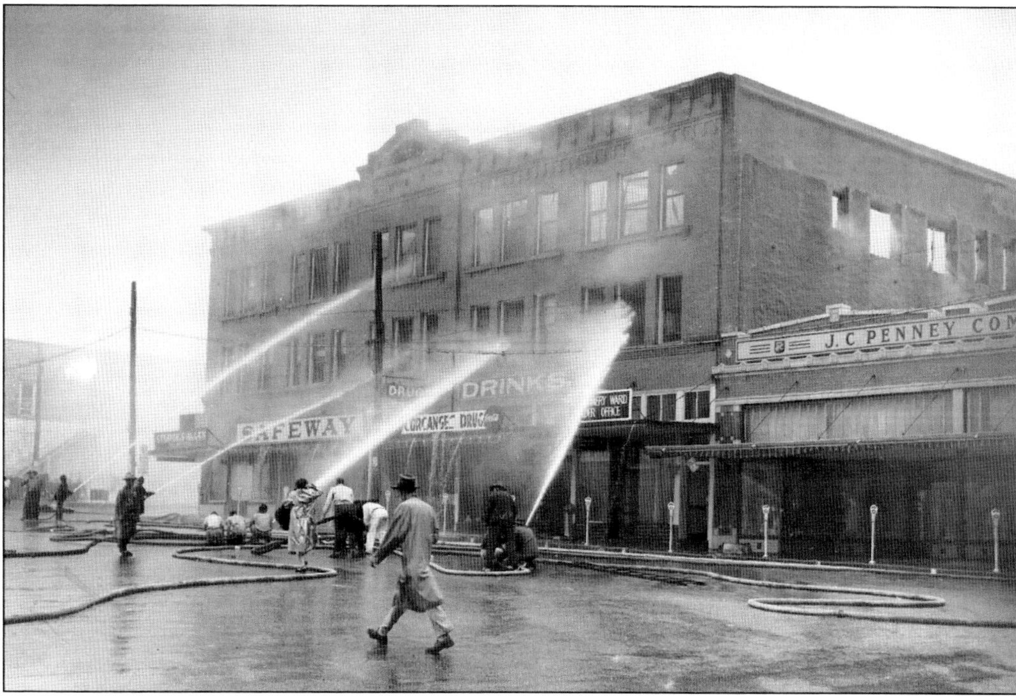

The final fire call for the city's first motorized firetruck, the old 1917 LaFrance, was the Kuteman Building in 1951. The old Carson and Lewis Hotel was replaced by the Kuteman Building in 1910. (Chamber of Commerce.)

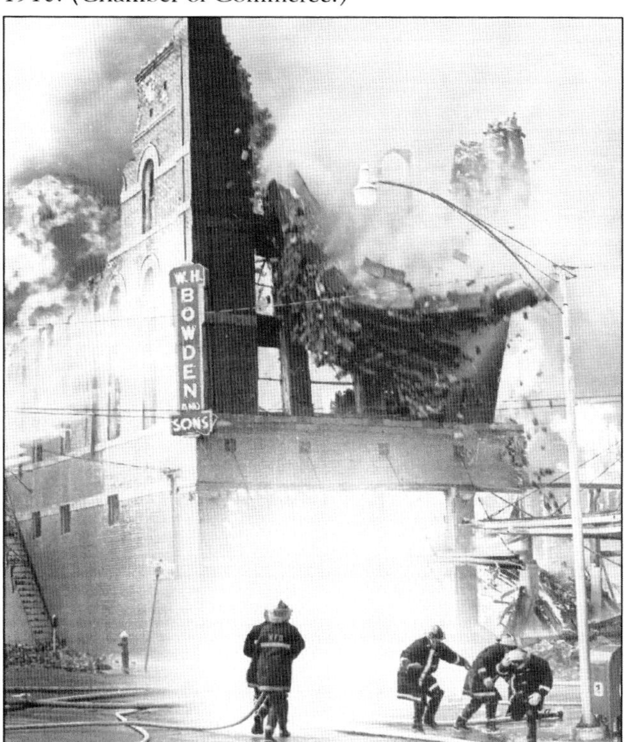

Built in 1902, the Lowe-Carter Hardware, Baker-Poston Dry Goods, and W.H. Bowden's and Sons Dry Goods building burned on the day before Easter in 1980. (Chamber of Commerce.)

Four

Homes and Gardens

Log cabins and clapboard homes were the beginning, yet storybook homes of gingerbread with fairy tale gardens are reality in Weatherford. The difference is the people! This wonderland of homes promoted fine art, artists, actors, singers, and even state and national politicians.

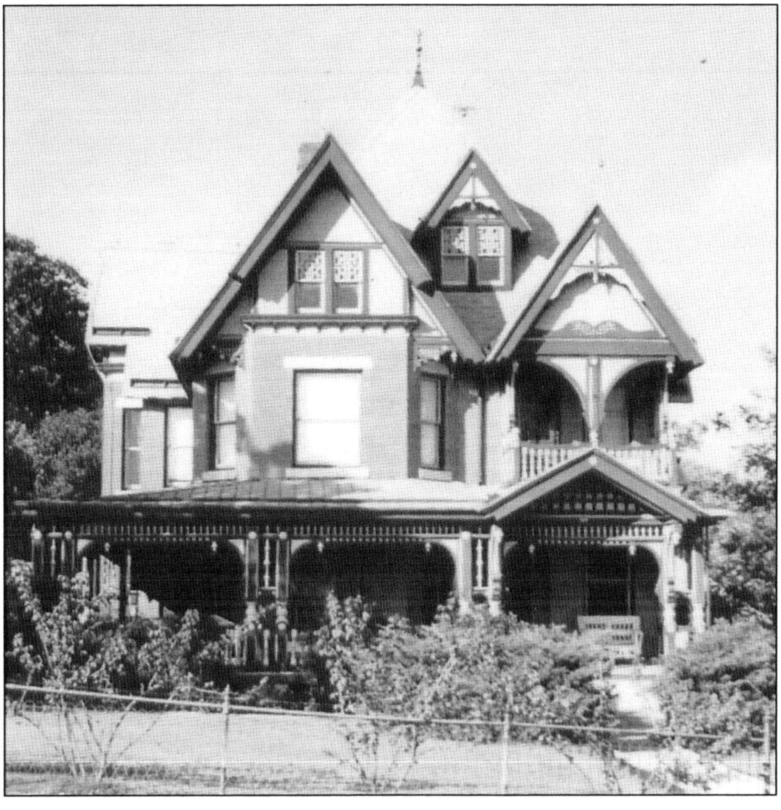

At 508 South Davis is the sole brick Victorian home in Weatherford. Cattleman-banker George S. White had it built in 1892. It is very striking with almost orange brick and green gingerbread details. The coach house had room for a horse stall and three carriages with servant quarters above. A pond, gazebo, and garden in a grove of large oak trees were part of an early campground. (Glenn Anderson.)

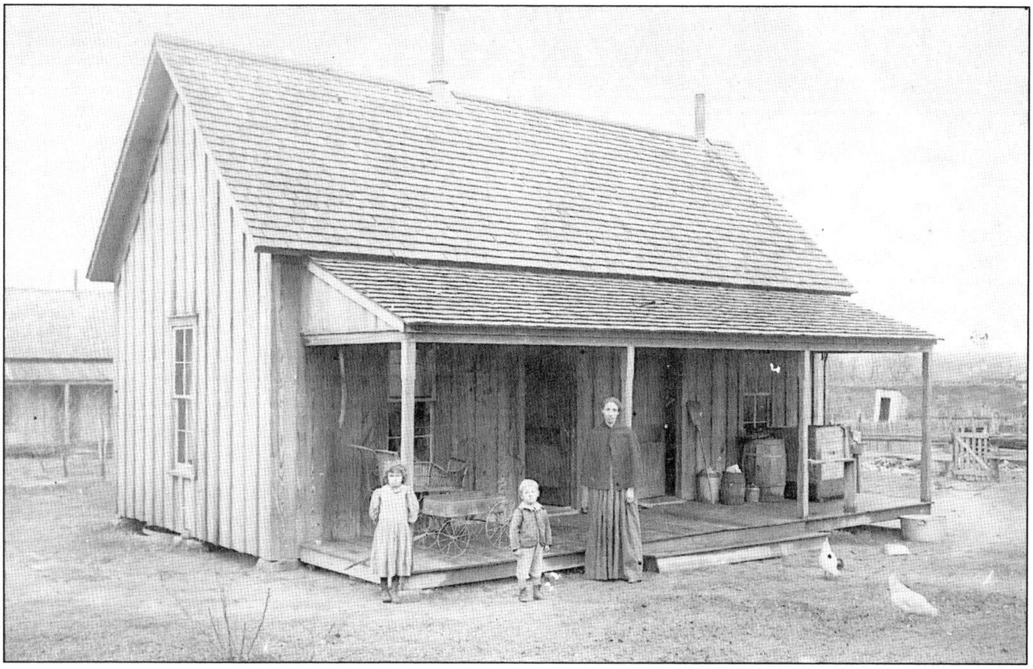

The Thomas R. Waters home at 406 Eureka Street is pictured in this 1896 photograph. Mrs. Laura Sisk Waters poses with her six-year-old daughter, Lee, and son, Berry. Eureka Street was very rural compared to its appearance today. (WL.)

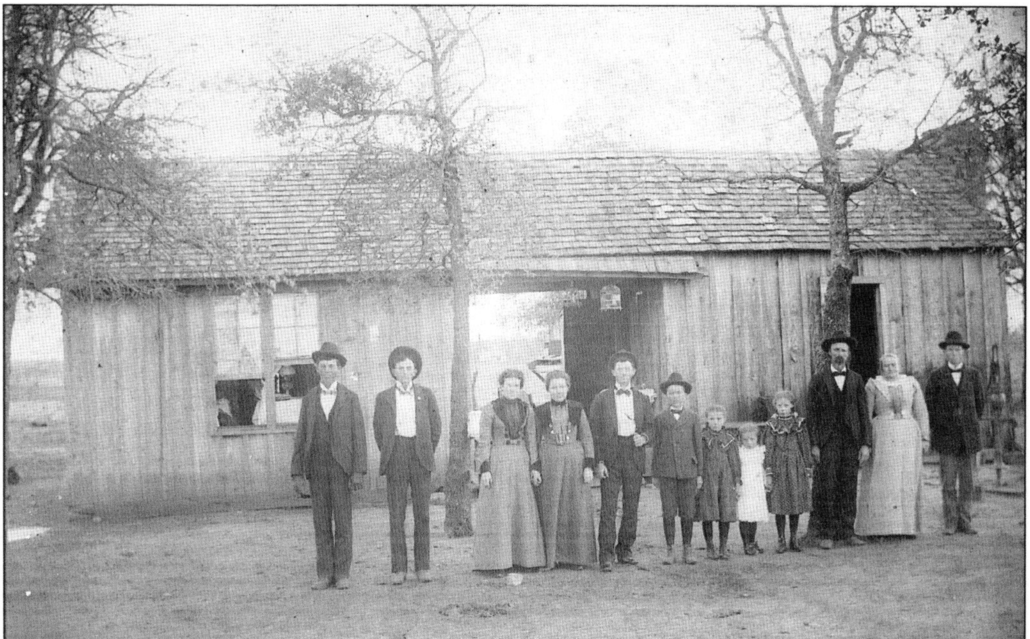

Sunday dinner brought the Scarlett and Huddleston families together. The "dog run" between the two rooms was also typical of the earlier log cabins. (Don Huddleston.)

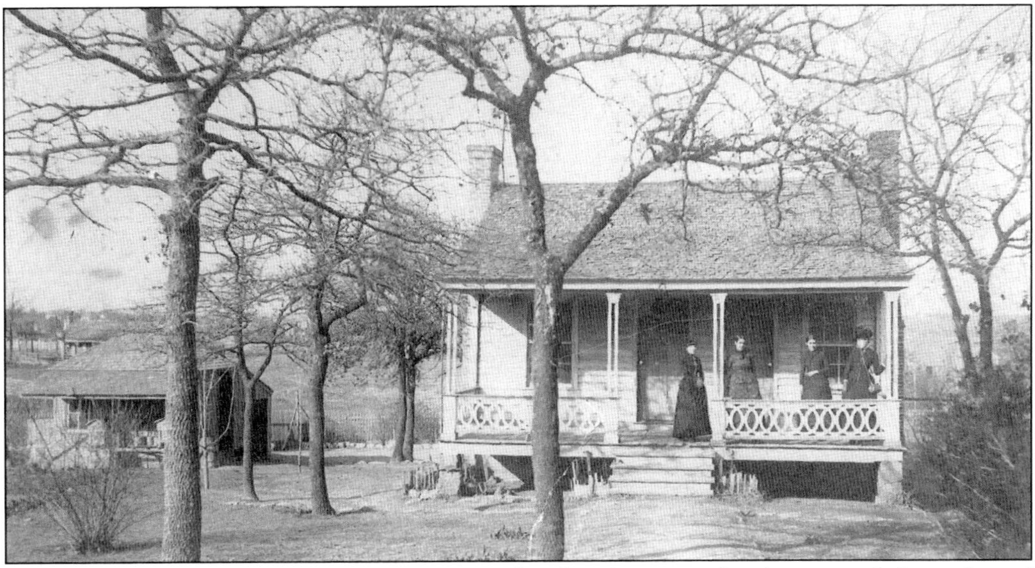

The C.C. Baker Transfer Company magnate first lived in a modest home, with his wife and three daughters. The three sisters taught music their entire lives. (WL.)

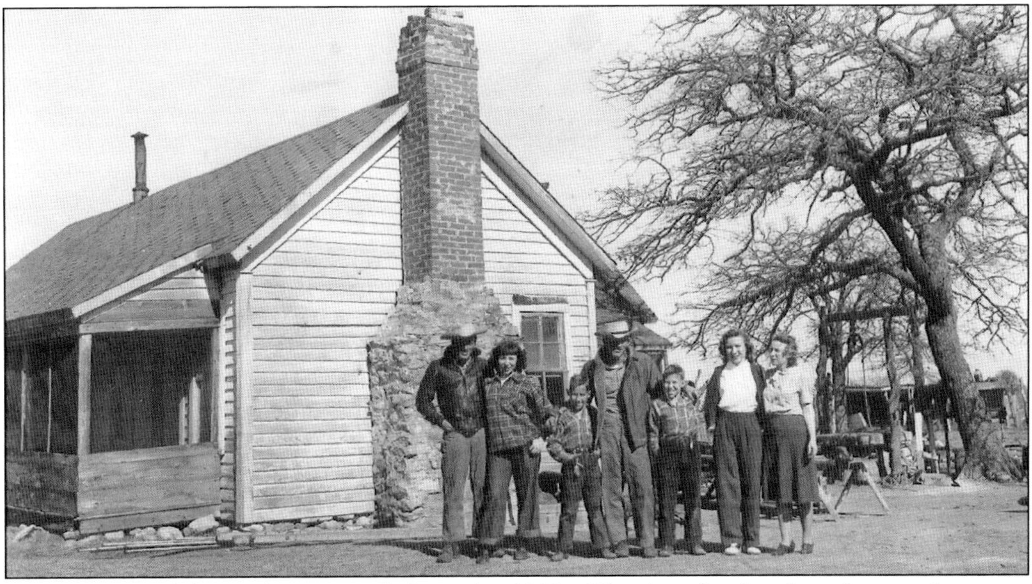

Ranch homes did not change much from the 1890s. The Ancelin family welcomes their new addition, Jim Guay, to Weatherford ranch life in January 1947. Jim is with his new bride, Mary Ellen Ancelin Guay, and David Ancelin, *Jean* Hartnett Ancelin, Donald Ancelin, Barbara Ancelin, and Daisy Hartnett Ancelin. (Mary Ellen Guay.)

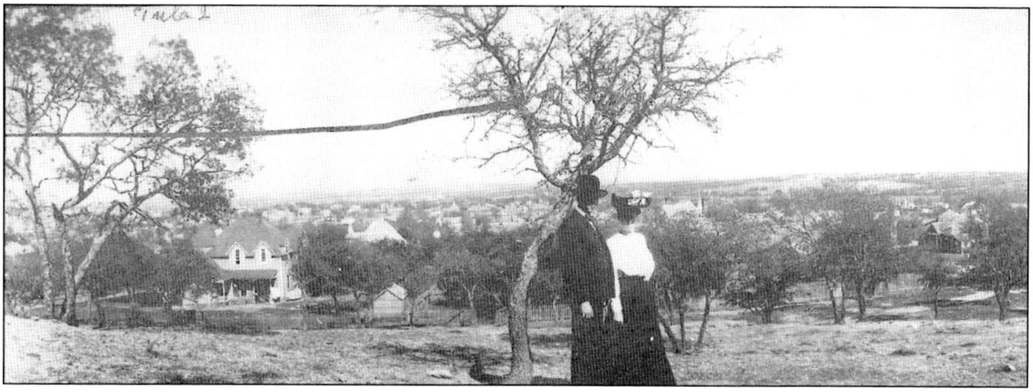

Looking northeast toward town, Sallie and Sam Taylor pose atop Oyster Hill c. 1900. The hill is so named for the fossils in the *caliche* rock formation. The hill was well known for "sparking." Governor Samuel W.T. Lanham's 1871 home is in the immediate left background. The final Civil War veteran to be Texas governor, Lanham served two terms. (Kirk Martin via James H. Doss.)

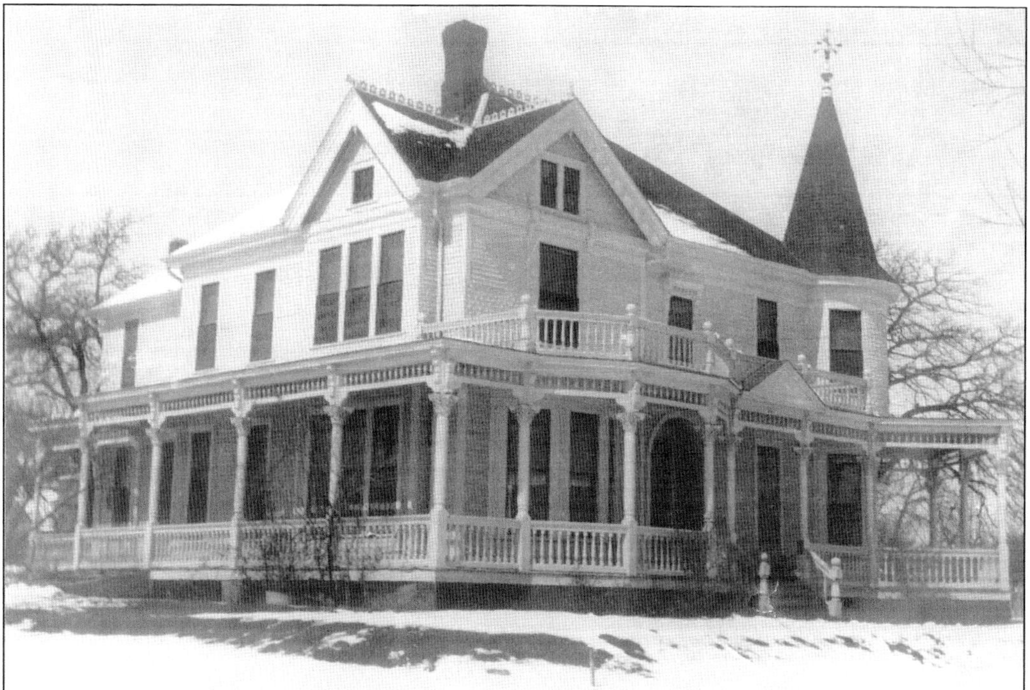

The hardware merchant John R. Lewis built this stately home at 904 South Main in 1899. With ten children, the family's Queen Anne-style home was just big enough. (WL.)

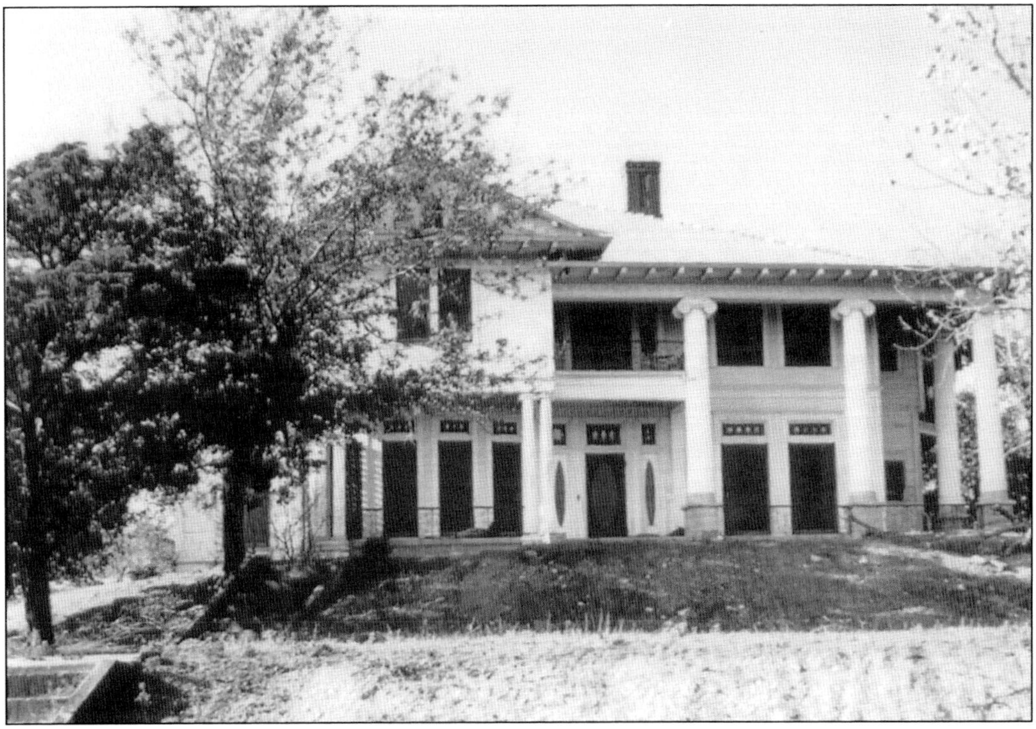

The late Dr. William M. Campbell's home at 201 West Rentz Street is on a hill overlooking Weatherford. Campbell Memorial Hospital is named in his memory. Built in 1902 by Weatherford pioneer Judge Walter F. Carter, the home has Victorian- and Greek Revival–style details. (Glenn Anderson.)

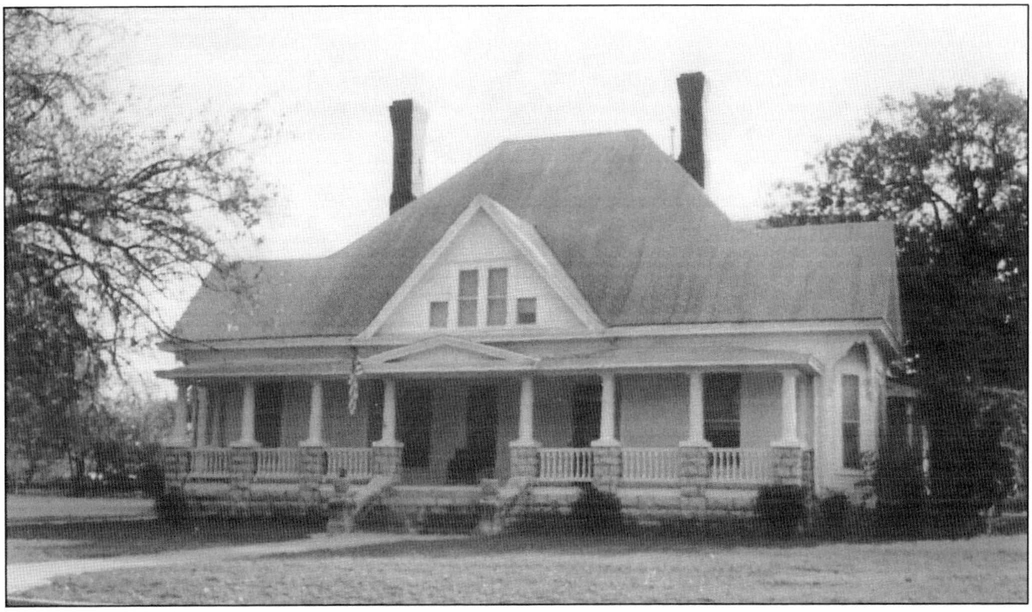

Dr. John R. MacKenzie was a prisoner of the Yankees in the Civil War. His family finally settled at 202 East Lee in 1900 just before his death. His nephew, Dr. Bill MacKenzie, practiced here. After his death in 1935, Weatherford College used the home for a boys' dormitory. (WL.)

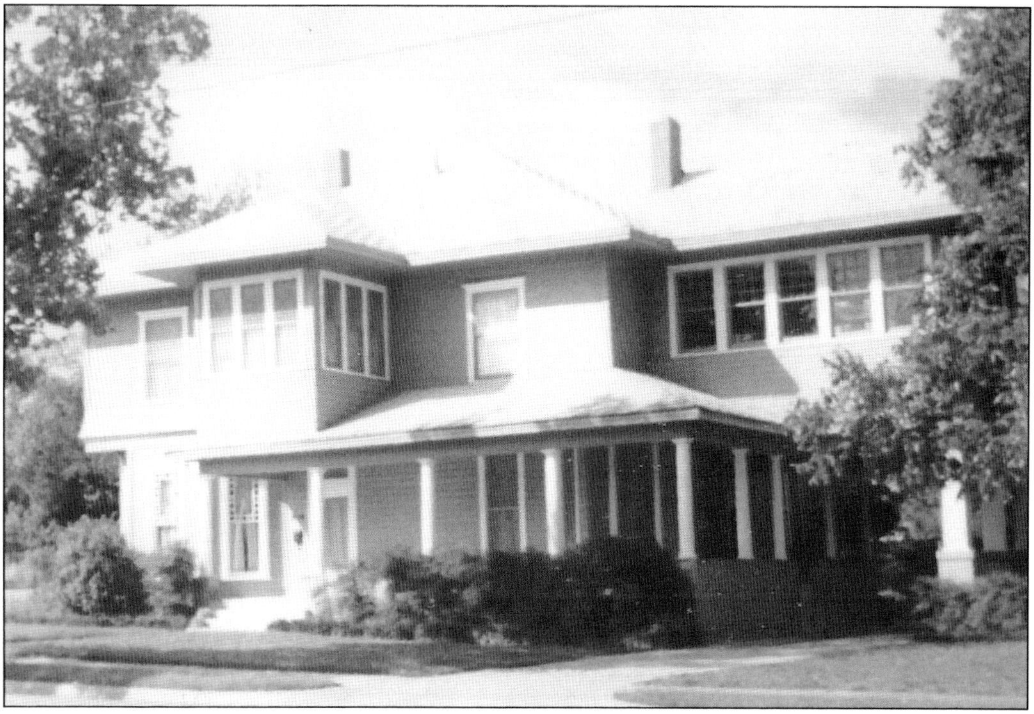

Actress Mary Martin was born at 414 West Lee in 1913. It was built by J.D. Baker in 1894. Upon purchase in 1907, Preston and Juanita Martin had a second story added. They moved in 1924 to West Oak. (Bernice Roberts.)

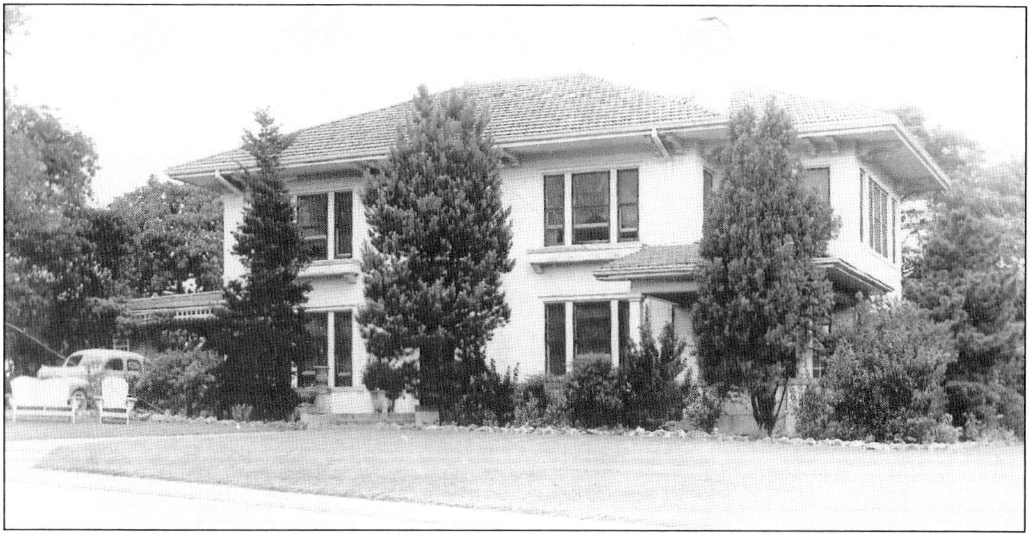

This is a photograph of Mary Martin's and, her son's, Larry Hagman, childhood home at 314 West Oak Street. It was built from cast concrete with 13-inch walls in 1918 by banker Robert W. Davis. It is said that a planter box out the second-floor window occasionally hid Mary's diary! (WL.)

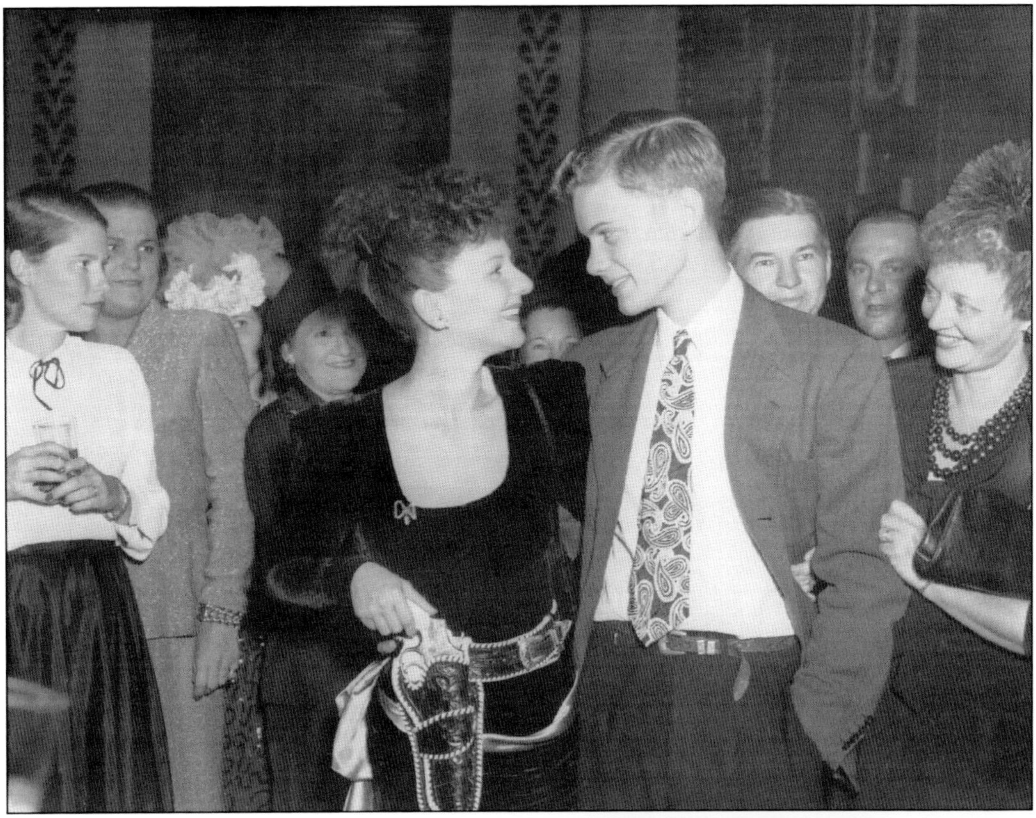

Promoting *Annie Get Your Gun* (1948), Mary Martin is met by her teenage son, Larry Hagman. Broadway and Hollywood kept her away from the hometown she often spoke of so proudly. (WC.)

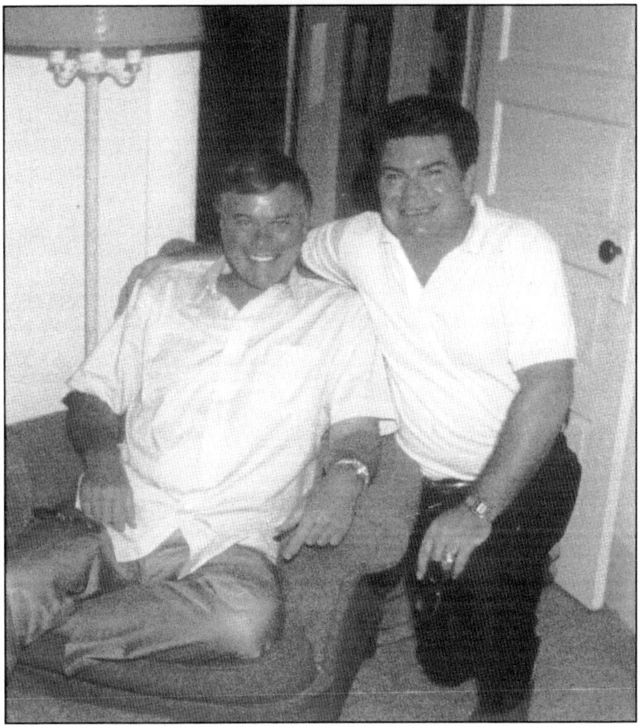

Larry visits with his brother, at Gary's home in 1985. Larry had his own turn in television with *I Dream of Genie* and *Dallas*. (Gary and Linda Hagman.)

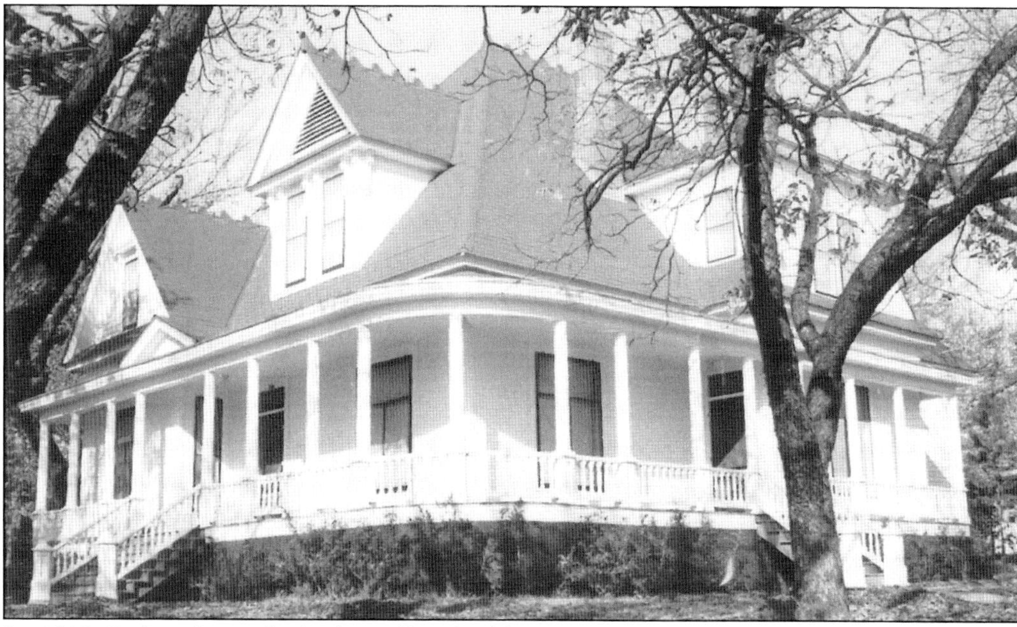

In 1902, Robert Lowe built the tallest building in town, the Lowe-Carter Hardware. His Victorian home was finished in 1899 at 202 West Oak. In 1939, his family sold the home to James C. Wright, whose son was later Weatherford's mayor, a U.S. congressman, and the Speaker of the U.S. House of Representatives. (Bill Witherspoon.)

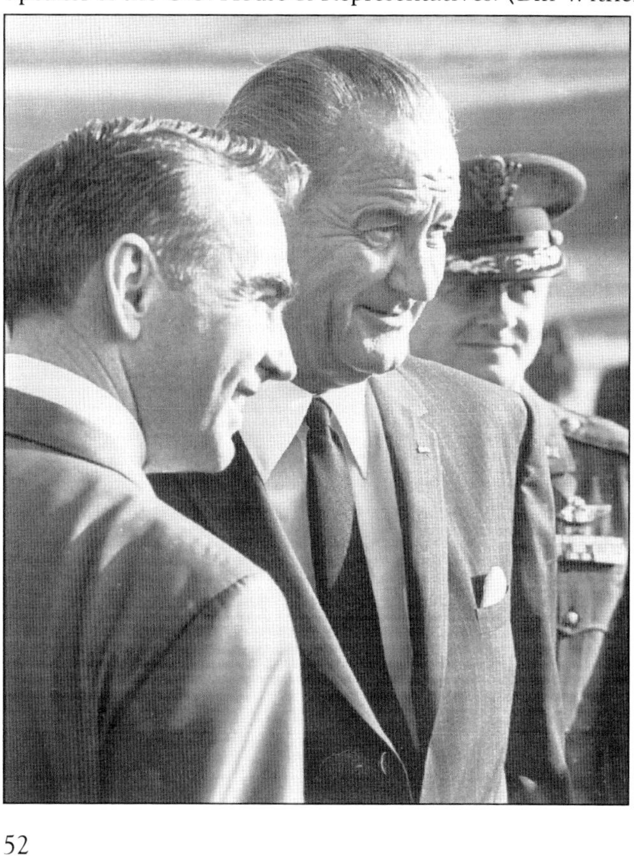

Congressman Jim Wright meets with the first U.S. president from Texas. (WC.)

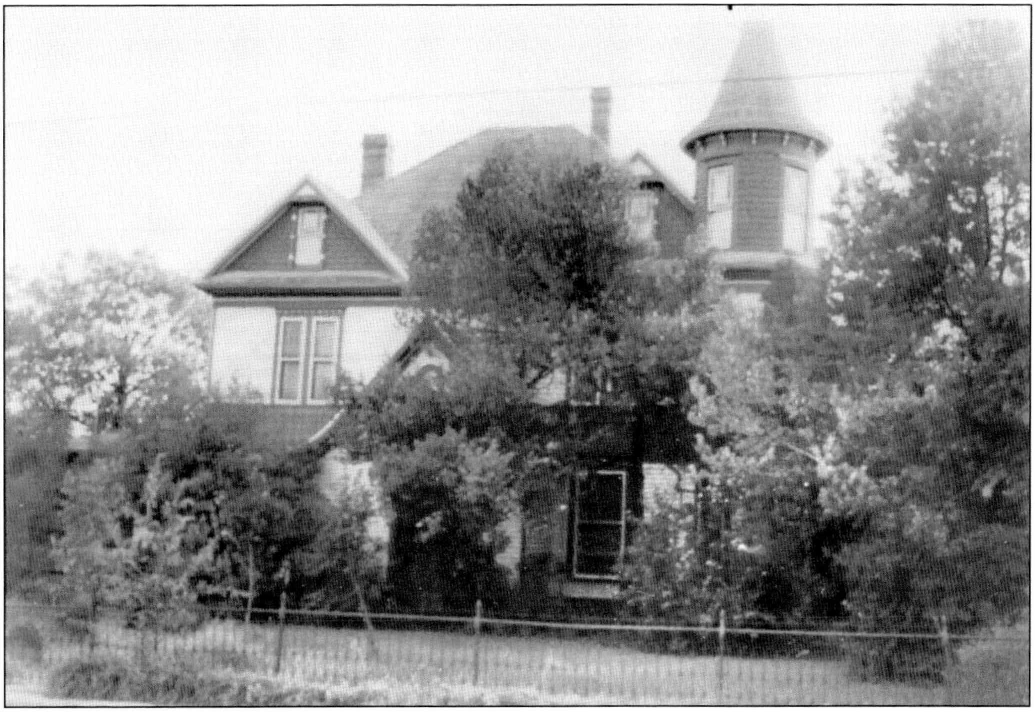

J.T. Cotton built this home at 208 East Oak in 1896. The Knights of Pythias orphans home is here due to his efforts. Their son, Fred Cotton, was the patriarch of Weatherford's history. Fred's daughter, Virginia Cotton Scott, still operates the Cotton-Bratton Furniture Store and Funeral Home, and former state representative James Cotton still lives in the family home. (Bill Witherspoon.)

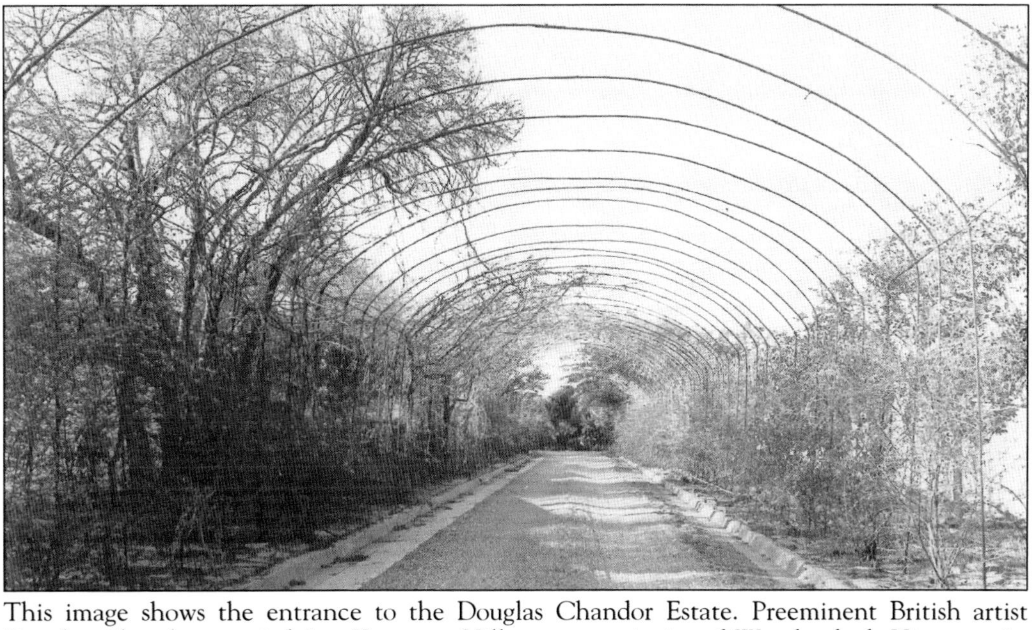

This image shows the entrance to the Douglas Chandor Estate. Preeminent British artist Douglas Chandor married Ina Kuteman Hill, concert pianist of Weatherford. His portraits include presidents, prime ministers, kings, and queens. (Chamber of Commerce.)

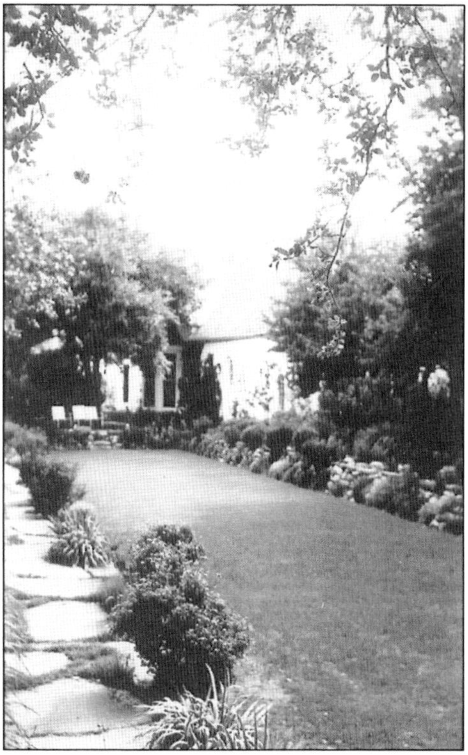

He designed "White Shadows," a beautiful 7-acre English garden, one of Weatherford's wonders, from the *caliche* rock. This view looks south toward the Chandor home's entrance across the bowling green. (Weatherford Heritage Gallery.)

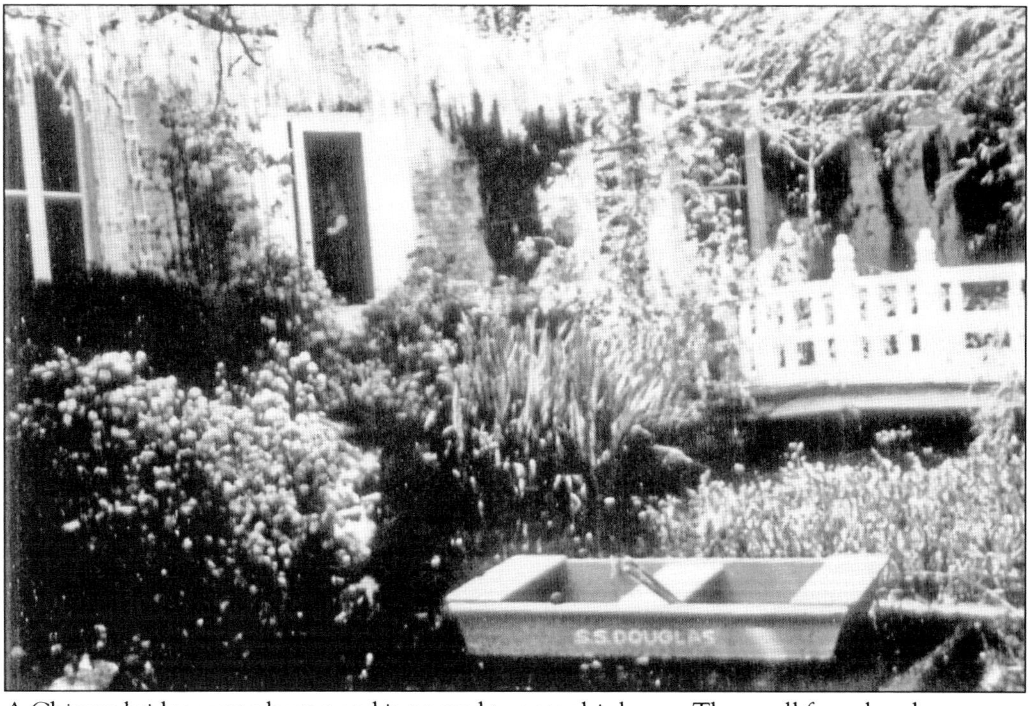

A Chinese bridge over a huge pond is crossed to enter his home. The small foyer barely prepares one for Chandor's huge studio, with a huge north window for ideal lighting, now a palatial dining room. Note the rowboat named S.S. *Douglas*. (Weatherford Heritage Gallery.)

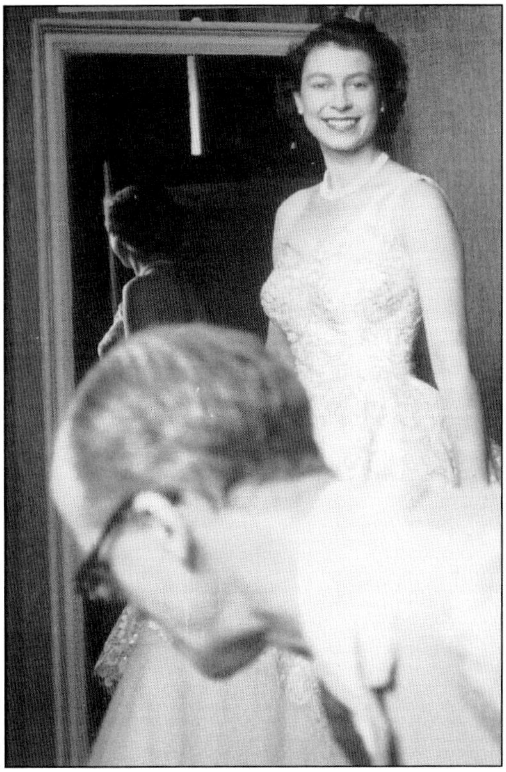

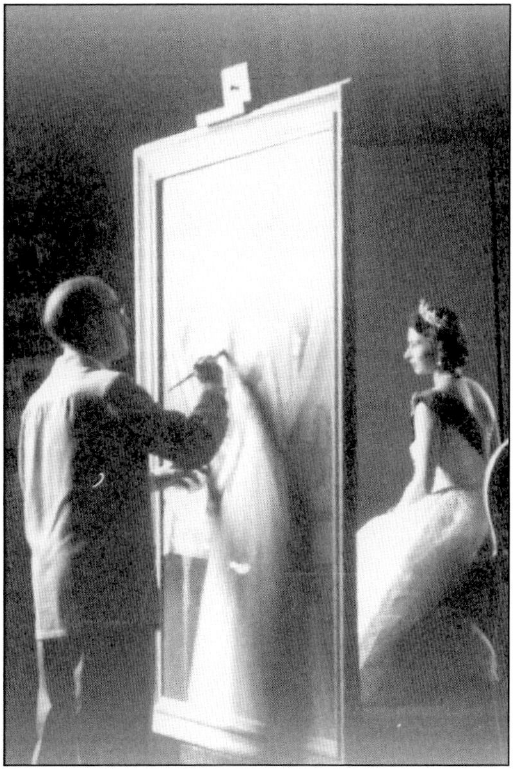

The young queen of England sits for her coronation portrait with artist Douglas Chandor, in Buckingham Palace. (Melody Bradford.)

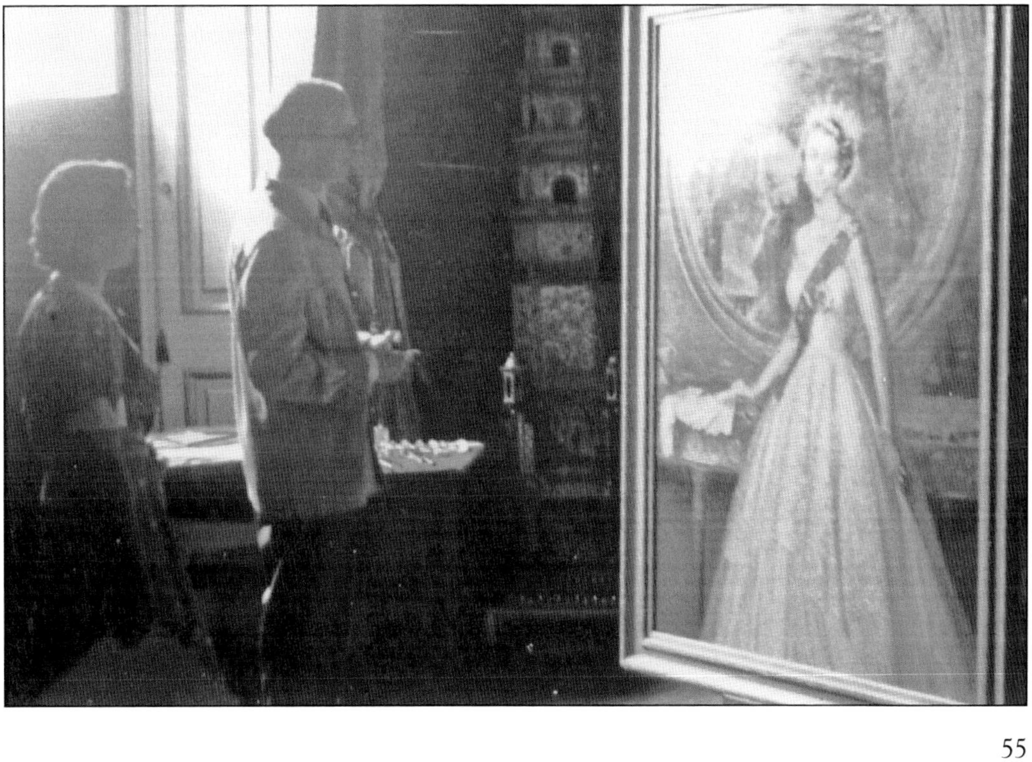

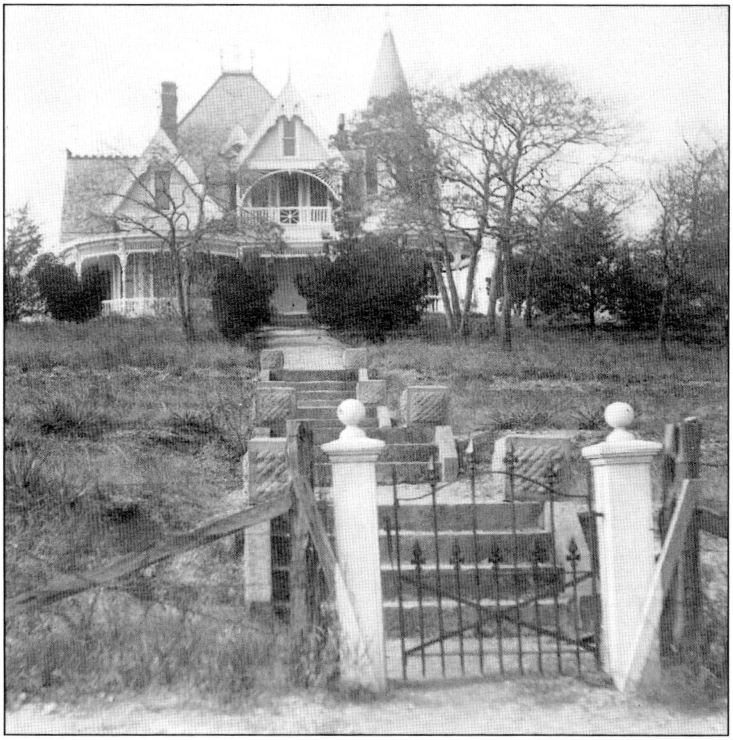

Sam Shadle Jr. was 18 when he took this photograph in 1915 of the W.E. Tate home at 808 South Lamar. The beautiful Queen Anne-Victorian arched home was built in 1897. (WL.)

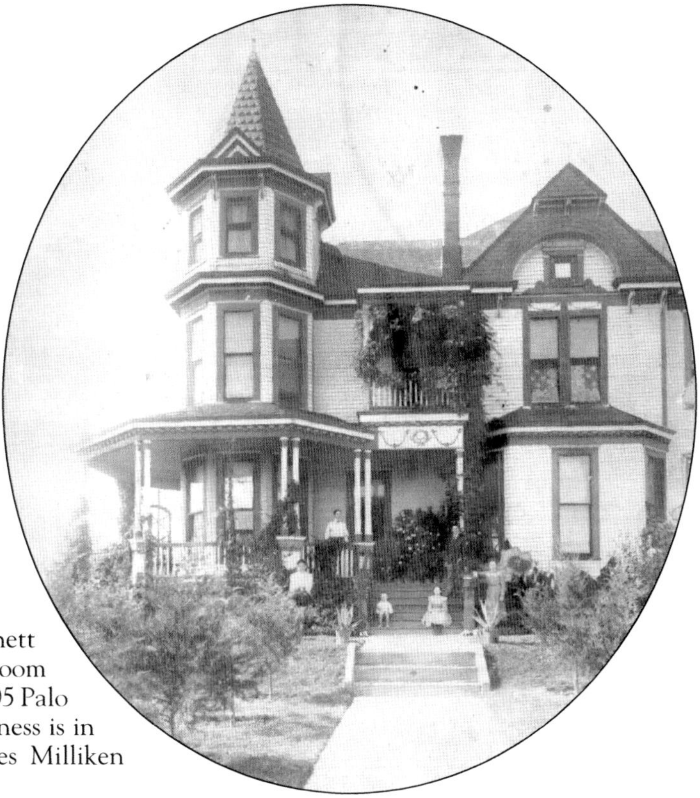

Wholesale grocer C.D. Hartnett built this large seven-bedroom Victorian home on a hill at 1105 Palo Pinto Street in 1896. His business is in its fourth generation. (Charles Milliken via Sylvia Eidson.)

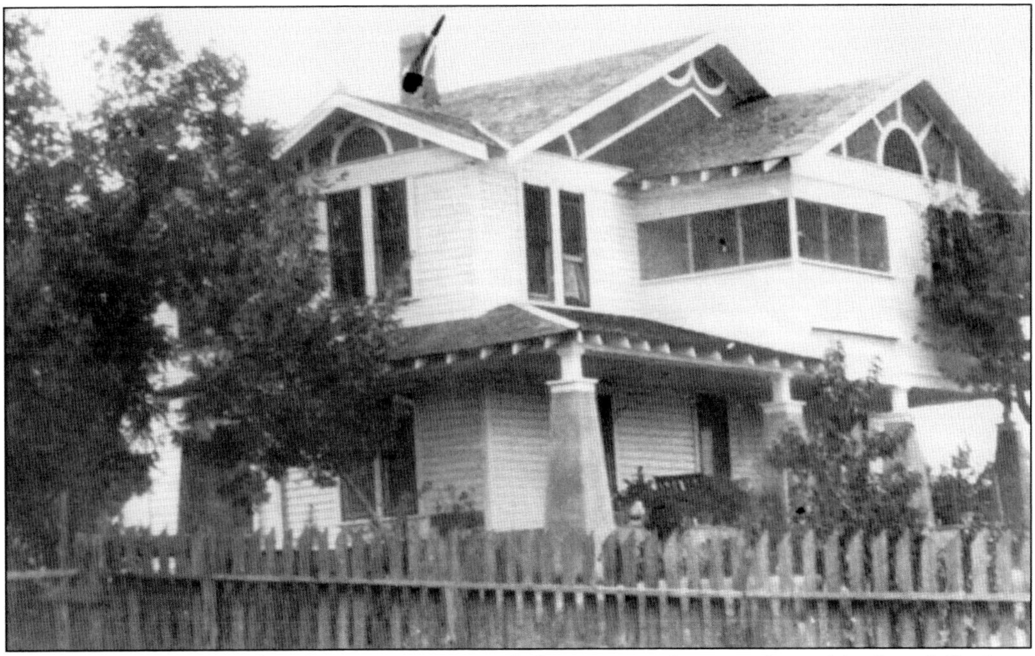

The home at 804 South Alamo Street is nestled in a quiet historical neighborhood. Built in 1898 as a Victorian home by M.S. Gordon, it was similar to the one he constructed next door. It was modified into a two-story Greek Revival style in 1915 by merchant J.W. Rummage, whose family lived here until 1940. (Bernice Roberts via Beth Lewellyn.)

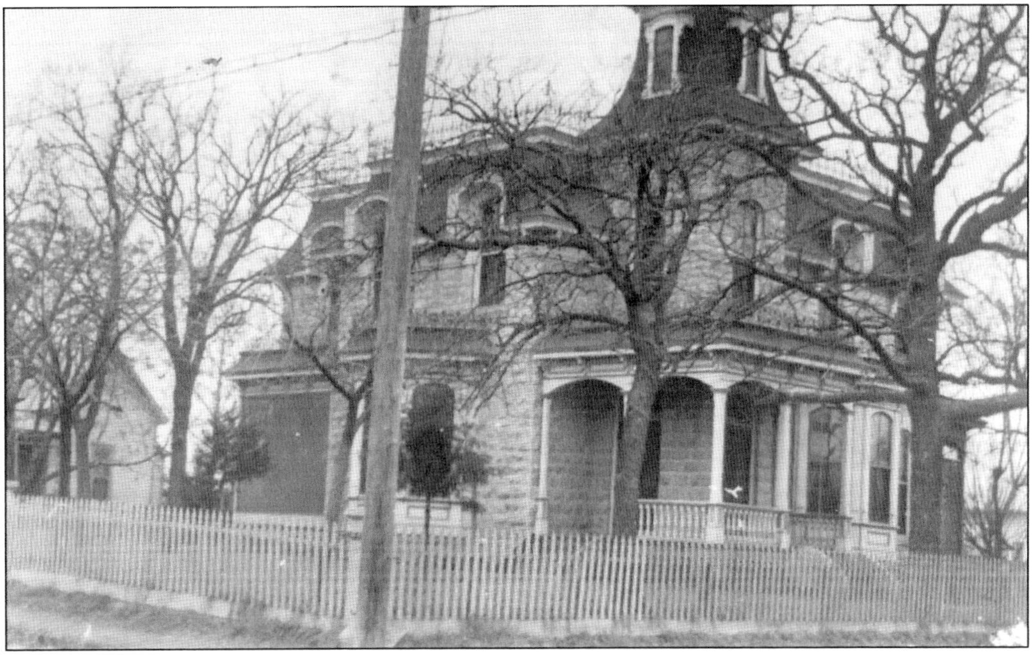

R.W. Kindel had 60 years of drugstore ownership and operation in early Weatherford. He was instrumental in civic functions, including bringing electricity to town. He finally had this palatial copper-roofed home built at 402 West Spring in 1881 and died here in 1931. Mahan Drugs took over his business. (Pat Bass.)

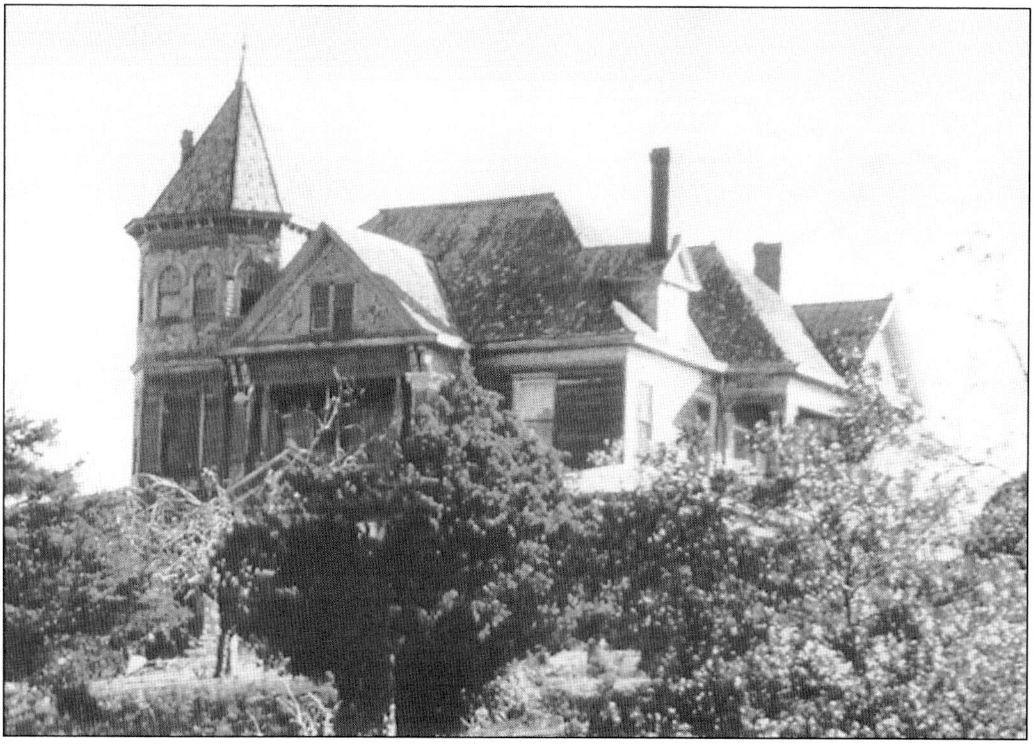

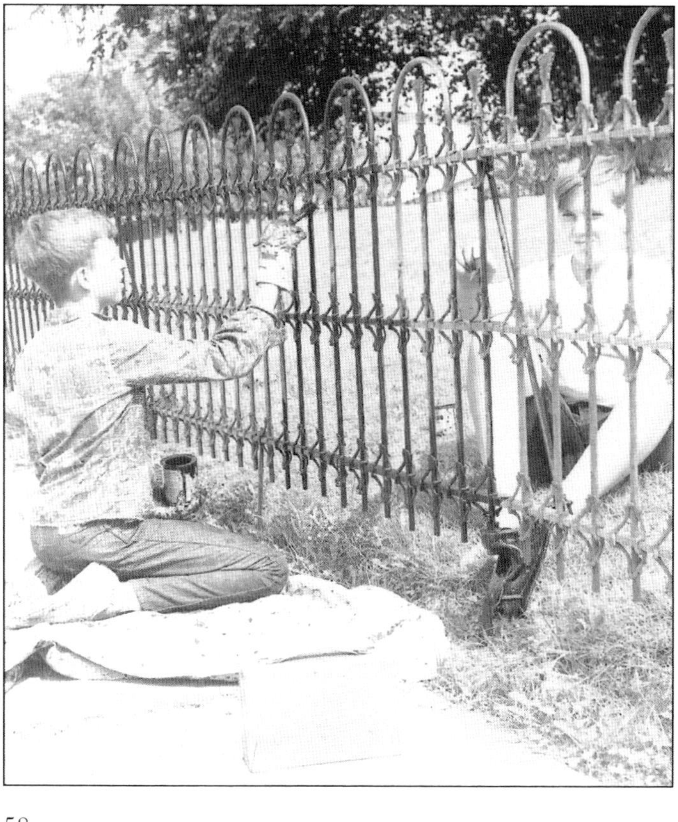

The Victorian-style Charles McFarland home was built in 1902. A tunnel led from the home for tornado protection. The sculptured Longhorn steerhead, made from tin, above the front entrance marked the interest of this cattle baron. This photograph was made just before the home was destroyed for a strip mall. (Glenn Anderson.)

After the death of Mrs. McFarland in 1934, the home (seen above) was closed. Its quick demise in 1974 shocked the citizens to care for the remaining homes of Weatherford. Upkeep on homes is worth it, but Mark Littleton and Mark Yoder may have had different opinions in June 1966. (Chamber of Commerce.)

Five

Dress Up

From work clothes to Sunday church dresses, the changes in style that embraced our lives were due in part to the change from handmade to factory-made clothing. Lace tatting and crocheting to purchased finery made wonderful combinations of adornments. The focus on a few Weatherford families gives insight into our daily life.

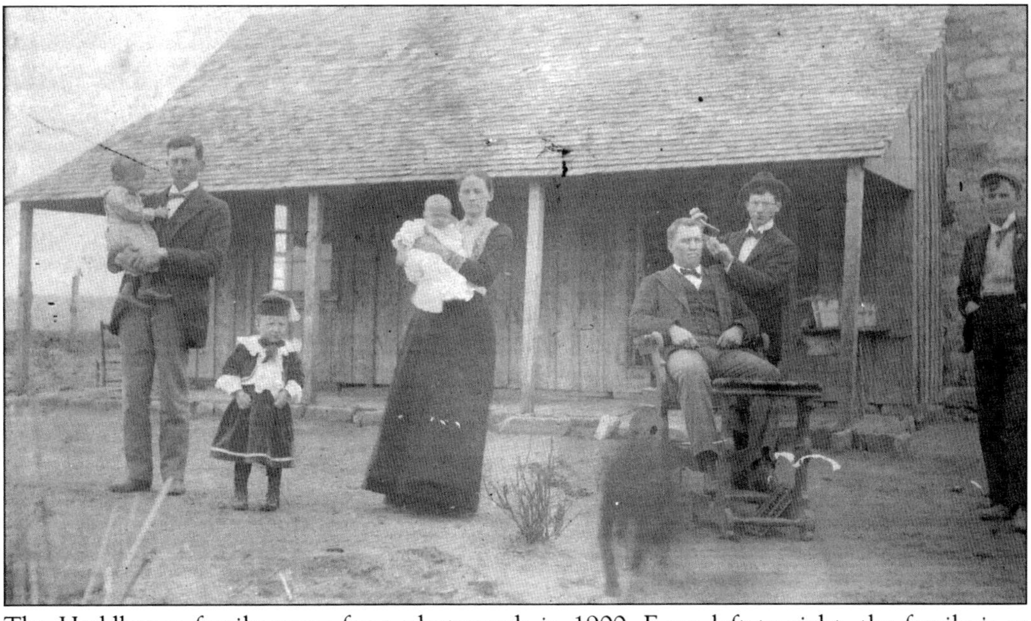

The Huddleston family pause for a photograph in 1900. From left to right, the family is as follows: Lee Varges, holding Escol; Lee's son, Bela, wearing a cousin's hand-me-down lace dress and a stylish fez; and Fannie, holding Leslie and adorned in a nice lace yoke and tucking with a pin. To Fannie's left, Escol's brother, Lawrence, a barber, gets a haircut from a friend, and, at far right, is their youngest brother, Jordon, who lost a bid for mayor in 1932. The clapboard house was typical for country houses at the turn of the century. (Don Huddleston.)

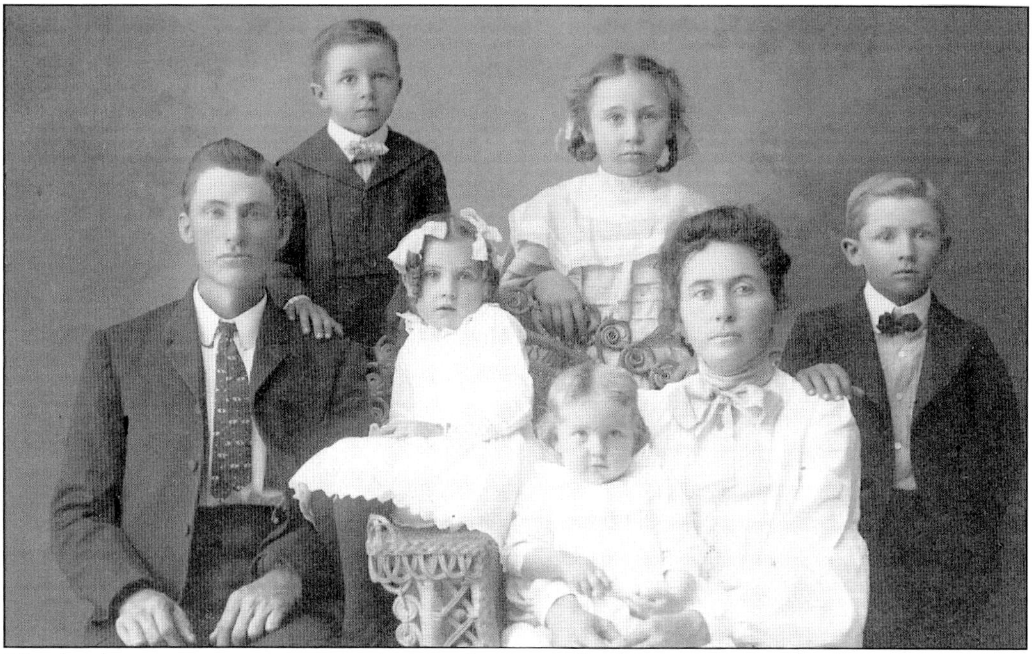

The family portrait was a treat in these early years. The finest was worn for this rare occasion. The setting included a wicker chair and fancy rugs. Seen here are, from left to right, William Prichard; Verdie; Vera; Mary Reural; baby Erma; William's wife, Laura Meniza Prichard; and Marvin. (Don Huddleston.)

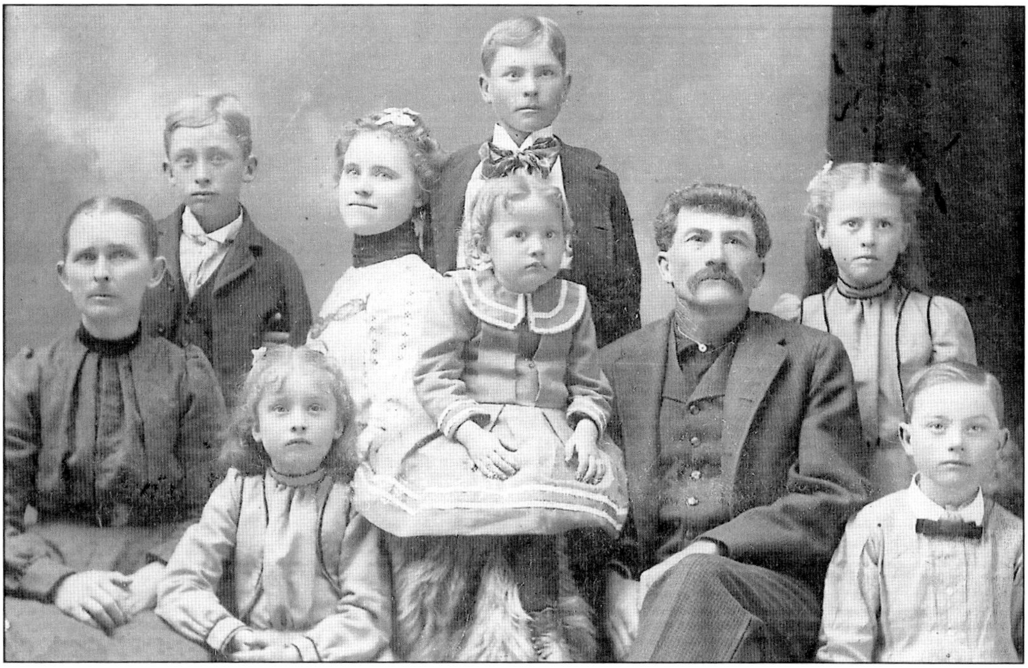

The similarity in dress styles with high collar suggest that Mrs. J.P. Davis did hand sewing or used a foot treadle sewing machine, invented in 1846, to provide most of the clothing. Long photographic exposure times gave preference to solemn faces. (Barbara Newberry.)

Their youth suggests that Fate and Beckie McMahan pose for their wedding photograph. It is unique that both are standing. Fate is in a four-button vest with a wide (for that time period) lapel coat. Beckie's high collar on her blouse adds flair to her tailored jacket. (Barbara Newberry.)

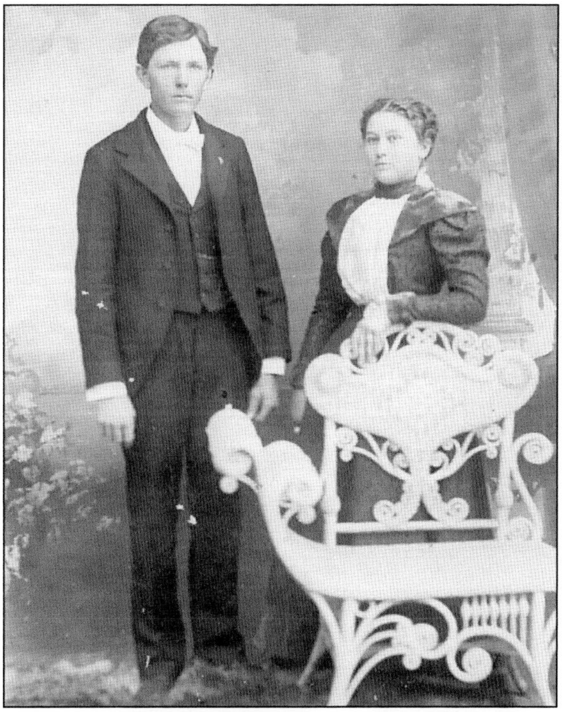

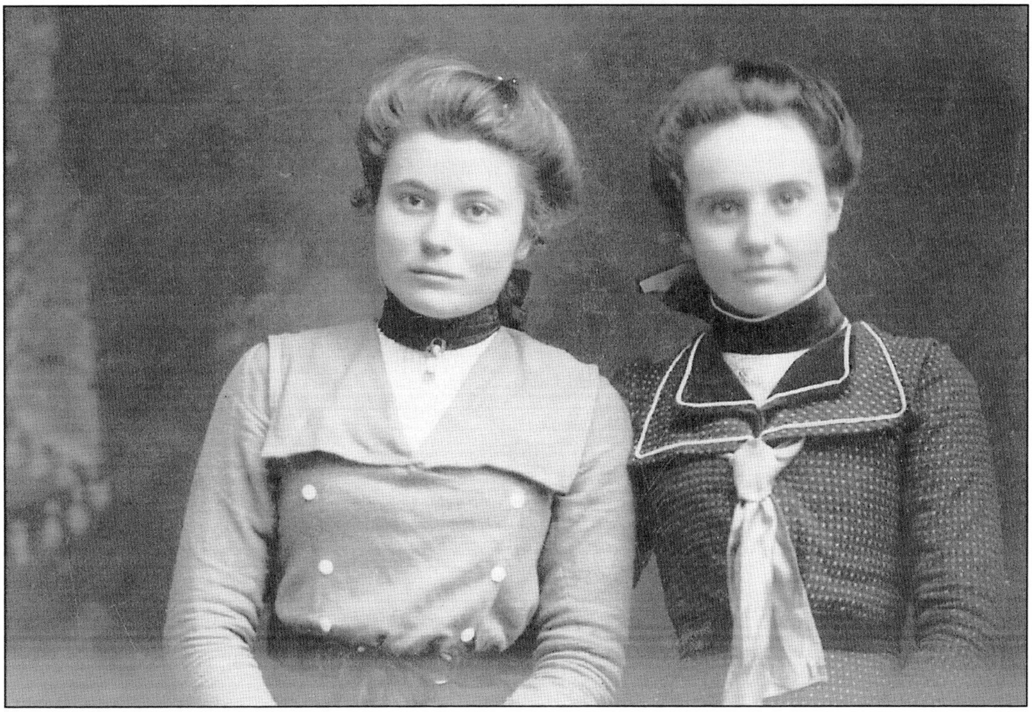

Young ladies seal their friendship with a memorable photograph. At left, a thin dickey is under Beulah Prichard McMahan's sailor-collar style blouse. A scarf and dickey adds color to Lela McWhorter's one-piece dress with double lapels. Both have added the tied silk chokers, then in vogue. (Barbara Newberry.)

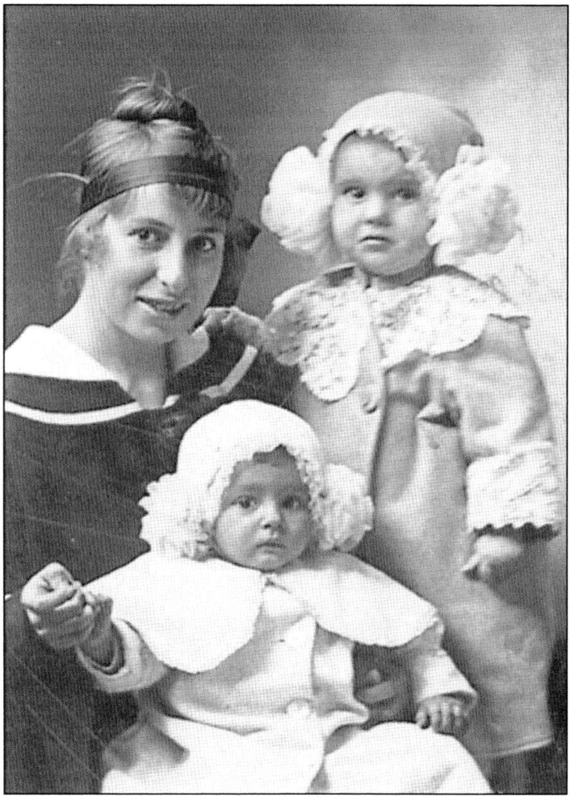

In 1915, Daisy Agnes Hartnett treats her nieces, Maurine White and Mildred Lanier, with a portrait. The babies have cute flowered caps and wide collared coats. (Mary Ellen Guay.)

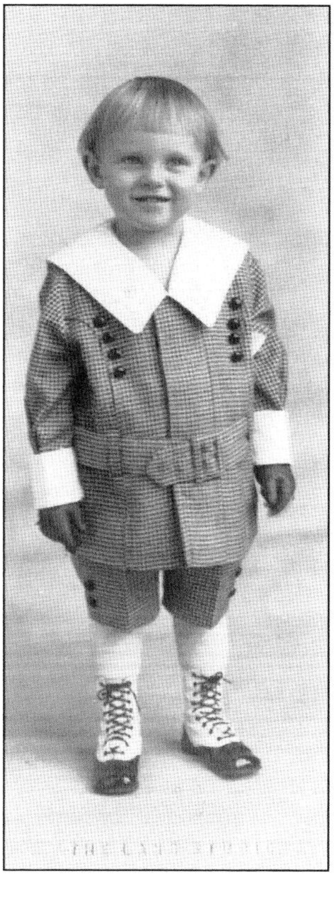

One of the Dan D. Hartnett's grandchildren, three or four years old, is stepping out like "Buster Brown." Wide collar, cuffs, belts, and spats were the stylish wear made famous by John Alexander Fox (1883–1961), of neighboring Peaster, Texas, who became the original "Buster Brown" in those shoe advertisements. (Mary Ellen Guay.)

The availability of box cameras brought photography into the home. In this 1917 pose with dining room chairs, Kathryn, Opal, and Ruth McGill, all have lace-trimmed dresses and bobbed haircuts. (Don Huddleston.)

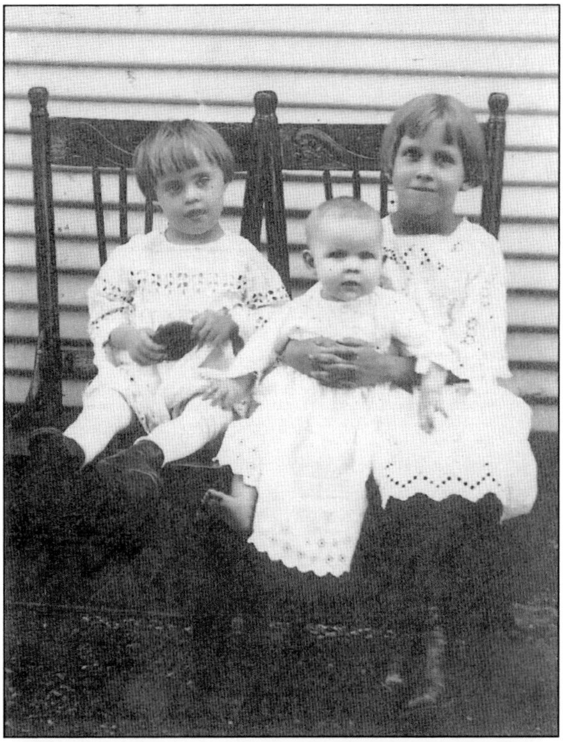

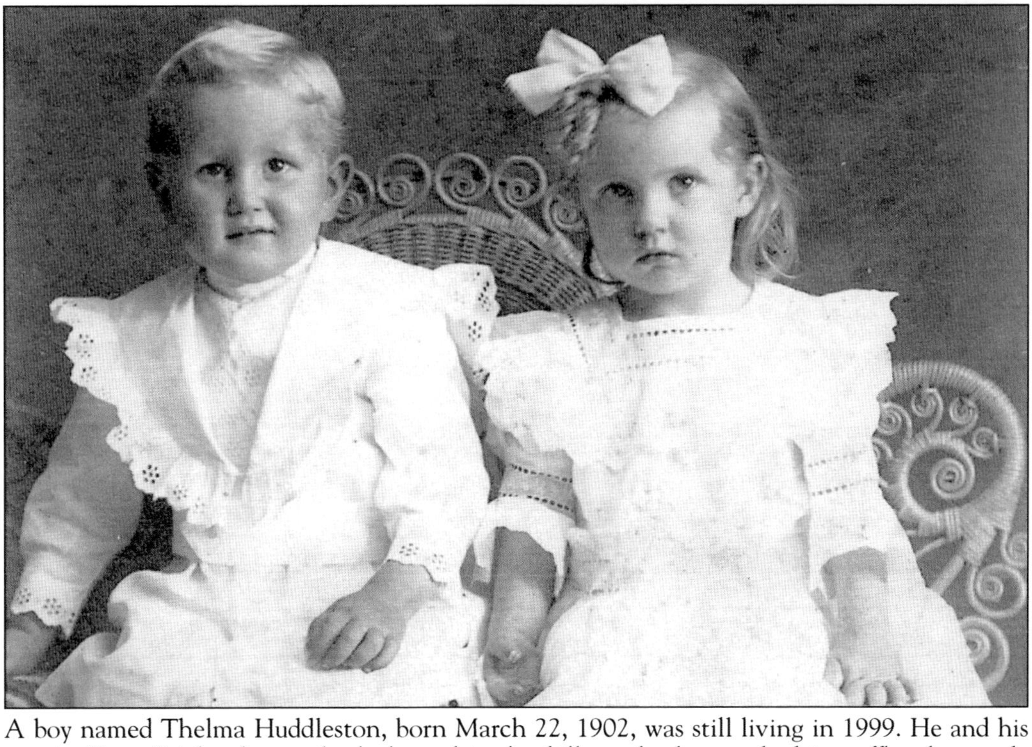

A boy named Thelma Huddleston, born March 22, 1902, was still living in 1999. He and his cousin, Erma Prichard, were both dressed in the frilly eyelet lace and white ruffles that made their mothers a darling photograph. (Don Huddleston.)

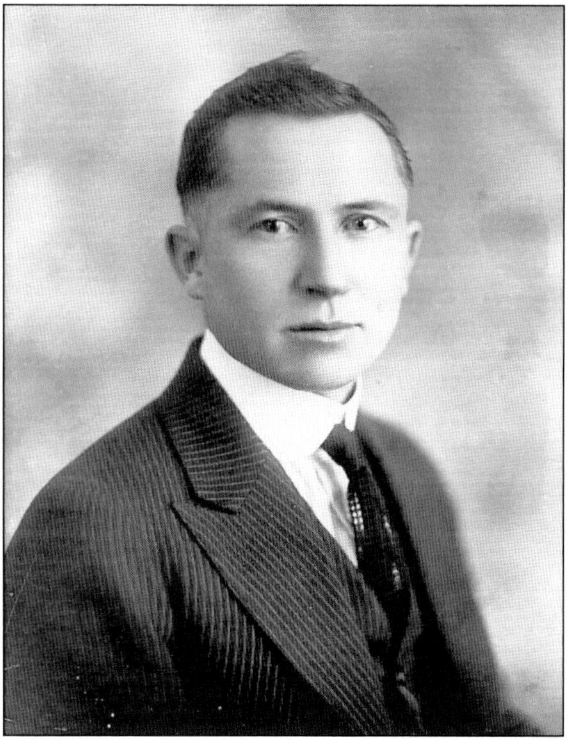

Marvin Prichard, now a young handsome man, poses in his new 1920-era suit. The add-on round corner collar, however, dates from 1913. (Barbara Newberry)

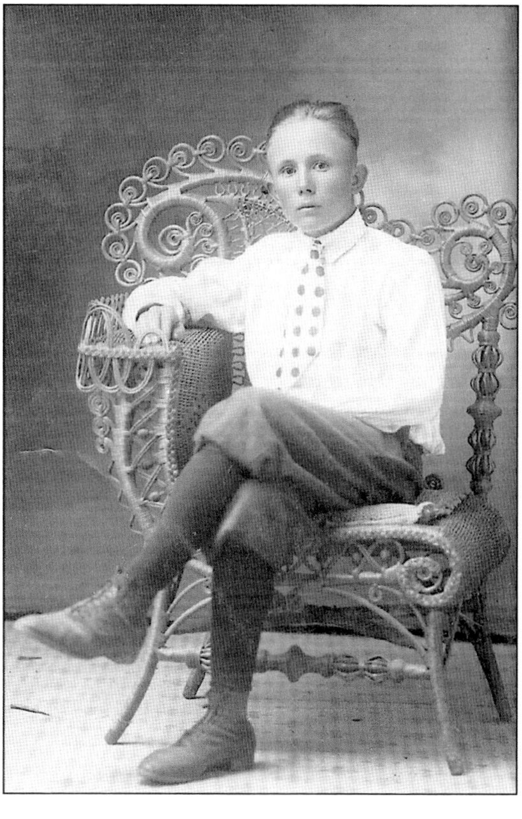

The strapping young Ewell McMahan gazes into the camera. Linen shirt, starched collar, knickers, and long stockings with high-topped shoes made a young man feel the hero that day. Love that wicker chair! (Barbara Newberry.)

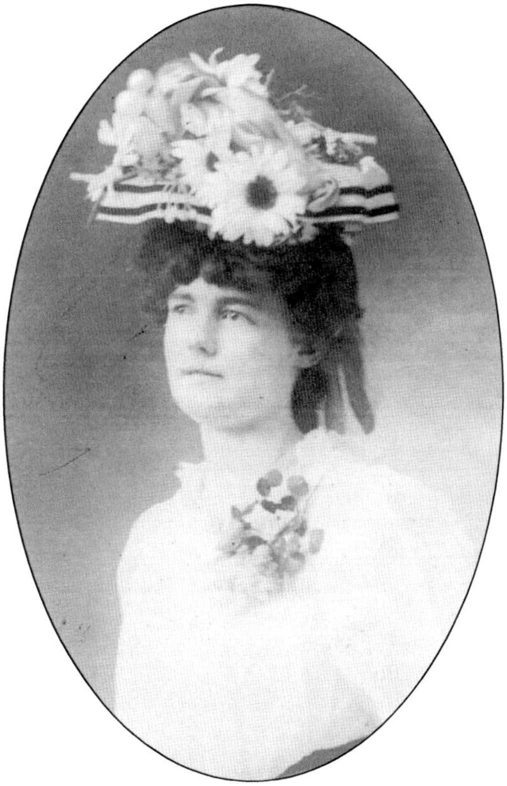

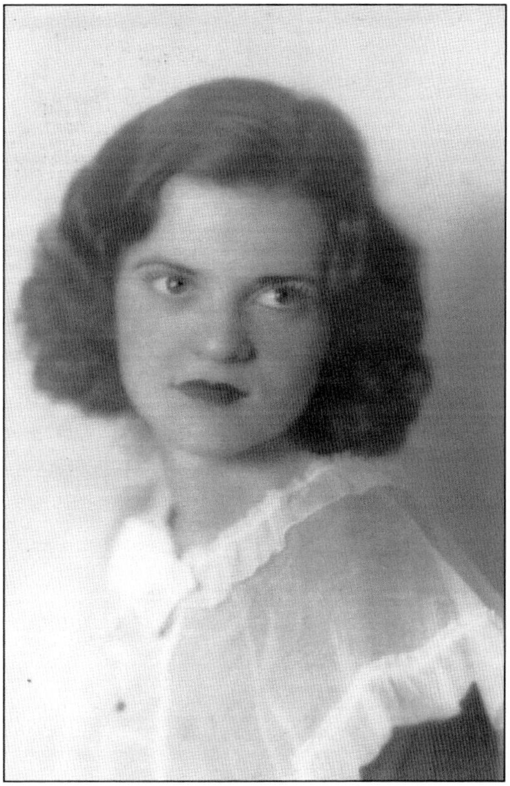

Left: Jimmy Josephine "Jodie" Huddleston, Weatherford telephone operator, in her whimsical white summer frock looks dreamy with her hair done with dangling "heartbreaker" curls. Her pretty hat perched on her head has a garden of flowers. (Don Huddleston.) *Right:* Miss Juanita Saul, Gary Hagman's mom, cuts a romantic figure in her beautiful coming-out attire, a dark dress under the wide voile collar. (Gary and Linda Hagman.)

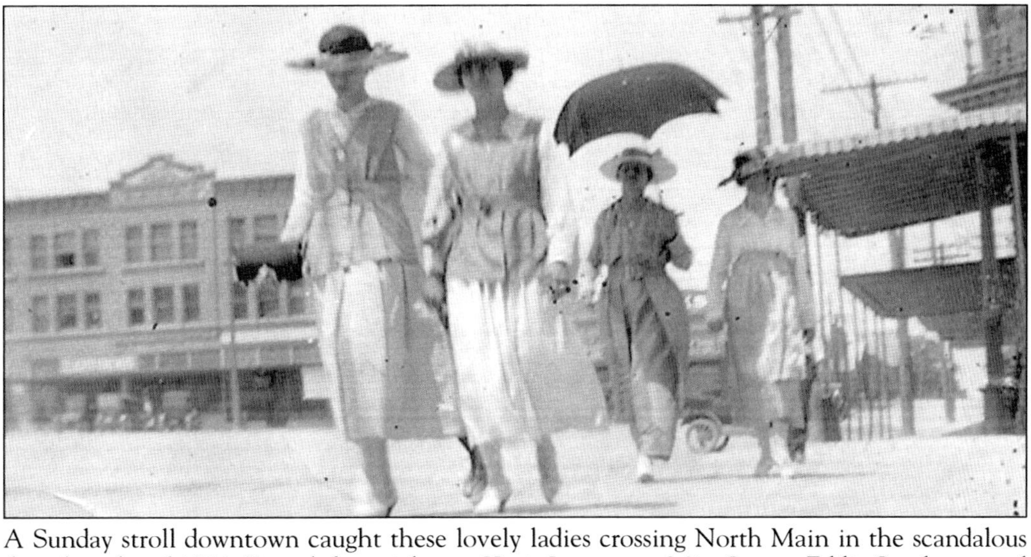

A Sunday stroll downtown caught these lovely ladies crossing North Main in the scandalous dress lengths of 1924. From left to right are Katie Lawrence, Miss Stuart, Eddie Stephens, and Fern Stephens Plemons. (WL.)

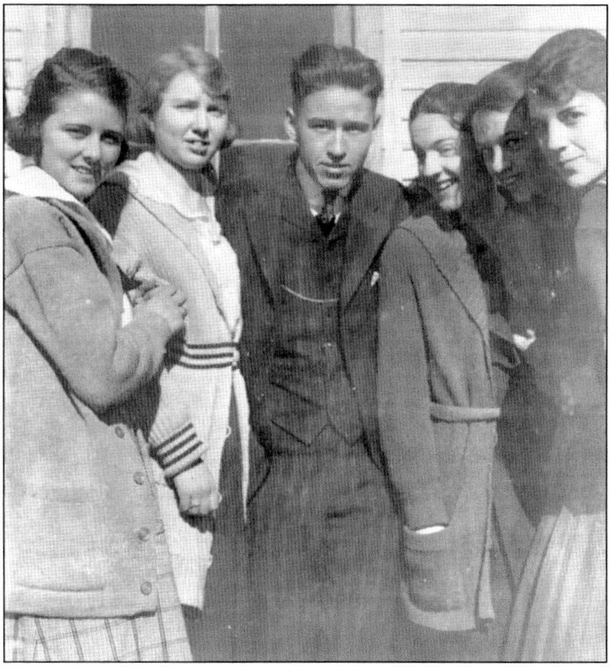

The Jazz Age begins early in 1919. Factory-produced clothes gave almost a uniform appearance. Grace Ragsdale, left, is with her Weatherford High School senior class friends Hillis Snoddy Hutchens, Carlos Milliken, Nona Holland Allison, Mary Barbour, Taylor Alexander, and Winnie Barker. (Bill Fant.)

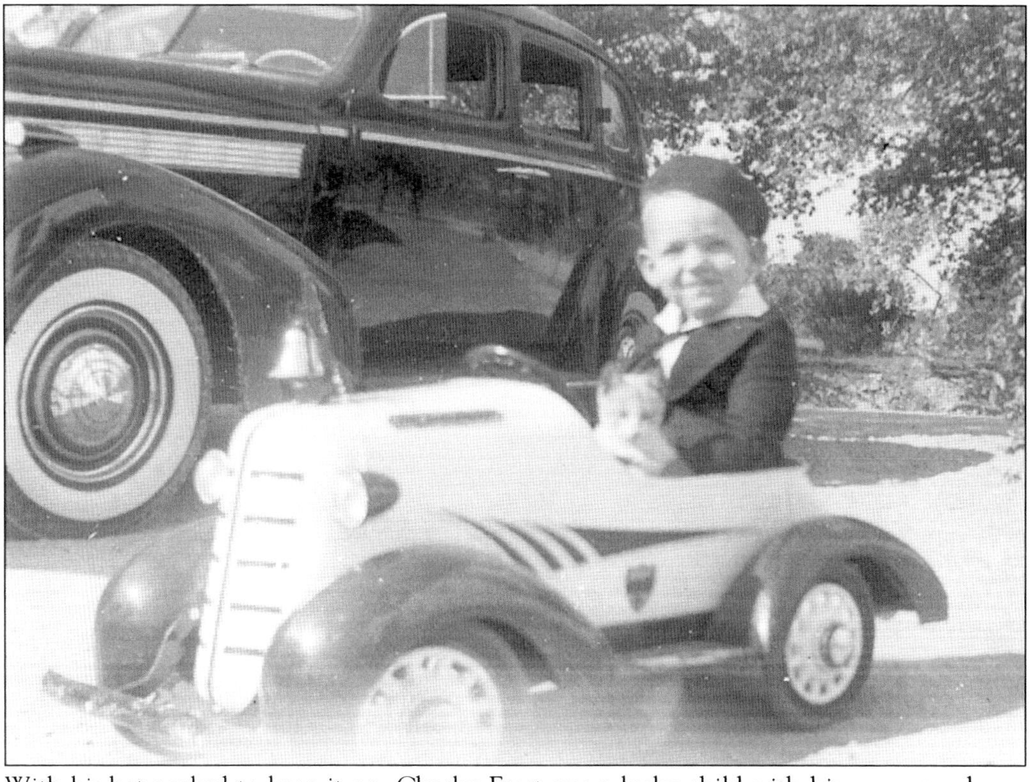

With his hat cocked to keep it on, Charles Frost was a lucky child with his own new dream push-pedal car, similar in style to his dad's car. Dressed for church, he gives his kitten a ride in the late 1930s. (Charles Frost.)

Six

Worship

As the churches grew so did the city. Immigrants and even slaves brought their faith in God, which helped with the harsh new life. The variety of sanctuaries reveals their faith as a community. Worship in Weatherford keeps our eye on the future.

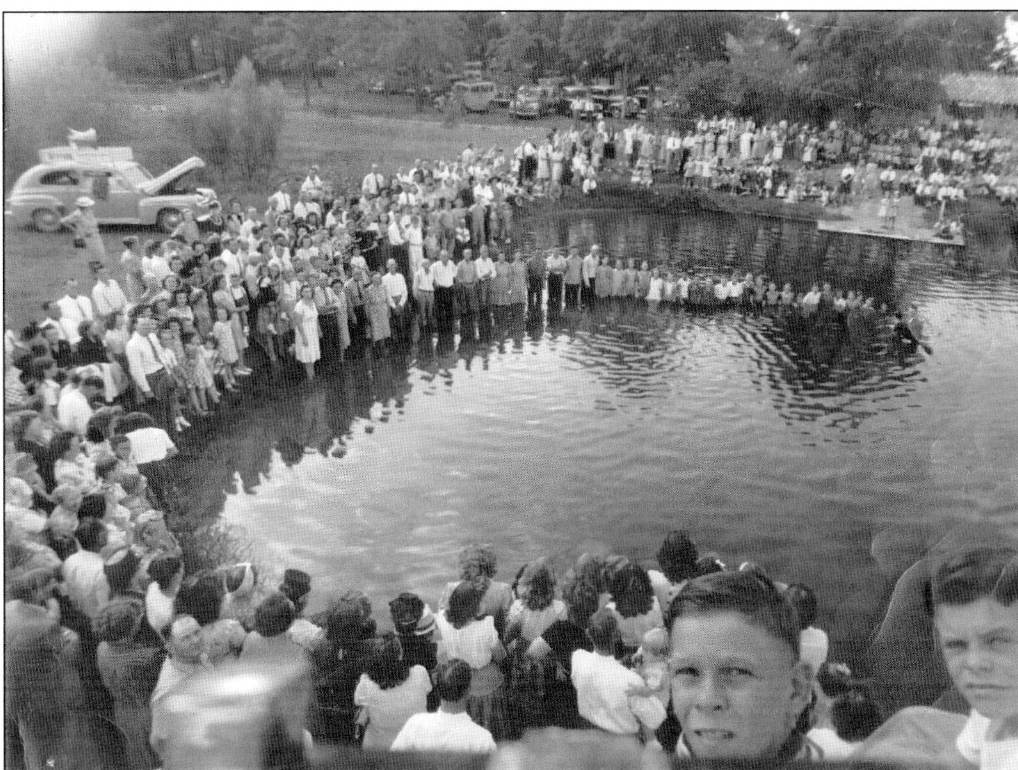

In August 1947, over 100 people were baptized at Holland's Lake during a three-week revival at York Avenue Baptist Church. Former Mayor G.A. Holland made his lake property a city park in 1935. (WL.)

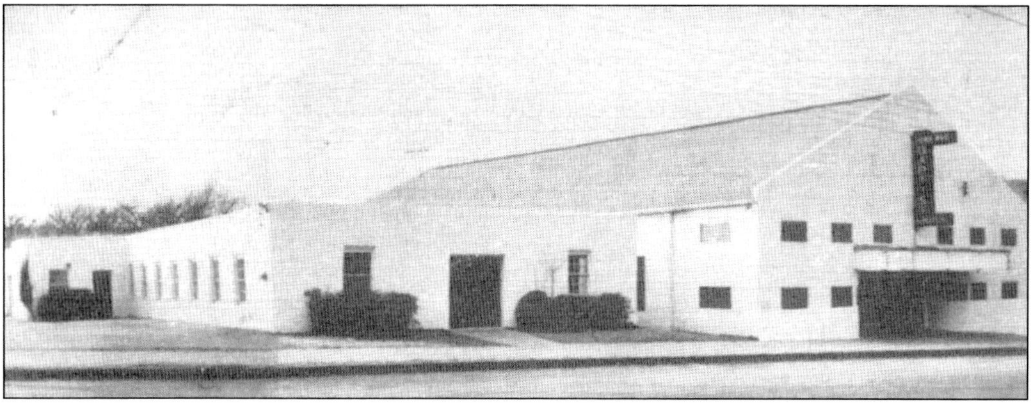

York Avenue Baptist Church was built on the site of the McFall Hotel. The church expanded in 1946 to the large auditorium on the right. The church grew again in the 1980s and moved to Santa Fe Drive. The old facility has been used for a weekly newspaper and a live theater. (WL.)

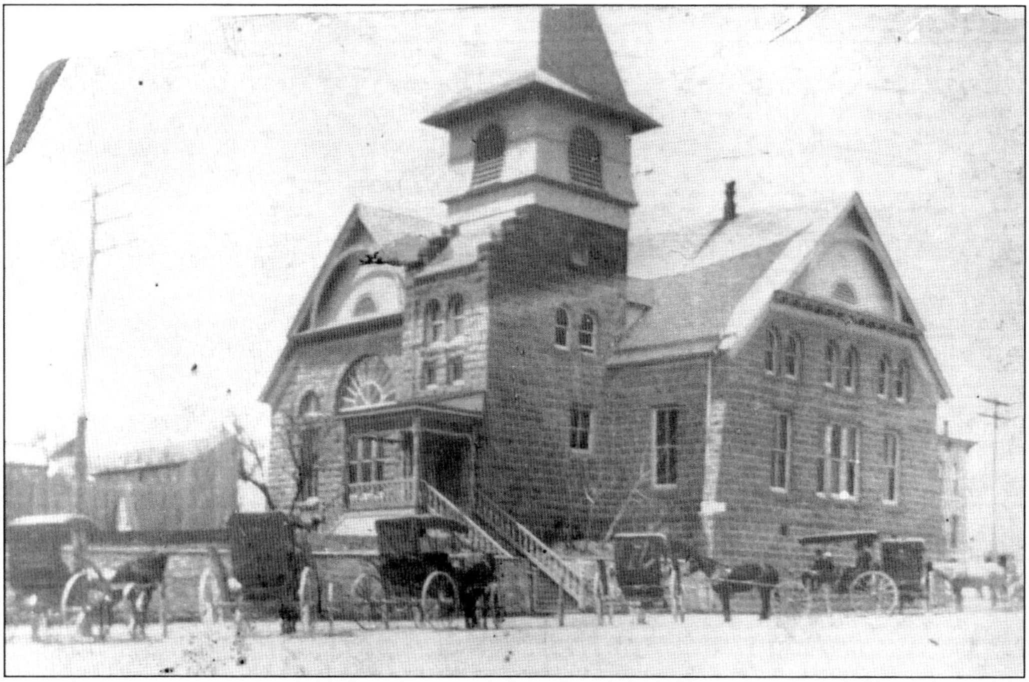

What became the First Baptist Church was organized in 1856 in a log cabin. The cornerstone of the above building was laid in 1895, the first service was December 6, 1896, and the building was replaced in 1960. (Martha McClung.)

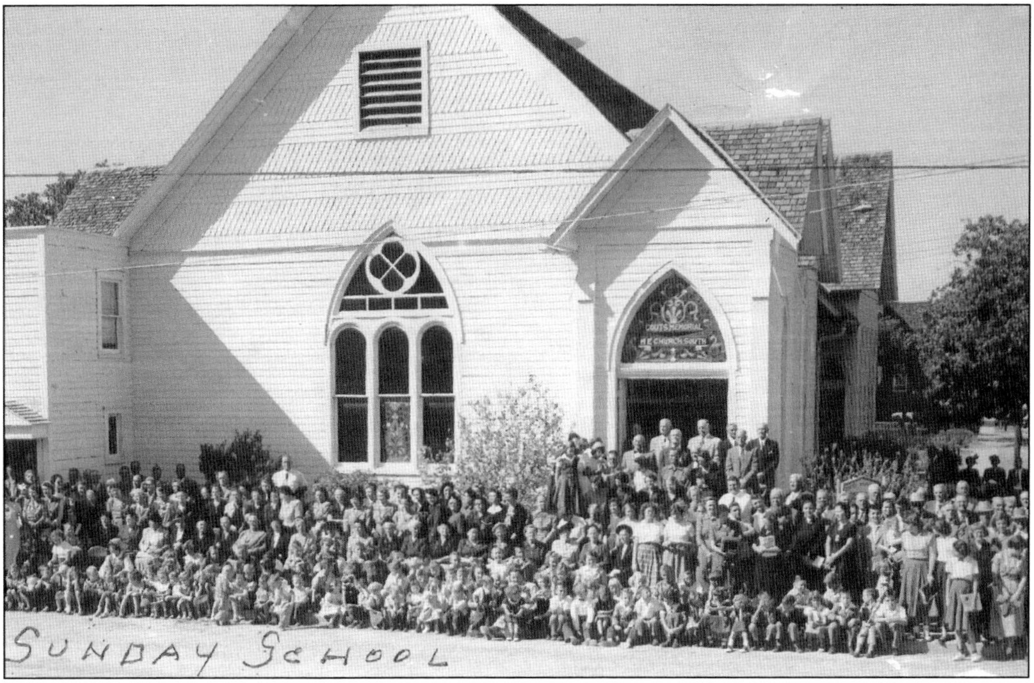

Couts Memorial United Methodist Church, located at 913 North Elm, is pictured here in April 1950 during a record-breaking attendance. This old building is now Galbreaith-Pickard funeral home. The church moved to 802 North Elm, across the street. (Couts Methodist Church via Larry Zellers.)

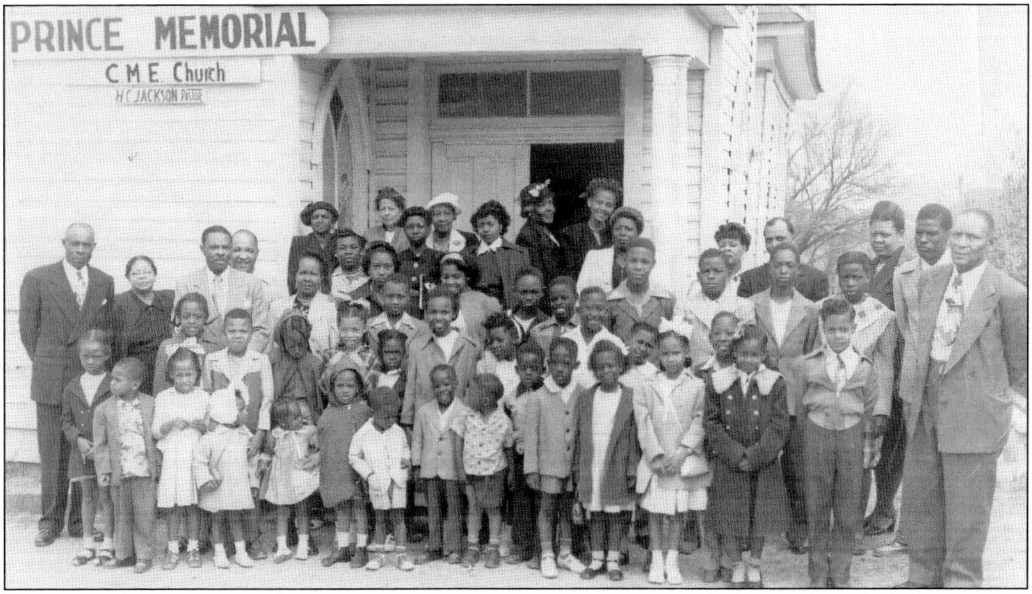

This photograph shows the modest Prince Memorial CME Church with a Sunday-school class in the late 1940s. It was built in 1871 and was honored by the Parker County Heritage Society tour of homes. Pastor Herbert Jackson is at left, and Mitchell Rucker, at right, was Sunday school superintendent. Rucker was a campaign worker for former U.S. Congressman Jim Wright. (Melvin George via Donald George.)

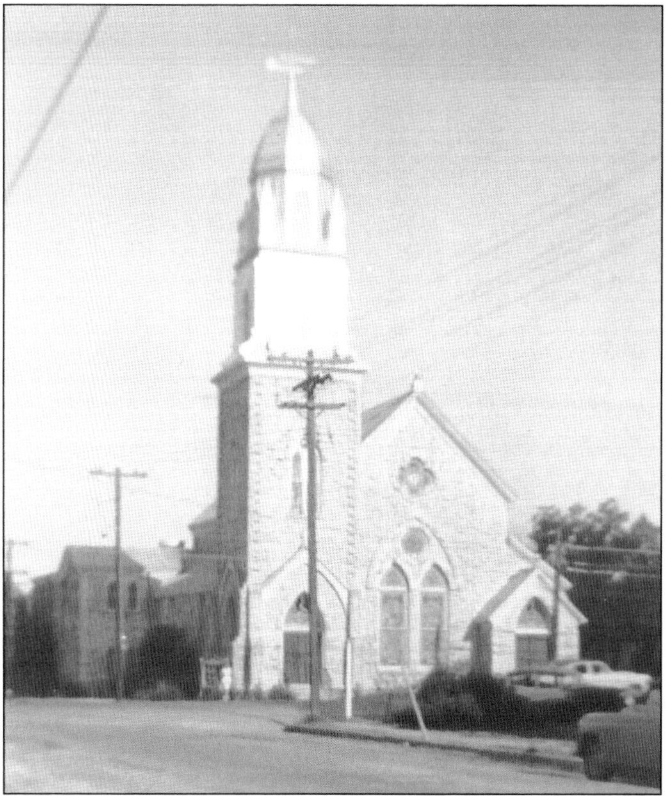

The stone First Methodist Church building at Church and Walnut Streets was blown down in 1884 in a storm. The current First United Methodist Church was completed in 1892. (WL.)

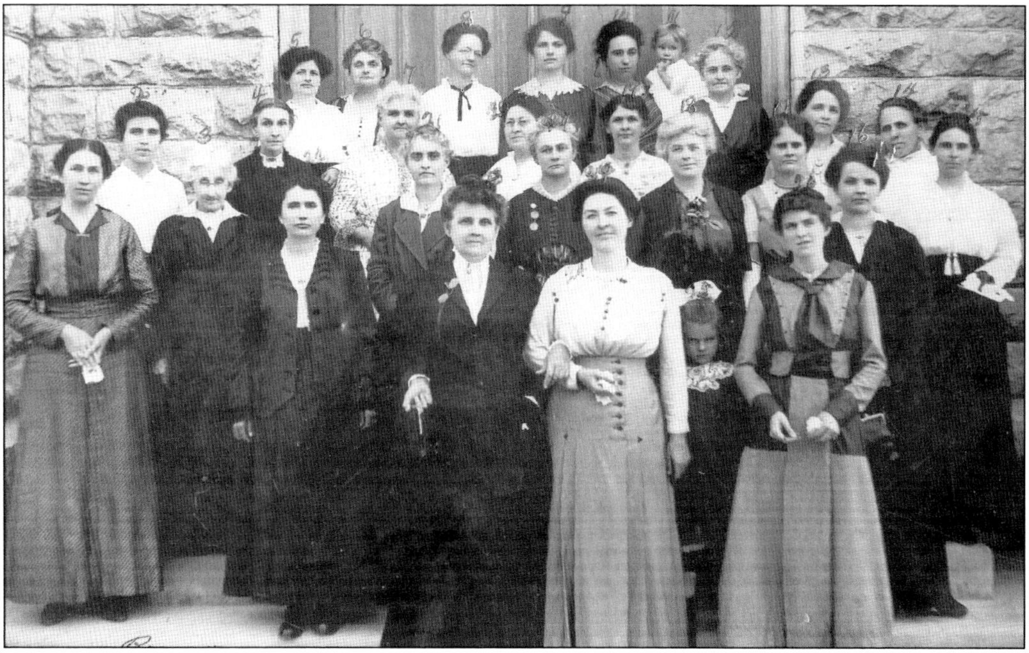

In 1921, the Women's Missionary Society from First United Methodist Church was led by Mrs. Nelms, the pastor's wife. (WL.)

Built in 1886 at 200 South Main, Grace-First Presbyterian Church steeple was often hit by lightning. Several lower steeples were tried on the building. (Grace-First Presbyterian Church archive.)

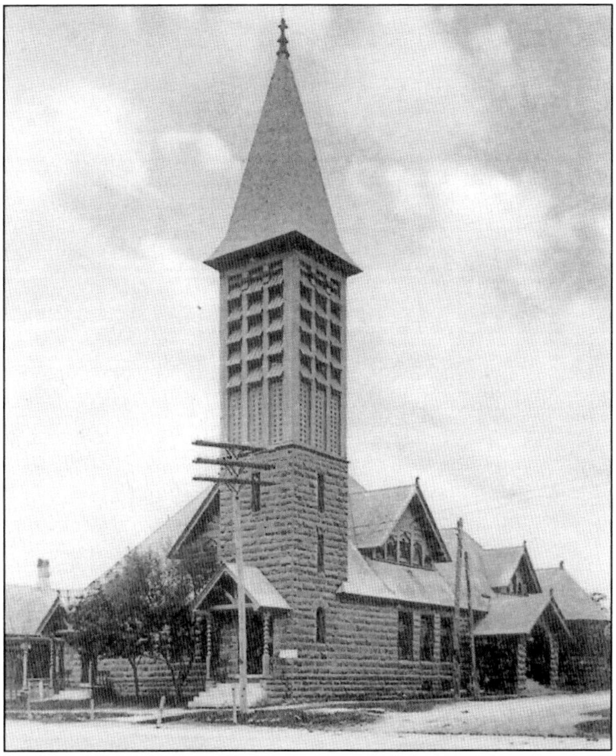

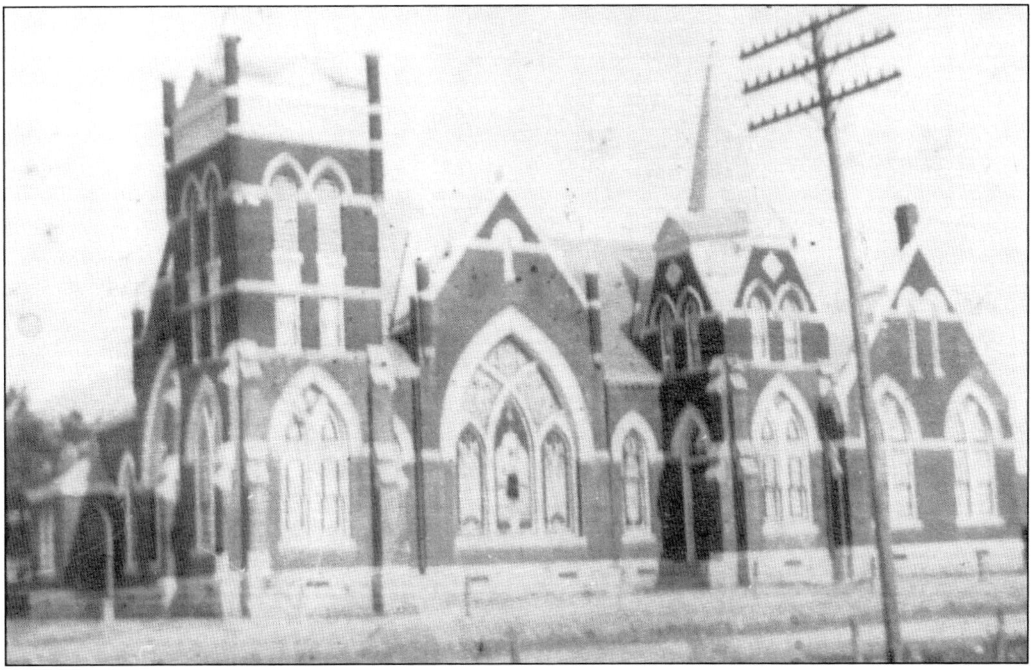

Cumberland Presbyterian Church, completed in 1902 at 201 Palo Pinto, sponsored the Women's Seminary. The church membership combined with Grace-First Presbyterian Church in 1906. The building was used by the high school for band practice until replaced by an auto dealership in 1948. (Grace-First Presbyterian Church archive.)

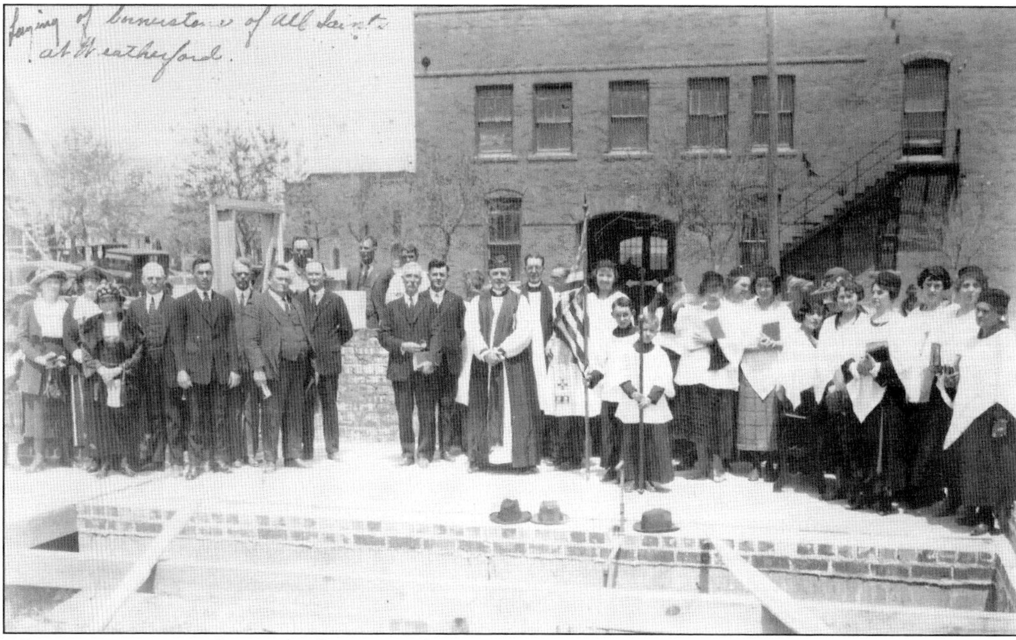

The cornerstone is being laid on April 18, 1923, at All Saints Episcopal Church, 125 South Waco. Bishop Moore from Dallas officiated with Rector Edward S. Barlow. Margaret C. Foat donated the land in memory of her daughter. (WL.)

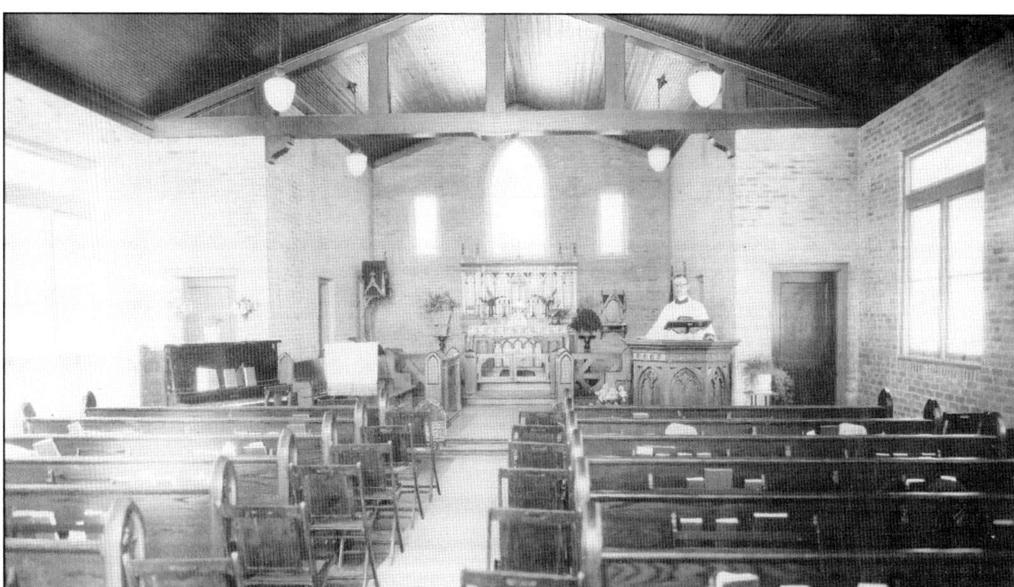

Rector Edward S. Barlow shows the new interior of All Saint's Episcopal Church in this 1923 photograph. (WL.)

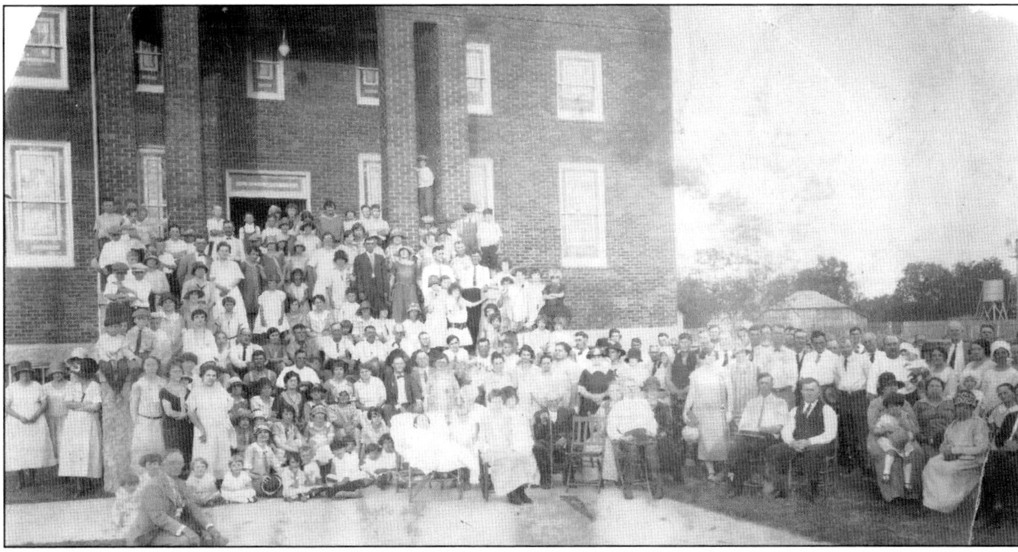

The groundbreaking ceremony on June 1, 1925, was for the youth tabernacle next to the main sanctuary of North Side Baptist Church, 916 North Main. Even invalid Etta Laycock, in her bed, was brought for the occasion. (WL.)

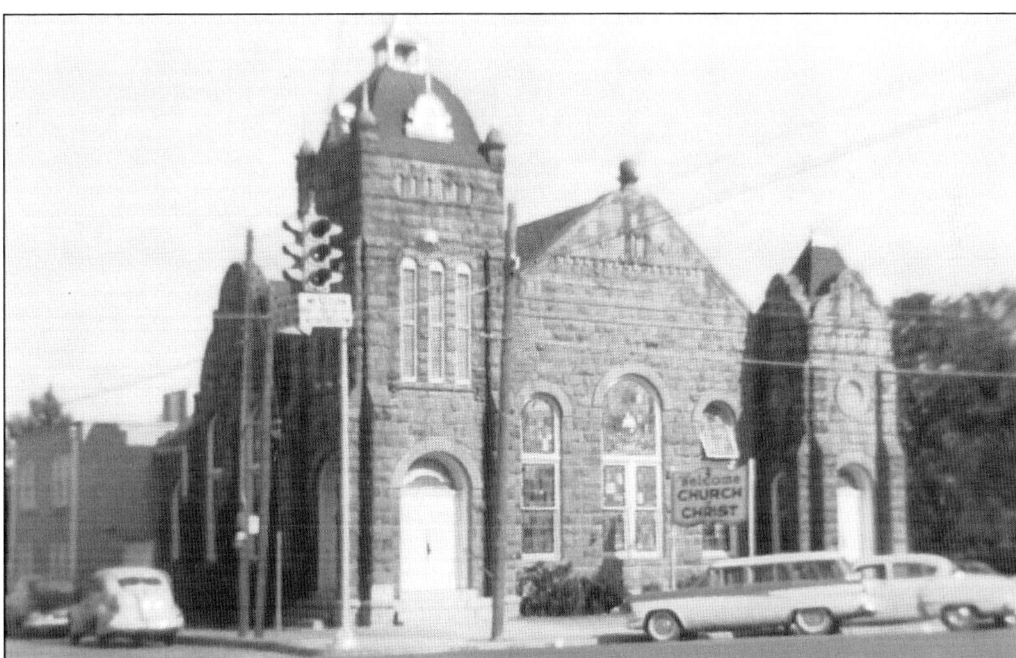

South Main Church of Christ is located at 201 South Main at the red light. A plank structure built in 1886, the Christian Chapel was replaced in 1904 by this sandstone structure. (WL.)

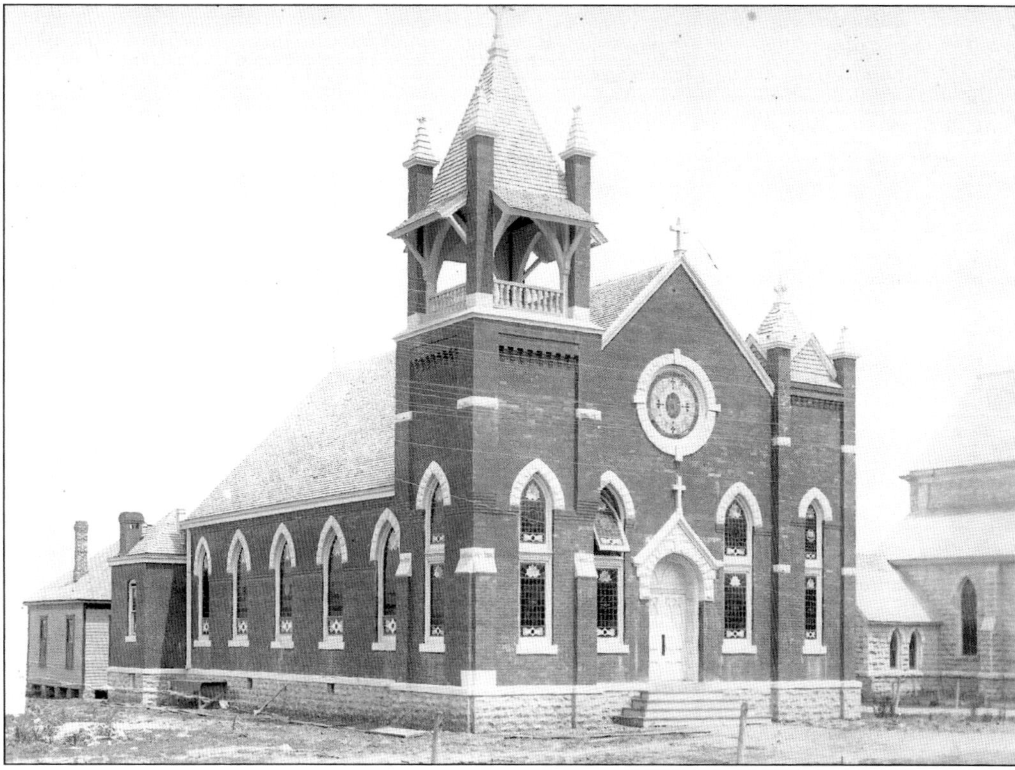

The new St. Stephen's Catholic Church was photographed by Henri Clogenson in 1902. The 1882 frame building burnt. In 1952, just prior to his death, famed local artist Douglas Chandor redecorated the interior. (Mary Ellen Guay.)

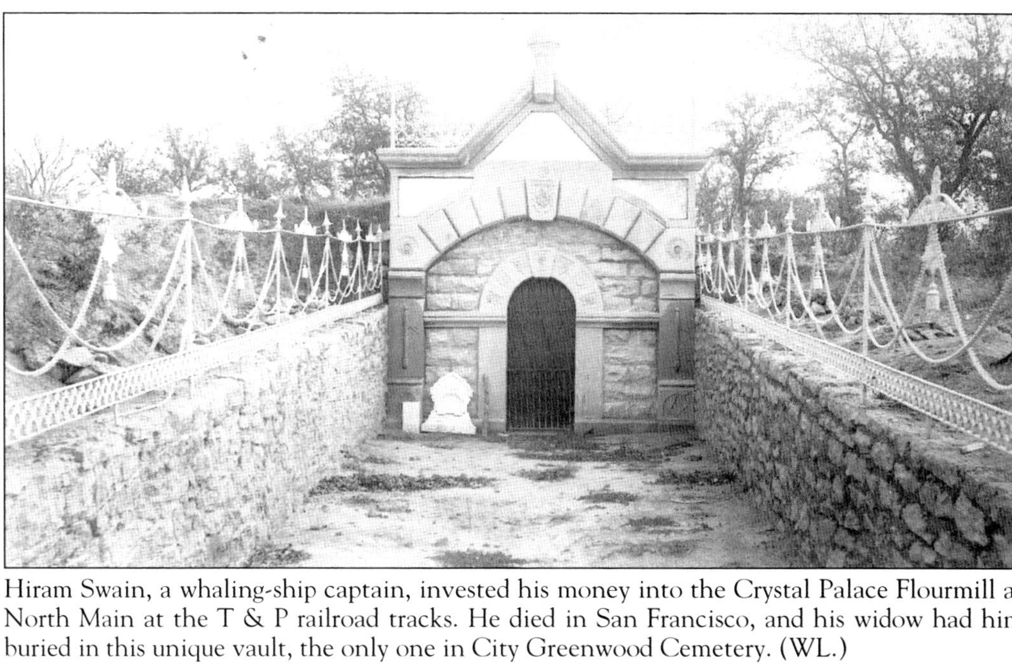

Hiram Swain, a whaling-ship captain, invested his money into the Crystal Palace Flourmill at North Main at the T & P railroad tracks. He died in San Francisco, and his widow had him buried in this unique vault, the only one in City Greenwood Cemetery. (WL.)

Seven

Education and Child Care

In the early years, churches and fraternal lodges greatly helped to educate and care for Weatherford's children. The first public school classes were held in 1860 in a blacksmith shop at 804 South Main. The cornerstone of the city's first school building, the Phoenix Masonic Lodge and Institute, was laid in 1869. Indians attacked some pioneers in route to the ceremony. As the city has grown, the number of schools have grown also.

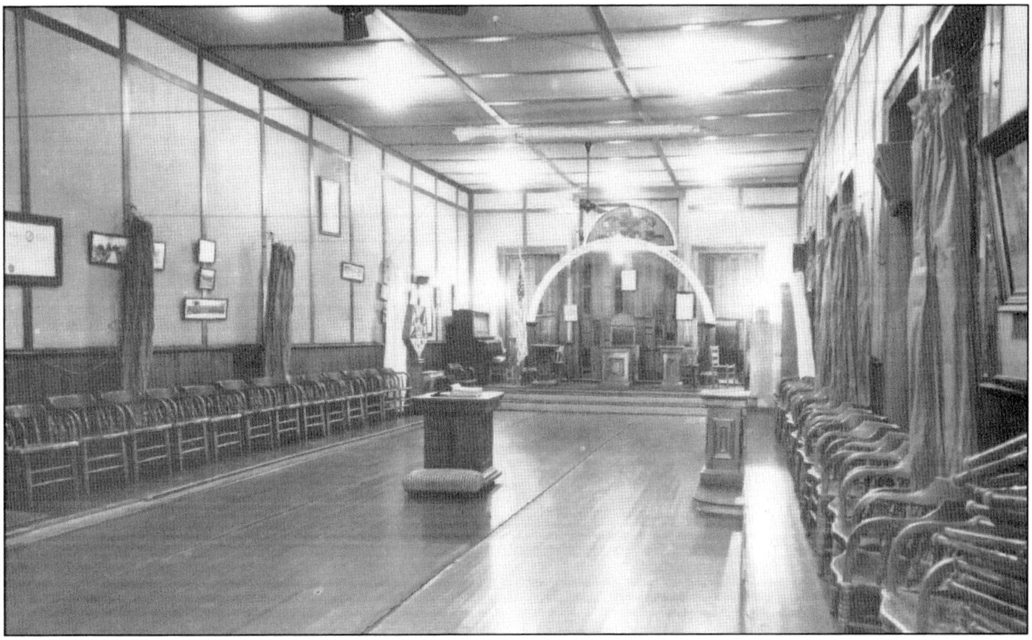

The second-floor interior of the next Phoenix Masonic Lodge building, 124 South Main, gives a view of what the first lodge interior may have looked like. (Phoenix Masonic Lodge 275 via Dexter Sammons.)

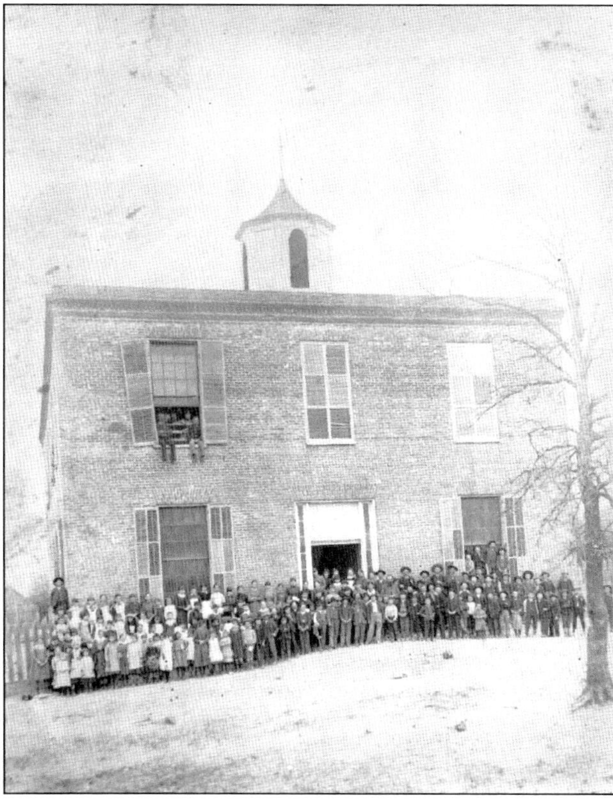

The Masonic Lodge and Institute is seen here in 1879. The Institute portion was leased in 1875 for all grade-school classes. The first class of graduates was in June 1876. The school moved to its new building in 1885. That fall, the first college classes were held. (WC.)

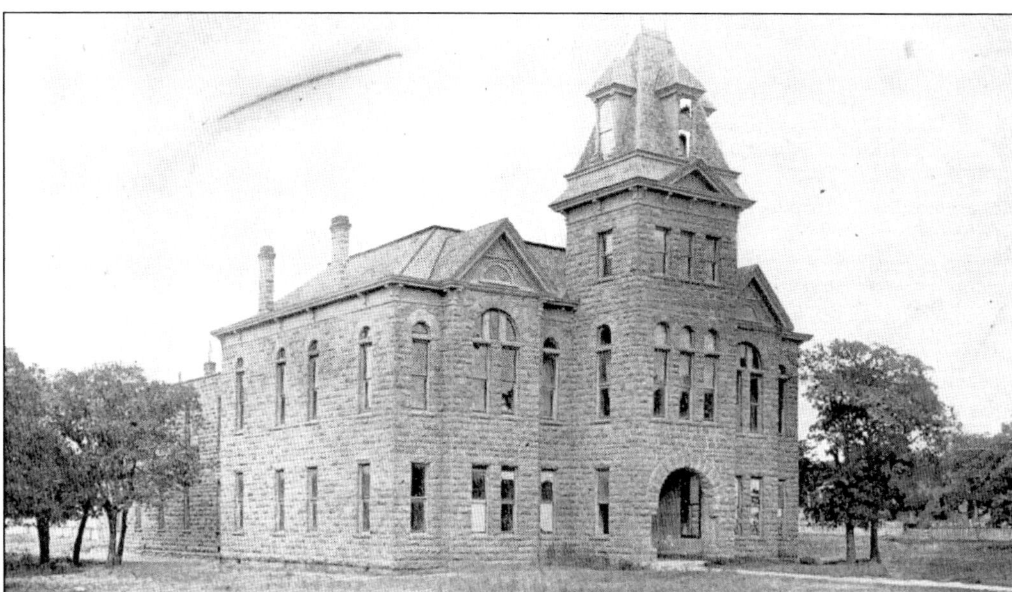

A contract was let in 1894 for an addition of classrooms in front of the existing brick building, a bell tower, and a uniform sandstone exterior was applied. The beautiful exterior gave character to "Old Main," as shown in 1924. (WC.)

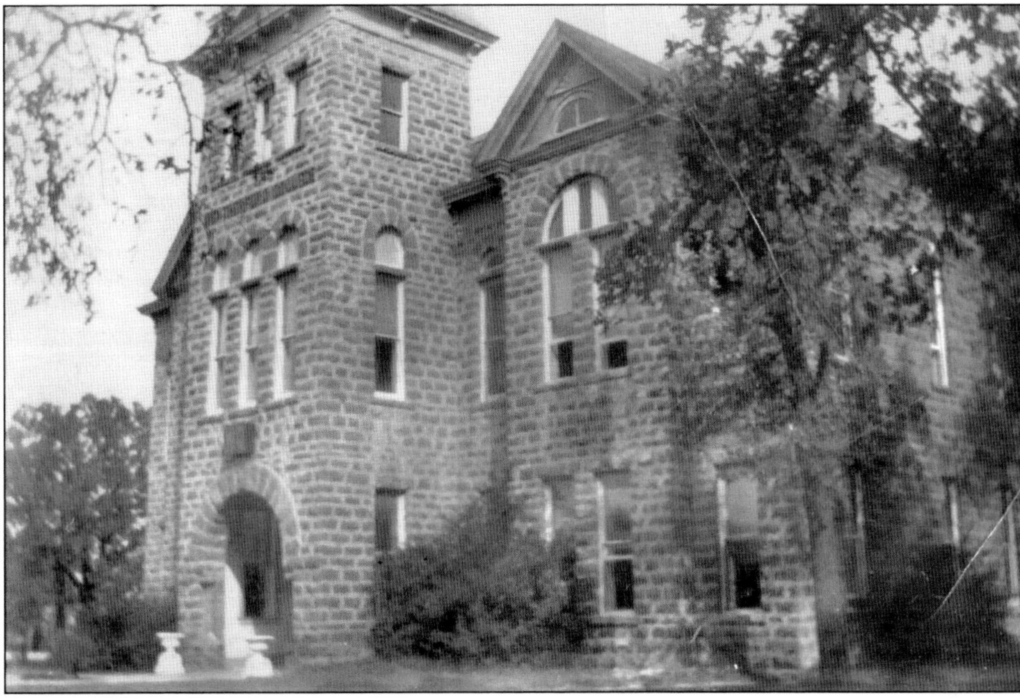

Weatherford College's "Old Main," located 407 South Main, is photographed here without the "bonnet" in the late 1940s. (Charles Frost.)

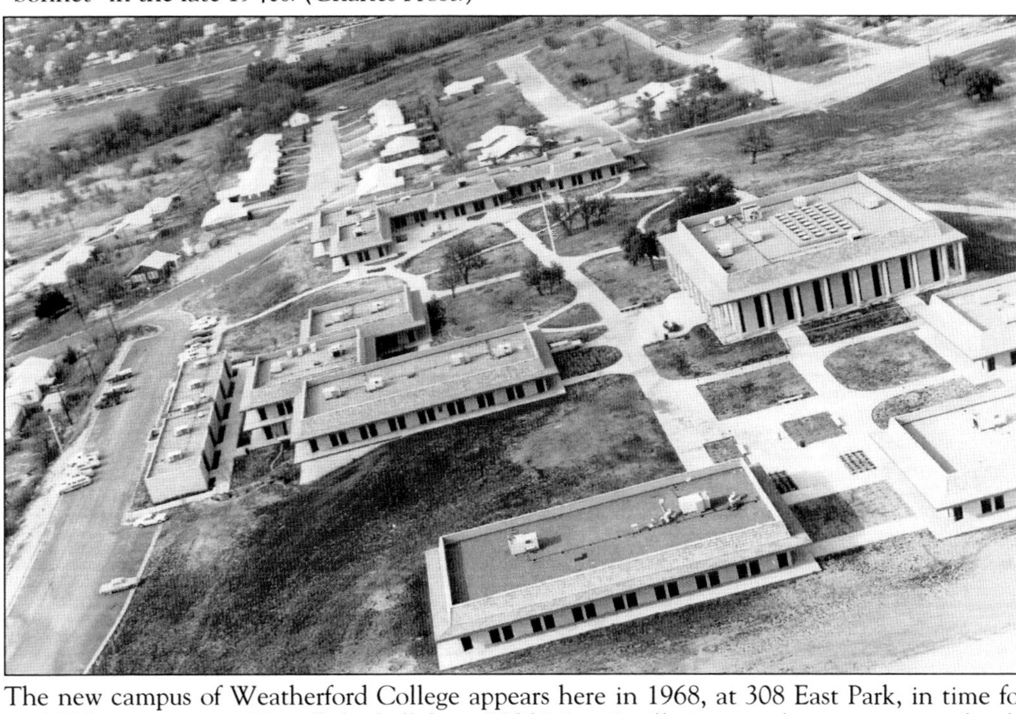

The new campus of Weatherford College appears here in 1968, at 308 East Park, in time for its 100th anniversary. "Sam," the bell from "Old Main," still rings on the new campus thanks to Vernon D. Parrott, former college president. It was named "Sam" by David Aiken in a 1964 college *Coyote* newspaper article. (Chamber of Commerce.)

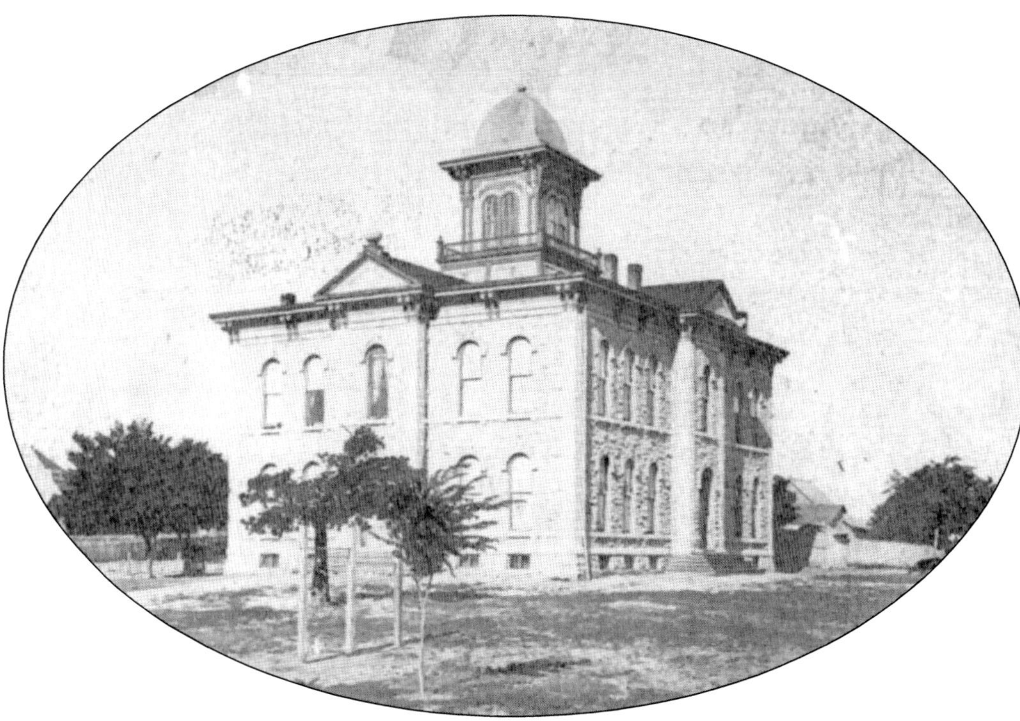

Weatherford "Central Free School," for all grades, was first used in 1885 in the 100 block of South Alamo Street. There were five graduates that year to receive certificates of completion. In 1894 the first diplomas were presented. As elementary schools were built, the Central School had grades 7th through 12th. (WC.)

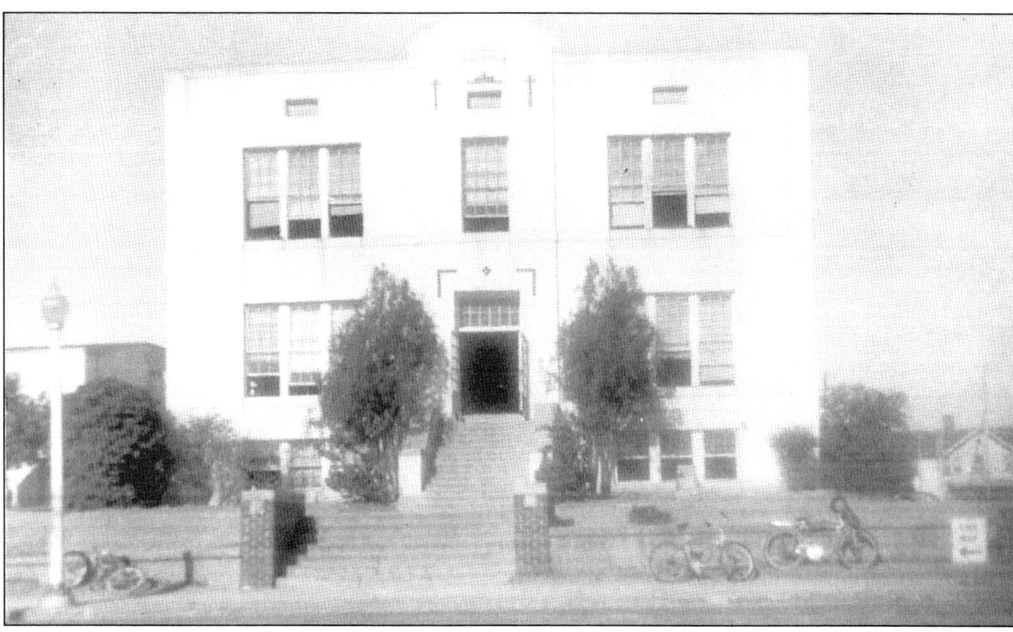

With more students, this addition next to the 1885 building was constructed in 1909, and it later became the junior high in 1921, when the red-brick building was completed. (WL.)

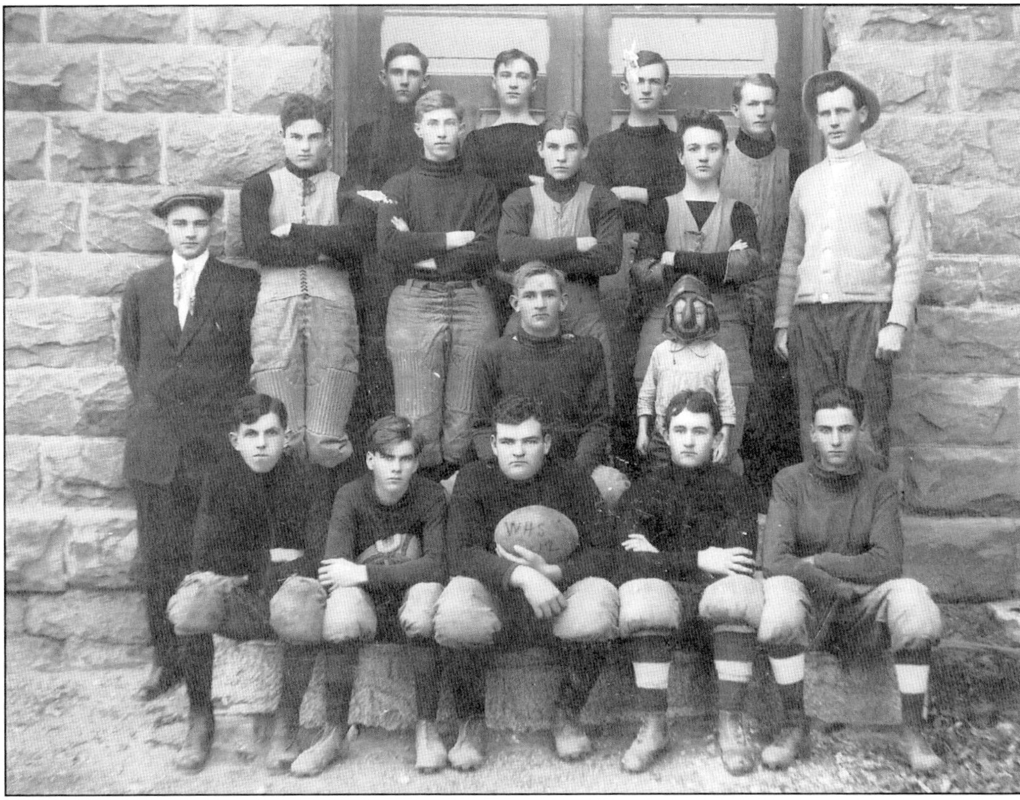

The high school football team is shown here in 1912. In the first game of 1913, the team beat Arlington High School by 47-0. (WL.)

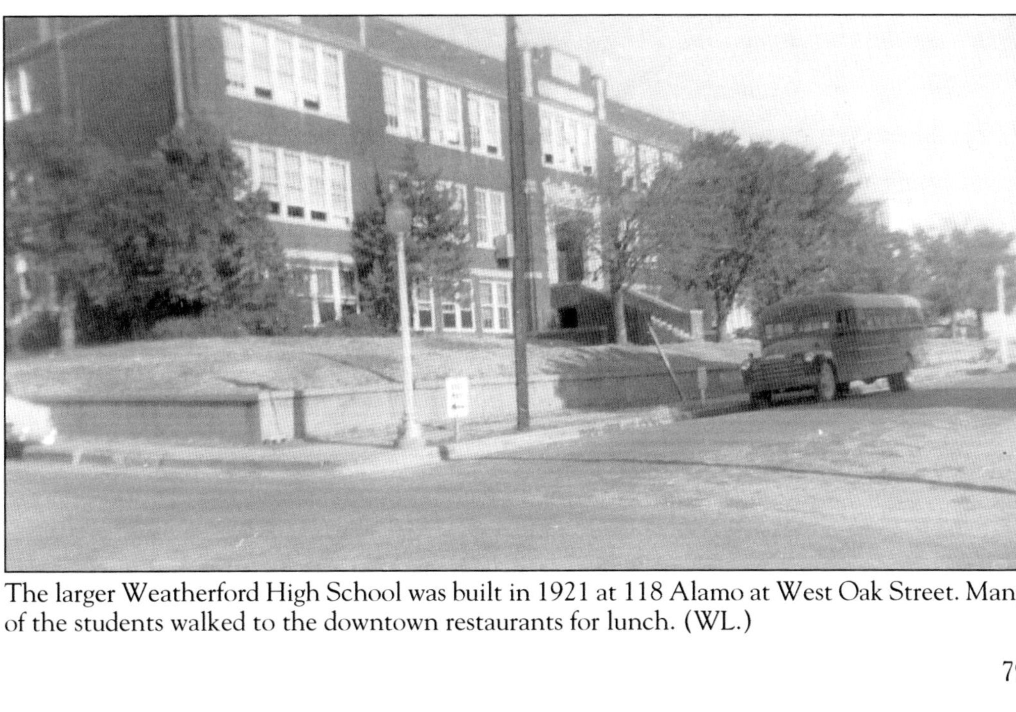

The larger Weatherford High School was built in 1921 at 118 Alamo at West Oak Street. Many of the students walked to the downtown restaurants for lunch. (WL.)

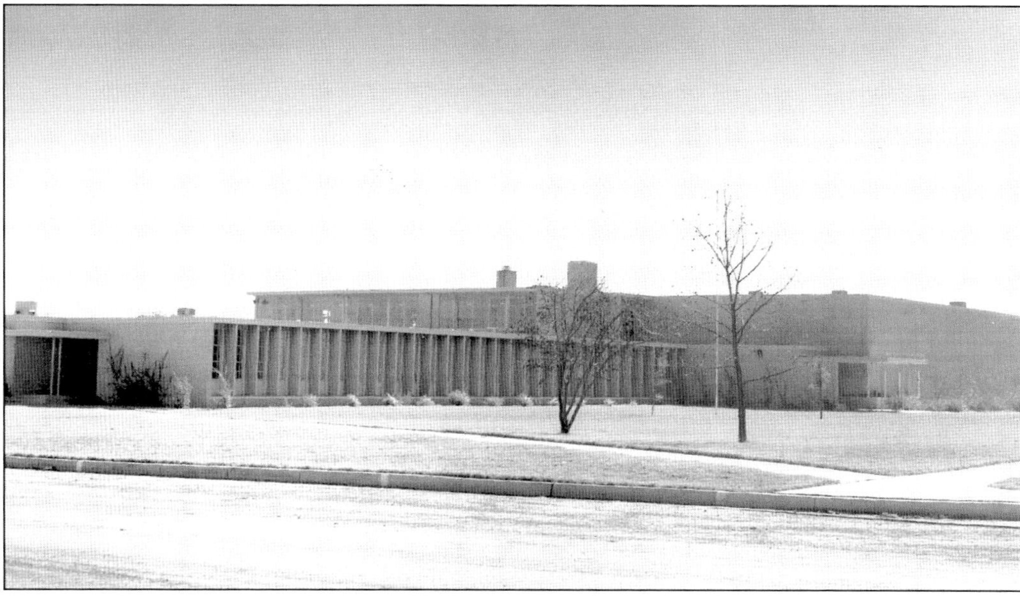

Weatherford High School appears here when it opened at 1007 South Main in 1957. Fast-food restaurants sprang up around the school continuing the tradition. (Chamber of Commerce.)

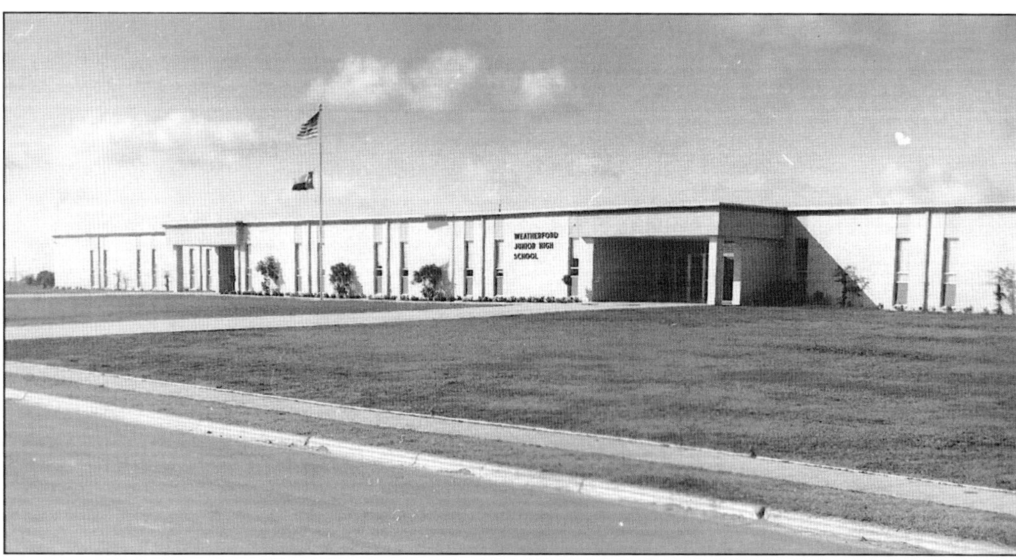

New in 1967, Weatherford Junior High School honored a school board member in 1990 by renaming the school Shirley Hall Junior High. It was built on the runway of the old Weatherford airport at 902 Charles Street. (Chamber of Commerce.)

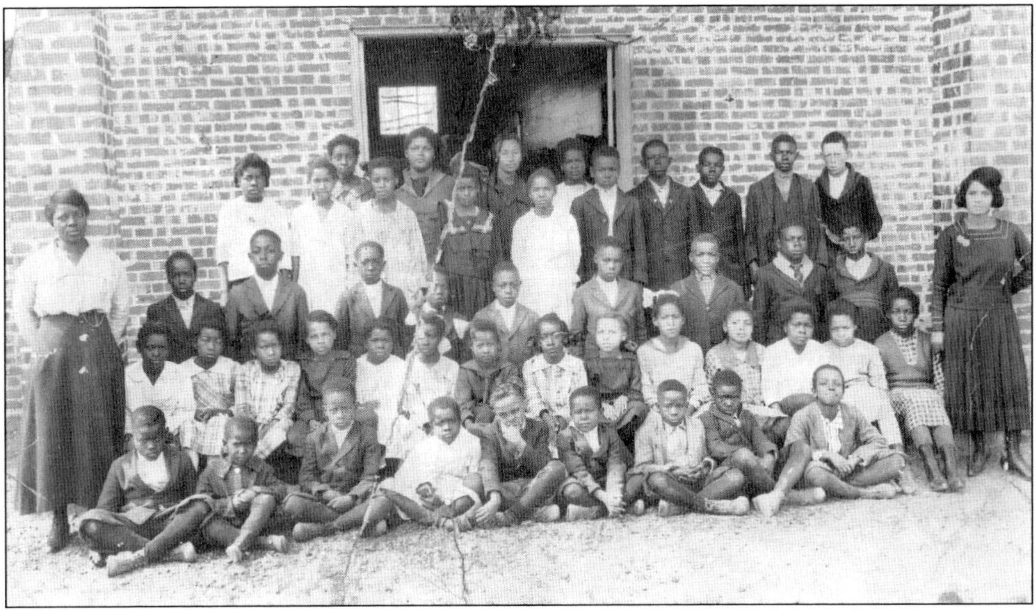

Weatherford Colored School (class photograph *c.* 1910–11) was renamed Mount Pleasant Colored School in 1936. At far left and right are teachers Clara Alexander and Ella Mae Rucker King. (Melvin George via Donald George.)

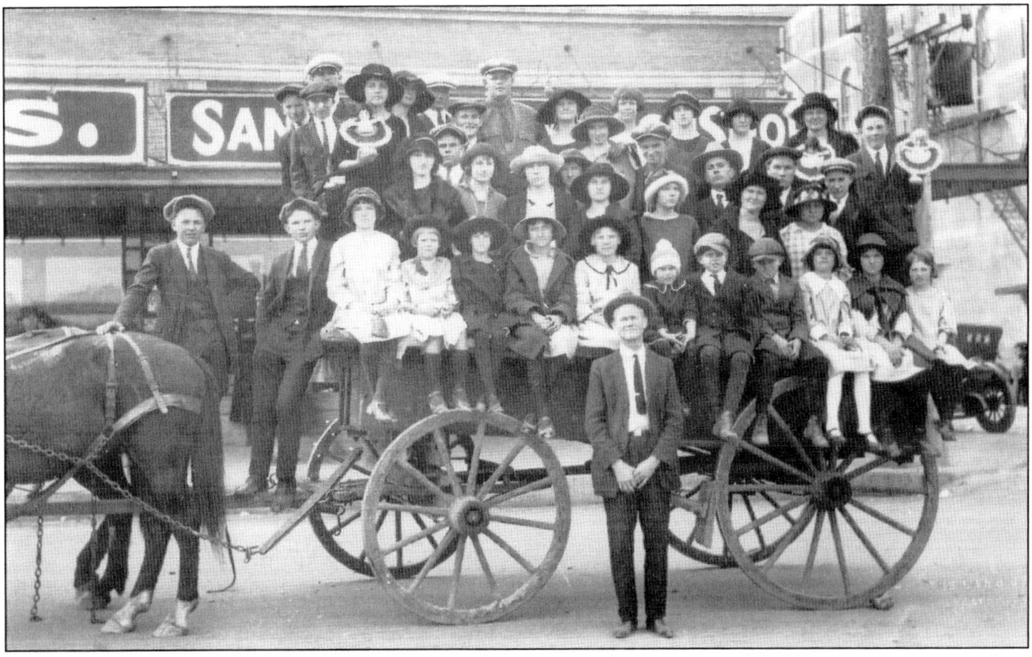

In 1924, Harmony, a small community in the county, had a school field trip to a carnival in Weatherford. Three children hold *Kewpie* dolls they had won. (WL.)

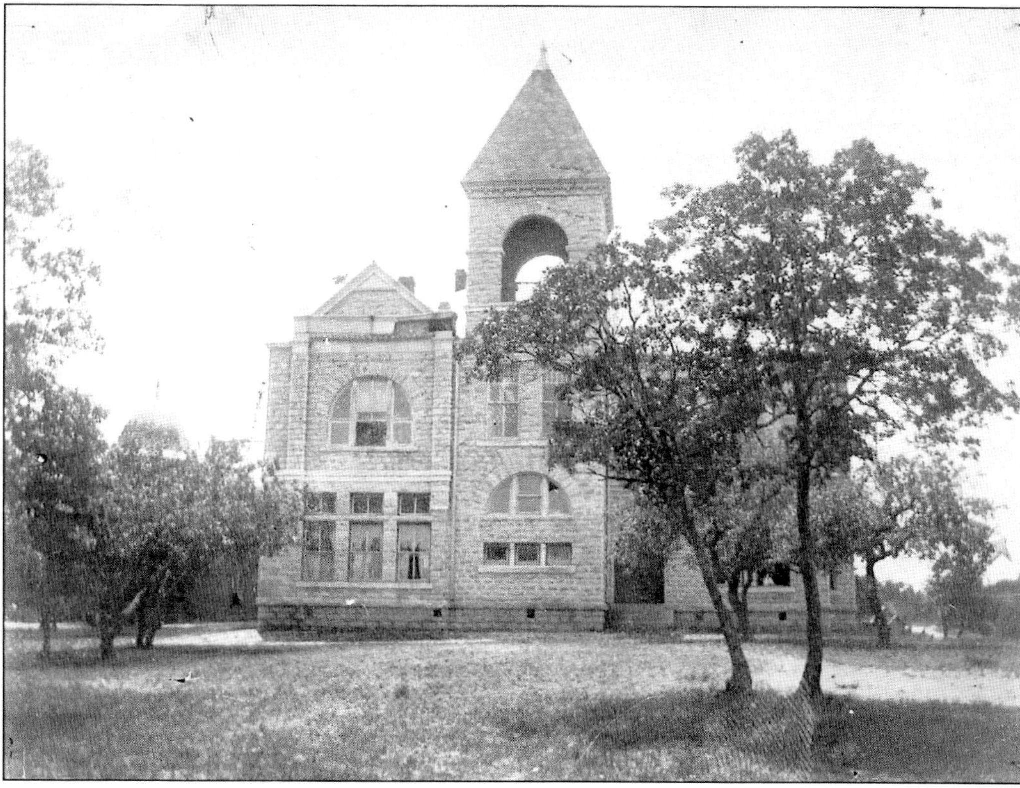

The Texas Fairmount Seminary, 1706 South Main, sponsored by the Cumberland Presbyterian Church, was a girl's school from 1889 to 1911, then a sanitarium and nurses school until 1929. (WC.)

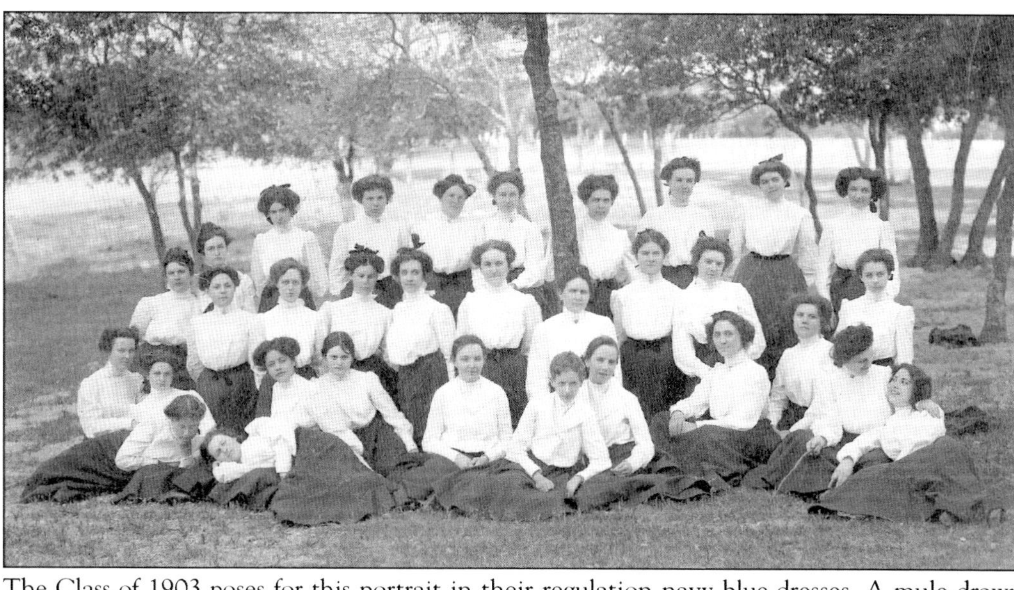

The Class of 1903 poses for this portrait in their regulation navy blue dresses. A mule-drawn rail trolley transported the girls to and from town. In route they were ordered to keep their eyes forward and hands clasped. (WL.)

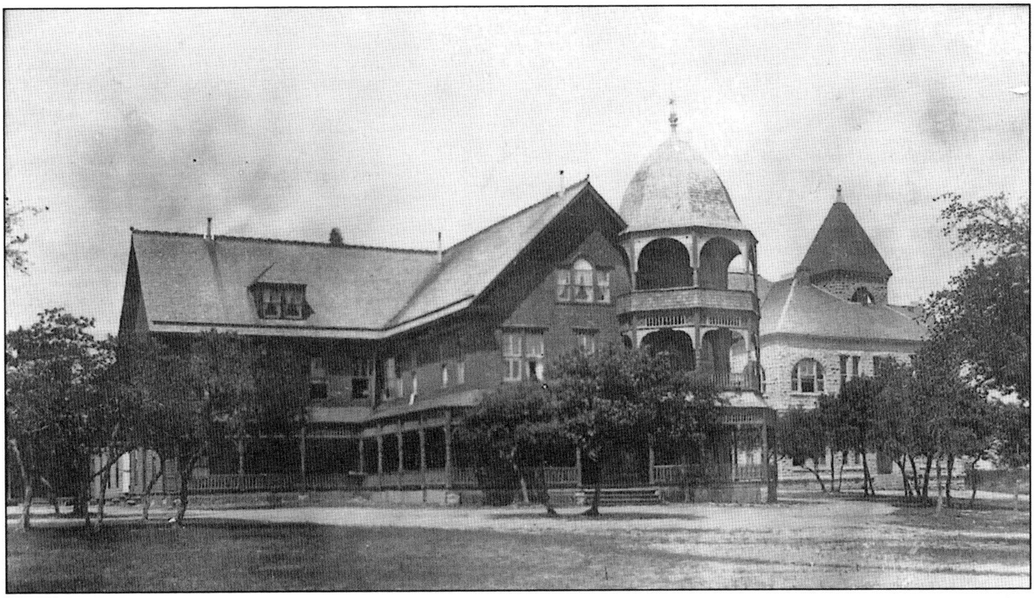

The original women's dormitory is visible on the left. The lecture hall is barely seen on the right. (WL.)

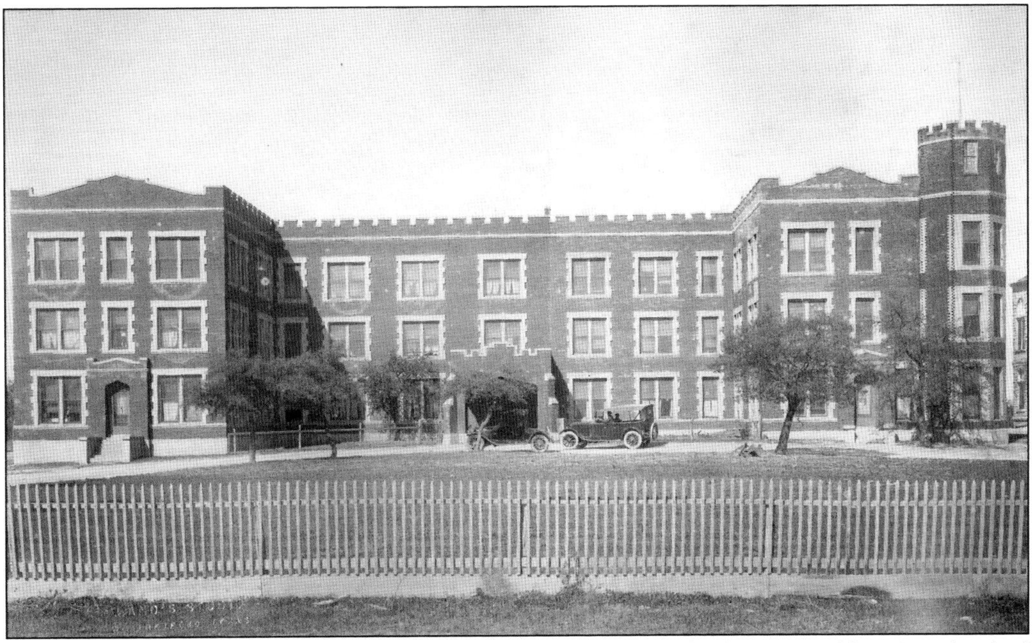

The dormitory was later replaced by this larger building. The facility was sold to Weatherford College in 1929 as a boy's dormitory. Emmanual Baptist Church is presently at this location in 1999. (WC.)

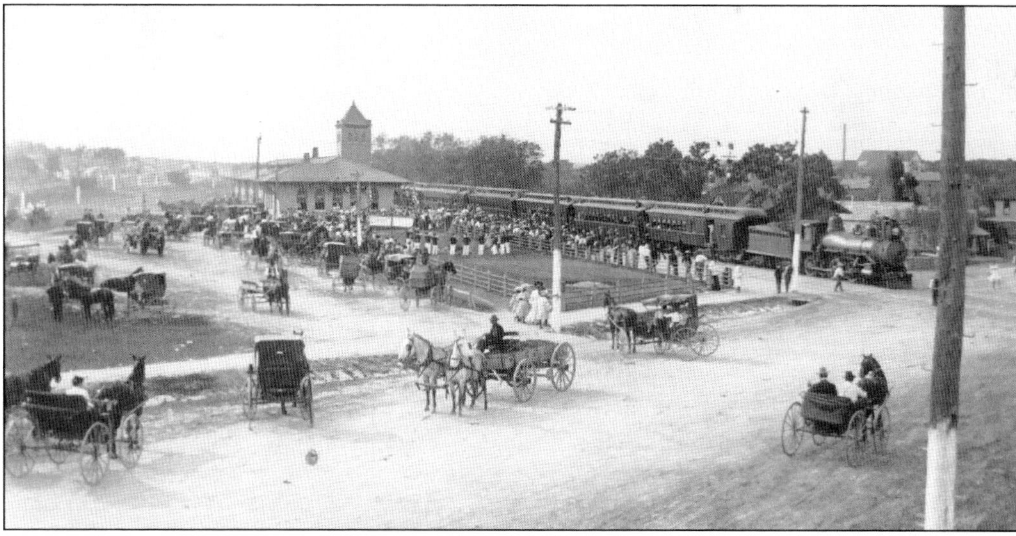

On April 26, 1905, dignitaries of the Knights of Pythias met at the T & P station to select a site for their projected national orphans' home. (James H. Doss.)

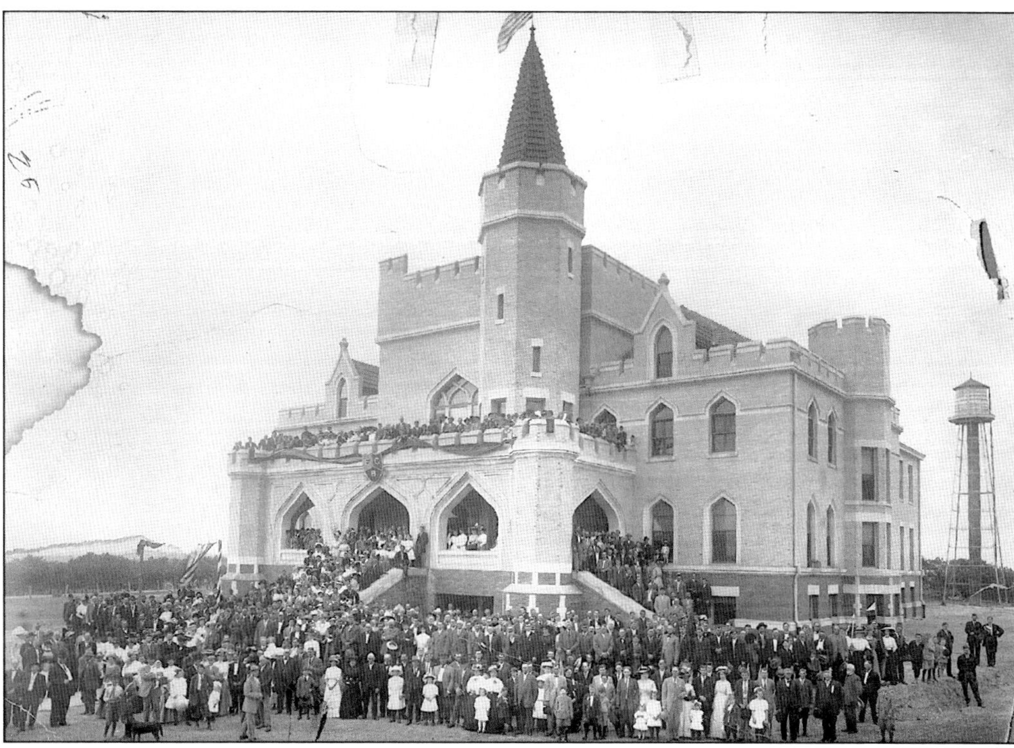

April 23, 1911, was the dedication date of the new Knights of Pythias Widows and Orphans Home. (Pythian home via Peggy Hutton, administrator.)

Eight

Transportation

Vehicles of the past and present moved Weatherford into the future. It brought our agriculture and cattle to market, and brought lumber and merchandise to make this community prosper.

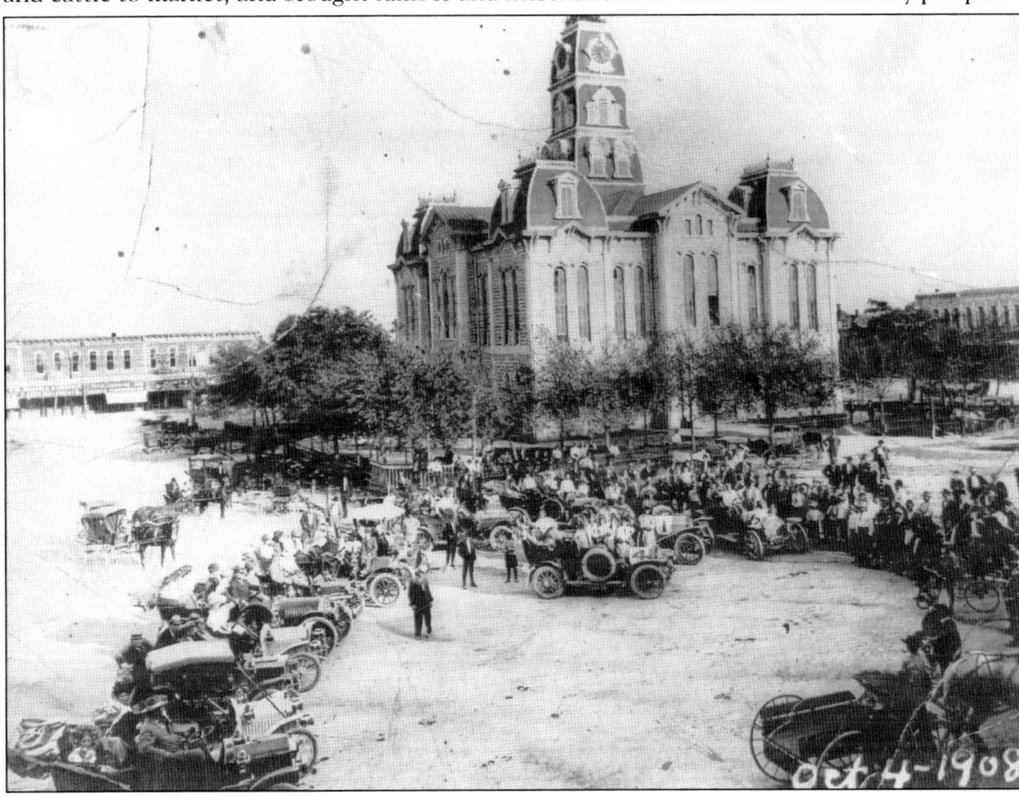

On Sunday, October 4, 1908, Weatherford was the halfway point in an automobile endurance race from and to Arlington, Texas. Three of the entrants pause for their photograph with most of Weatherford's cars. A year later the City laid down oil to keep the dust down from so many cars. The perimeter of the square and a portion of North and South Main were paved in 1919. (WL.)

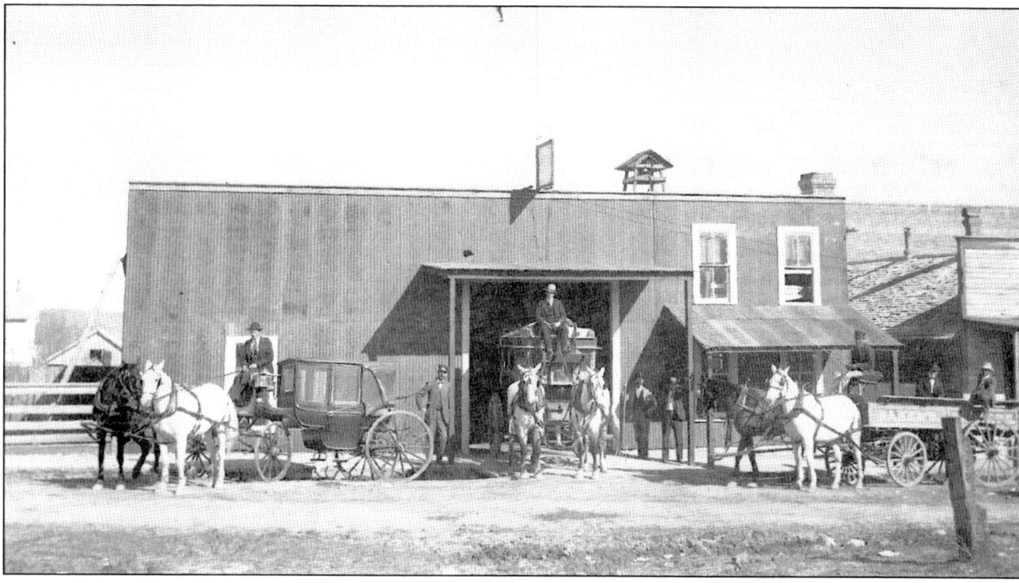

C.C. Baker Transfer Company office and stable on West Dallas Avenue was in back of the family home at 303 West Spring. For decades, they provided the main transportation within Weatherford. (WL.)

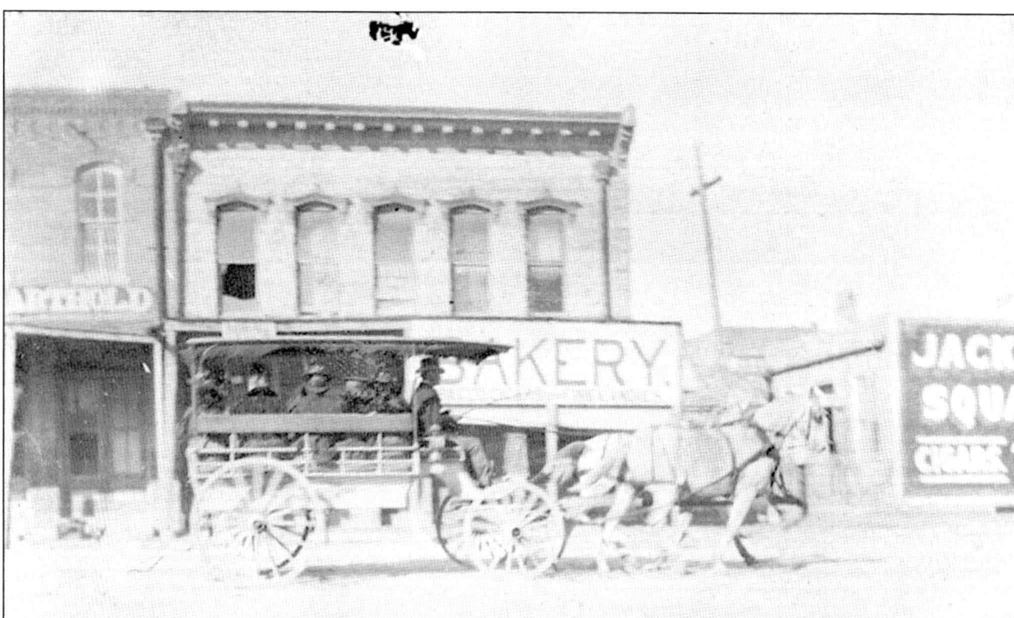

The Baker Transfer tokens, the size of a half-dollar, were printed, "Good for 25 cent Ride." The taxi is on North Main at Spring Street headed for the train depot with hotel passengers. (WL.)

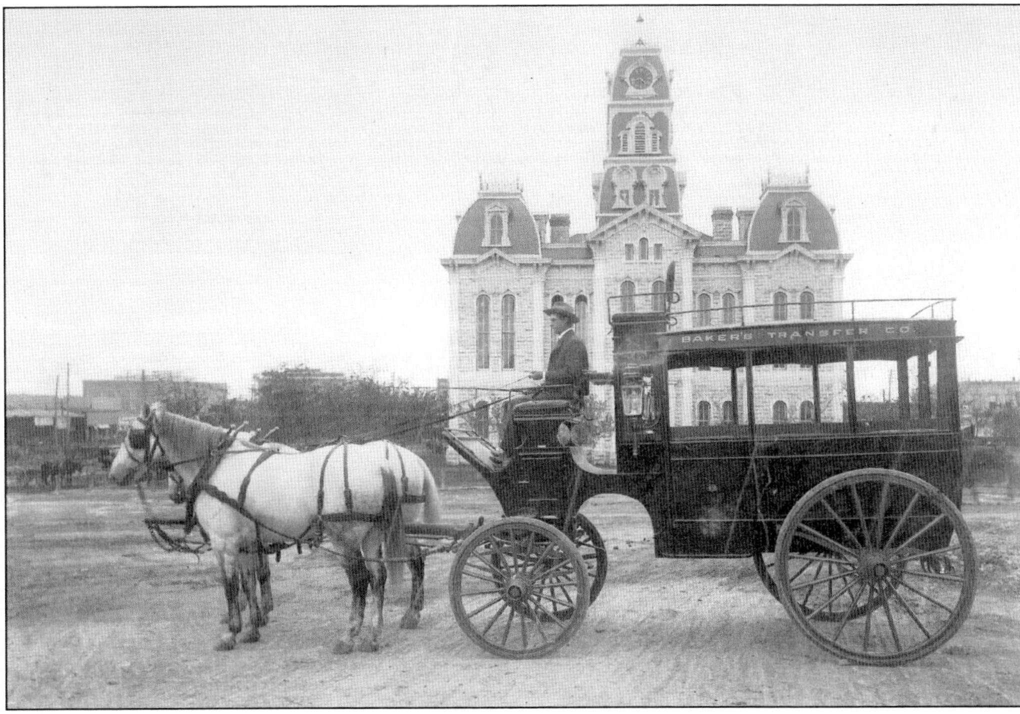

C.C. Baker's landau carriages were the limousines of that day—their rubber treads helped. Rich merchants and cattlemen had their streets widened to help turn the carriages around. (WL.)

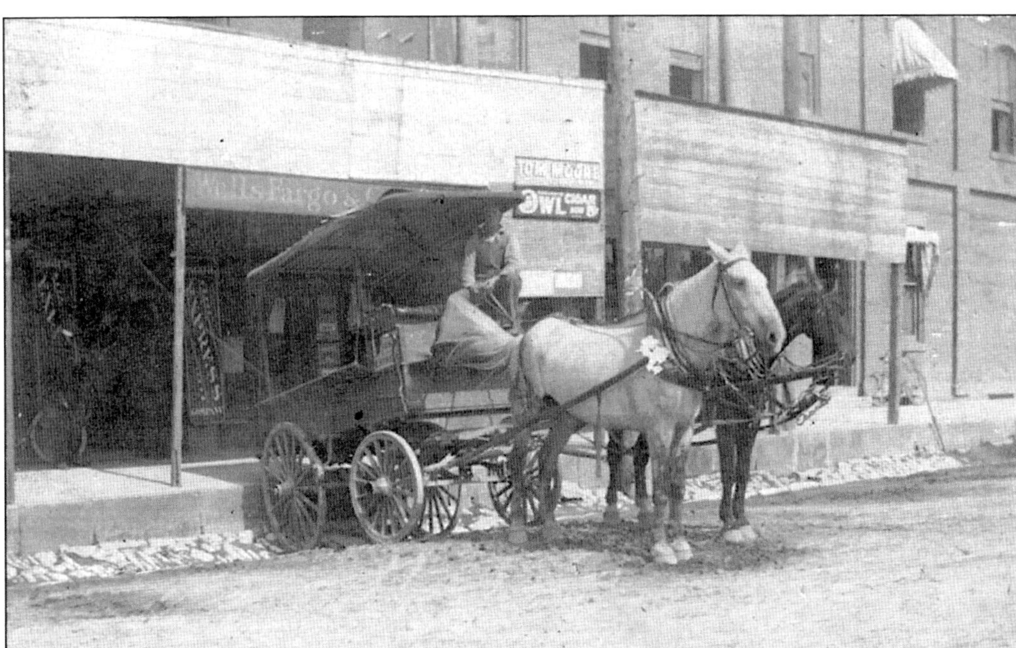

The Wells Fargo Freight Co. at 112 North Main accepts a Baker Transfer delivery. (WL.)

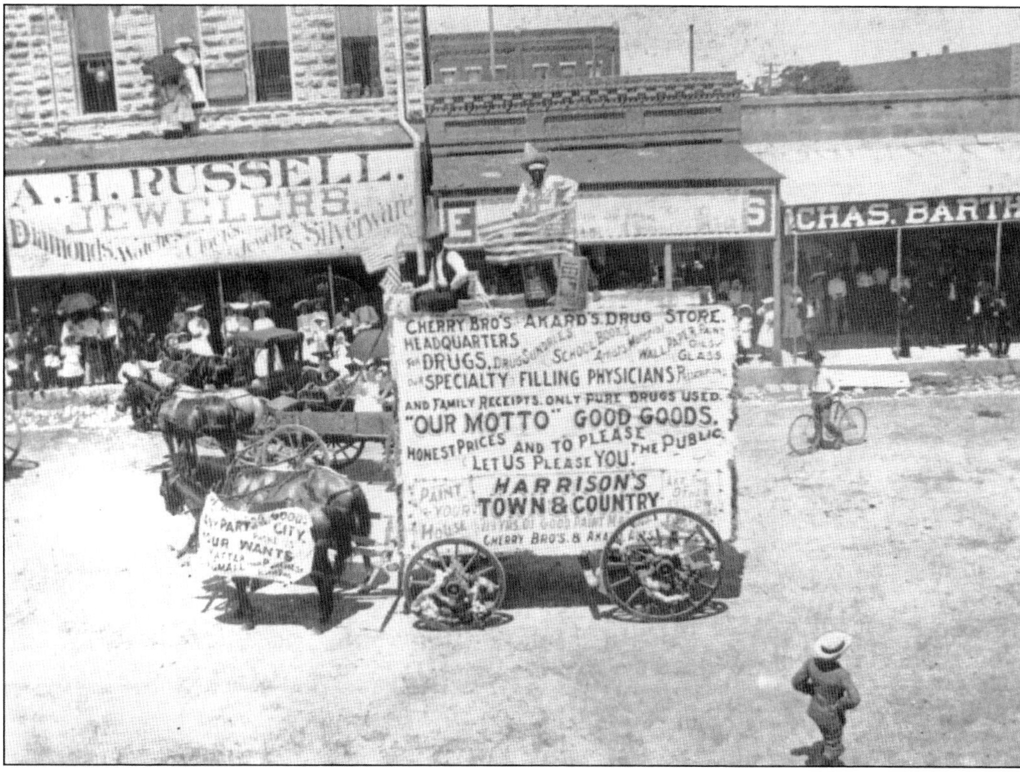

A parade advertisement is on North Main. Charles Barthold's men's clothing store operated here from 1878 to 1928. (Martha McClung.)

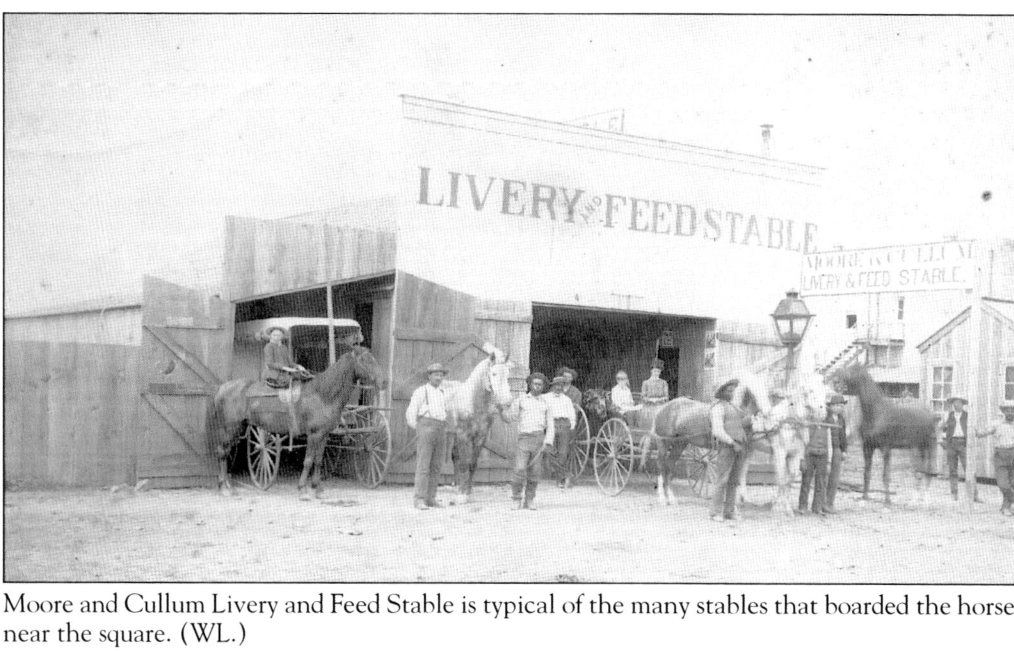

Moore and Cullum Livery and Feed Stable is typical of the many stables that boarded the horses near the square. (WL.)

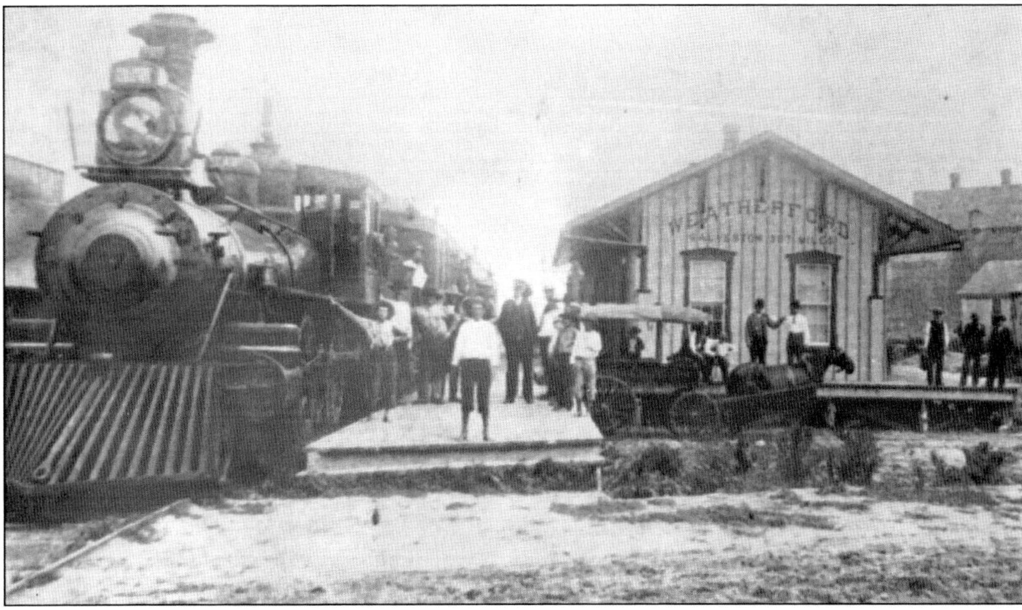

The first Santa Fe passenger train arrived at the new depot on November 1, 1887. The depot was at 319 North Main and advertised "Galveston 357 Miles." It was replaced by a huge stone building after about 20 years use. (Martha McClung.)

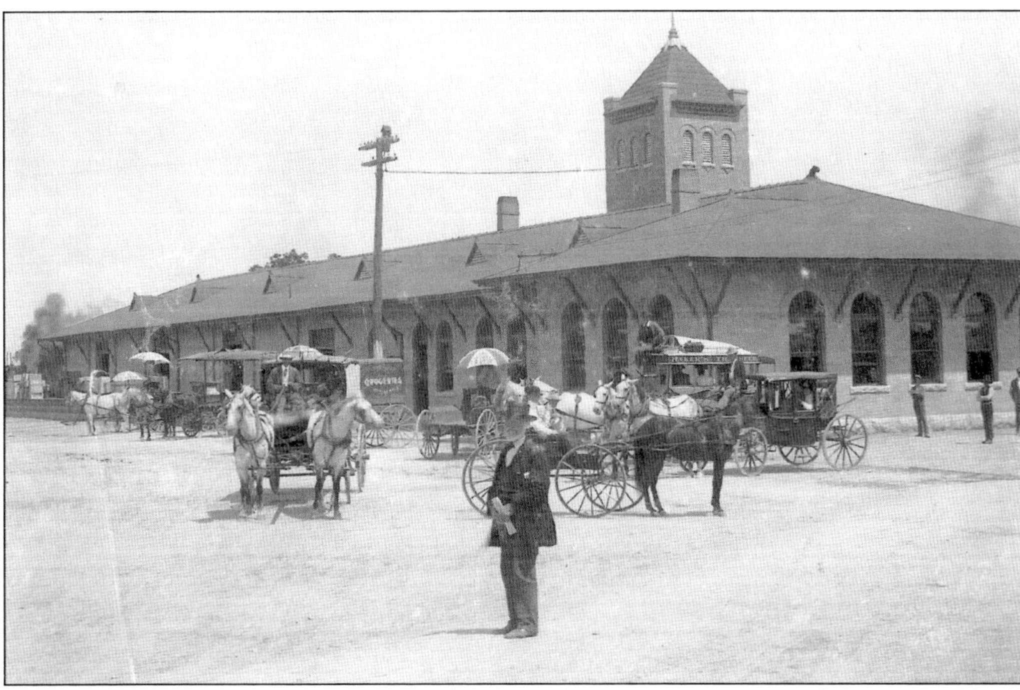

Wagons and carriages, including C.C. Baker Transfer, await a train's arrival at T & P Railroad Depot. (WL.)

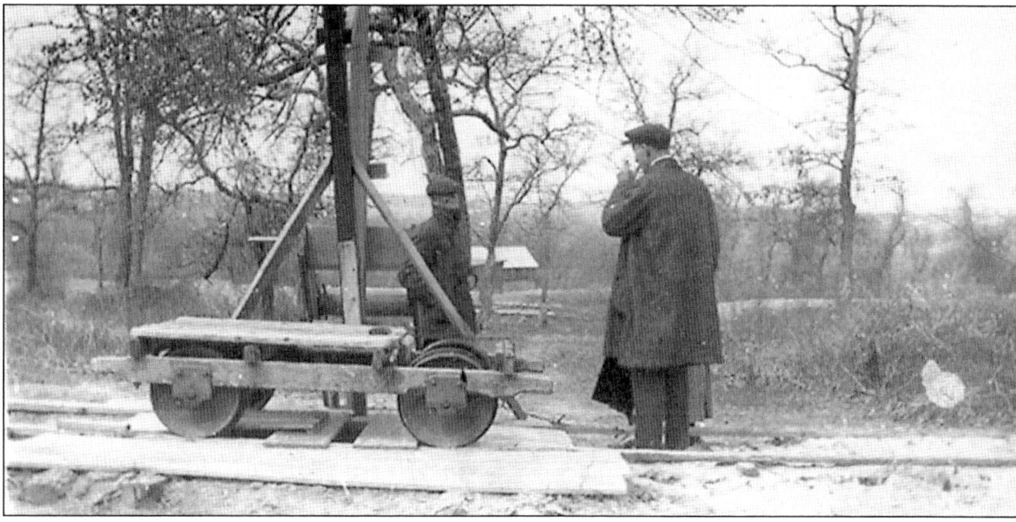

In 1916, Remy Ancelin, right, is pictured with a railroad-section worker. (Mary Ellen Guay.)

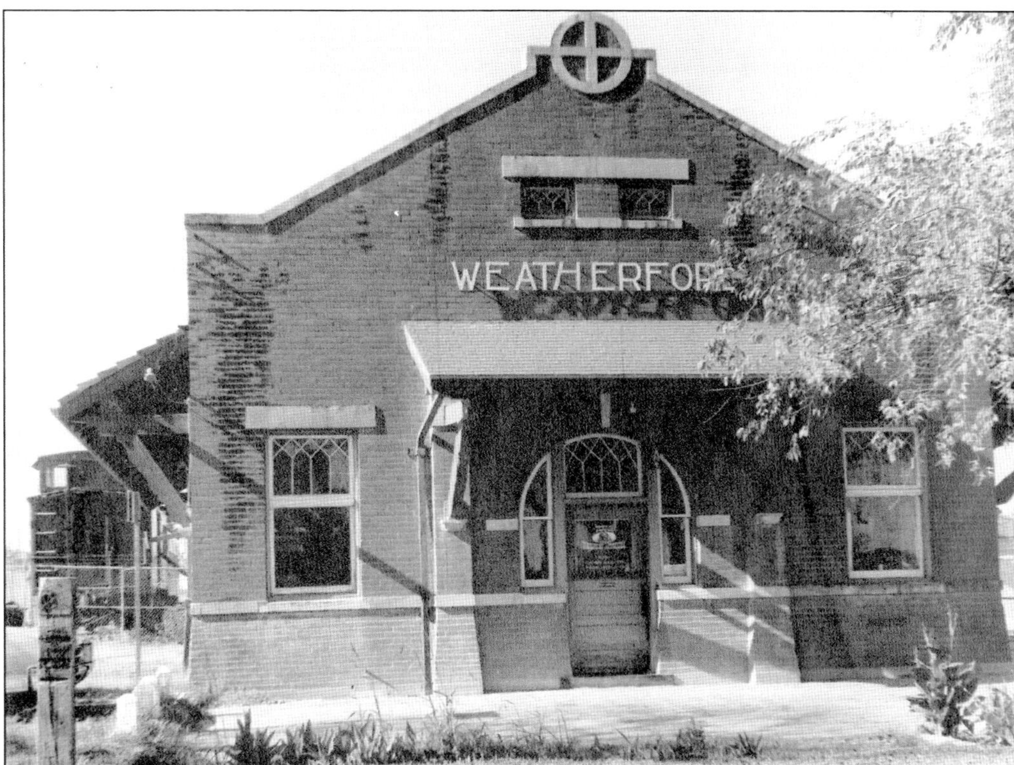

The second Santa Fe Depot was completed in 1910 at 401 Fort Worth Street. Weatherford was given the deed to the depot in 1959. It housed a railroad museum in the 1960s, and later the Chamber of Commerce. (Chamber of Commerce.)

All Aboard! Ted Frost takes the train to points east. The T & P and Santa Fe railroads operated passenger service until the early 1950s. Tourism further increased to Weatherford when major highways replaced the old coast-to-coast Bankhead Highway. (Charles Frost.)

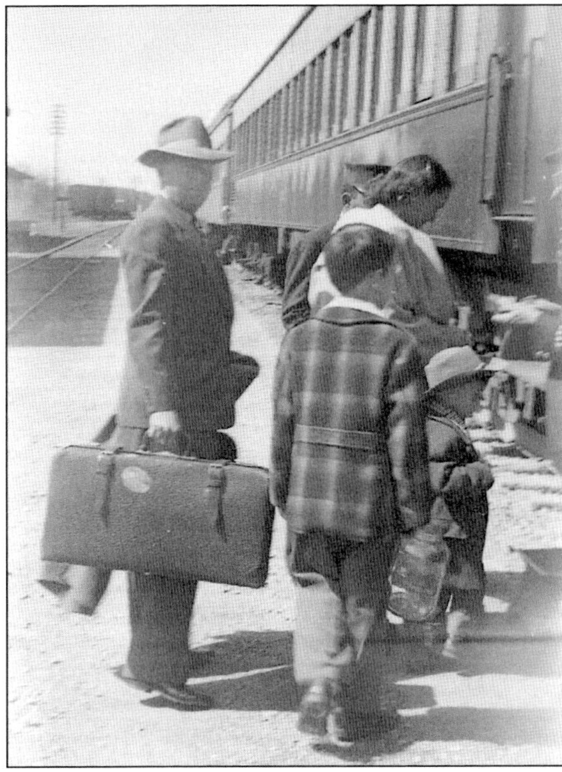

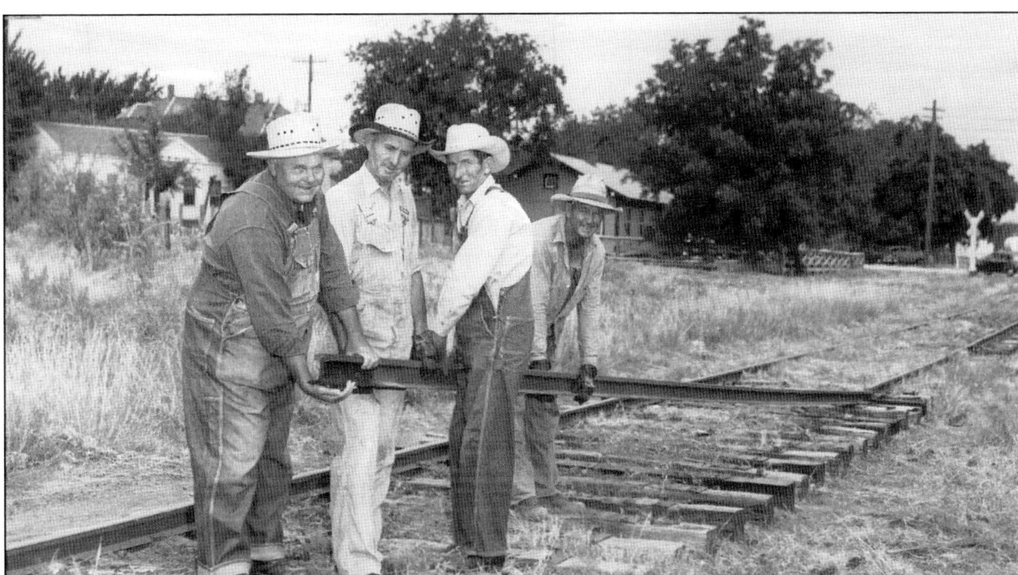

In the late 1950s, the Santa Fe began to remove its rails under supervision of longtime section foreman, Bill Meeks, left, who poses with his crew. (Lynn Harris.)

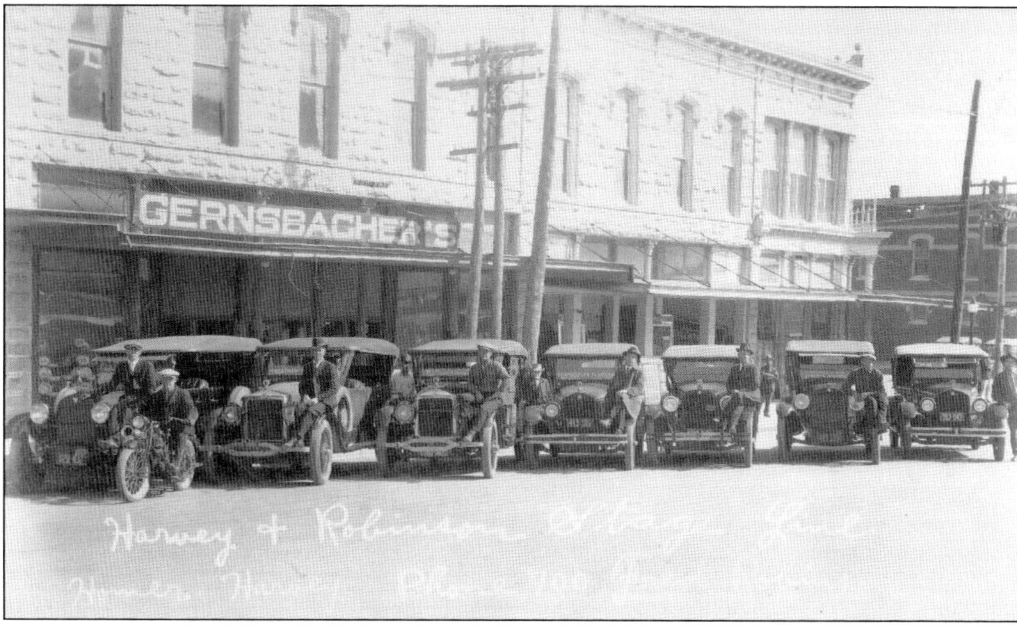

The Harvey and Robinson "Stage" Line operated between Fort Worth and Weatherford. Owners were Fred Robinson, left, and Homer Harvey, third from left. The Princess Theater, 104 Dallas Avenue, between Gernsbachers and Citizens Bank, was showing a Rudolph Valentino movie. (WL.)

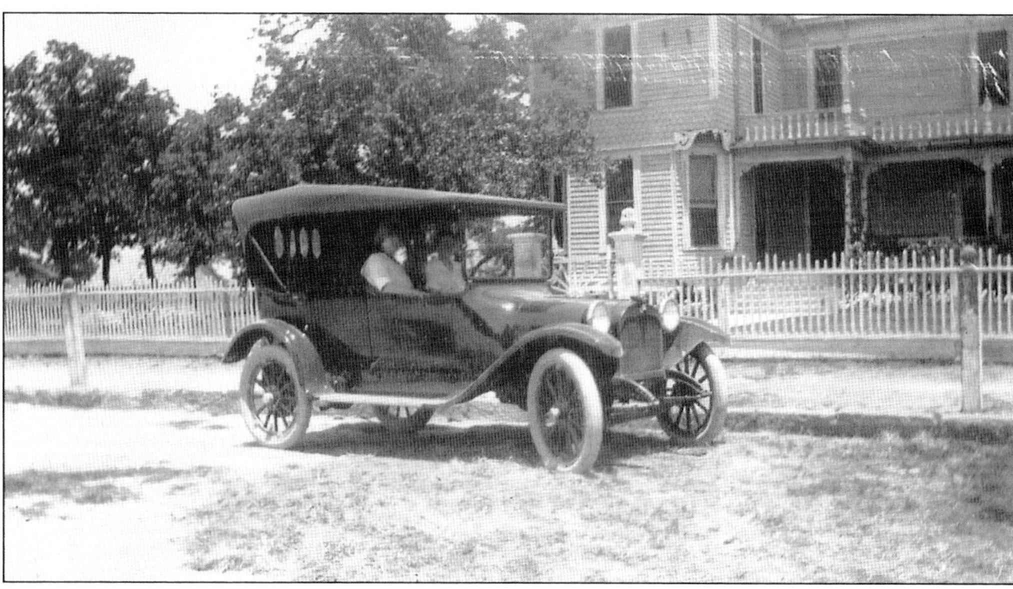

Dan D. Hartnett, a successful retail grocer, got a new 1914 Dodge Brothers car with a steel body and baked-on enamel. (Mary Ellen Guay.)

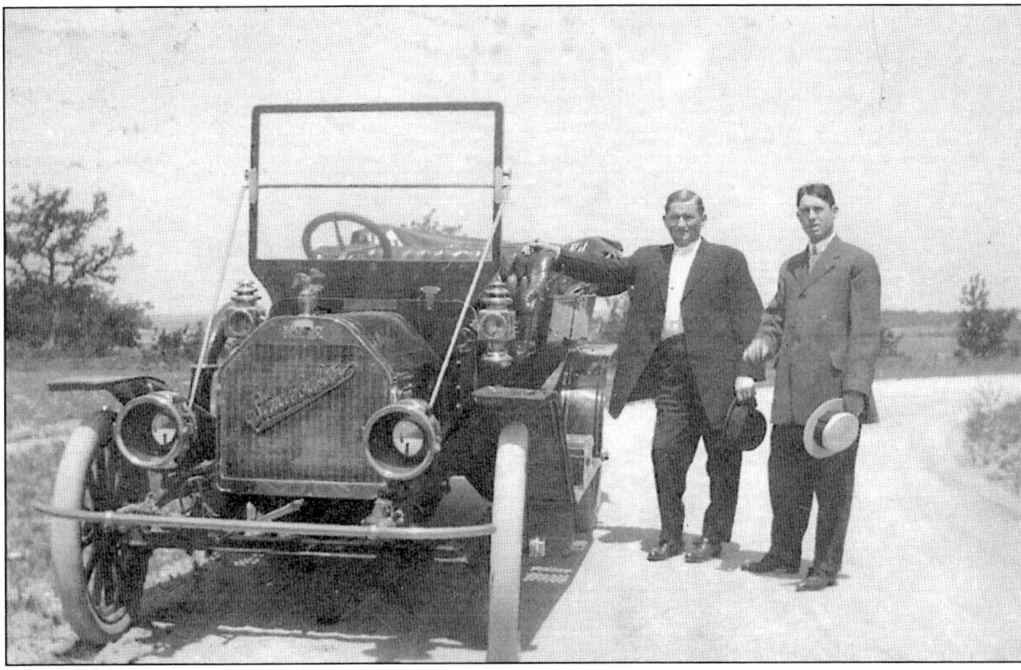

In July 1906, Harry Baker looks over a new Studebaker. Charles Fant, right, went car hunting. Below, Charles parks his new 1911 Hupmobile "touring car" on the square. (Bill Fant.)

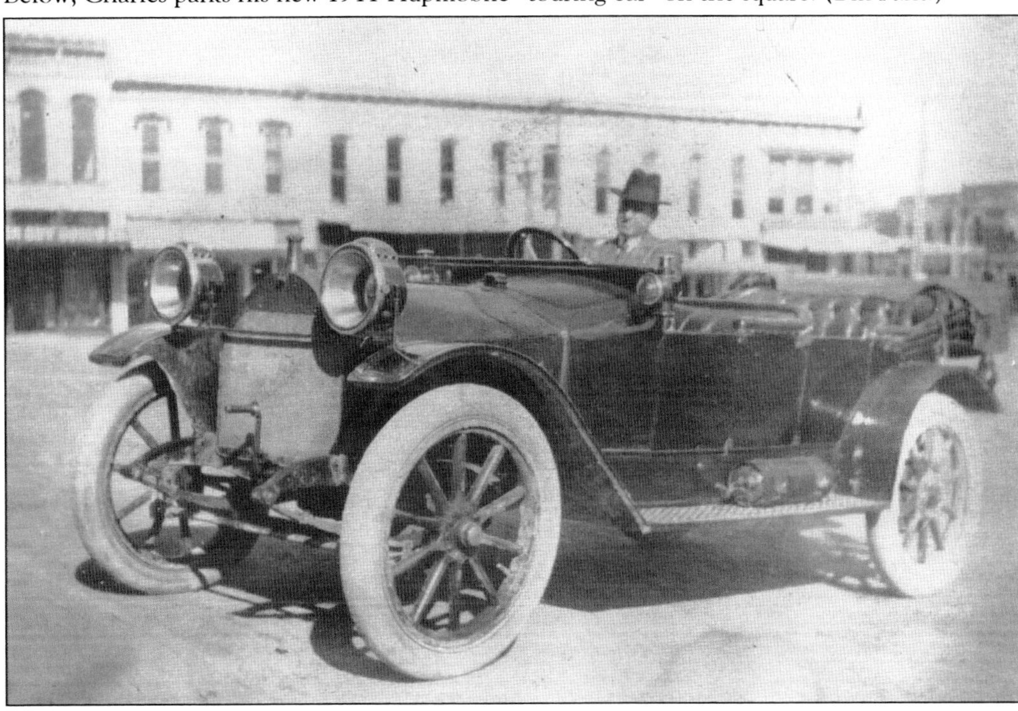

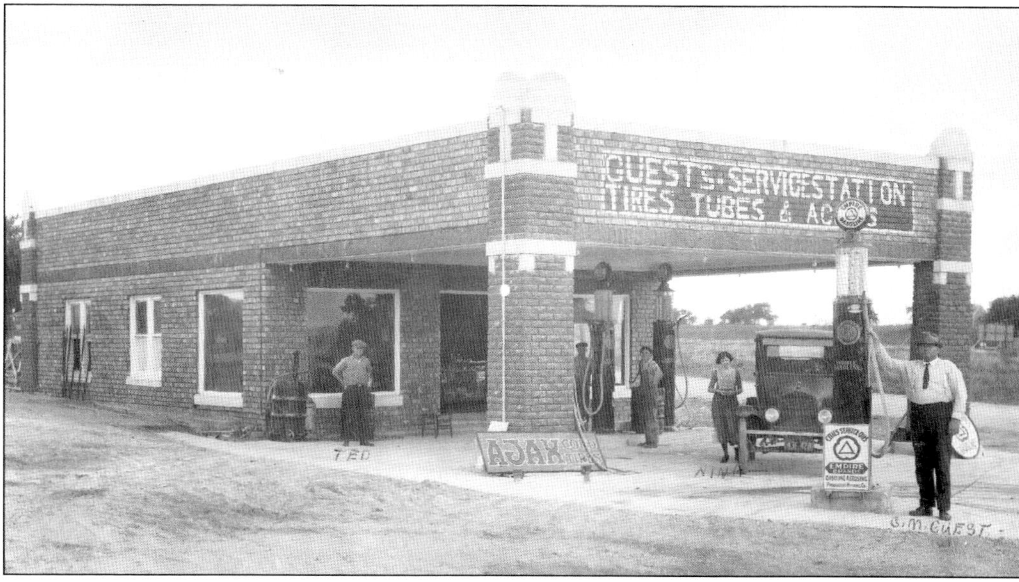

To go west in 1921, Guest Service Station, 1125 Palo Pinto at Bowie Drive, was the final fuel stop in town. Owner C.M. Guest poses in front. The station was converted into the Guest Motel in 1948 and operated until June 1982. (Charles Frost.)

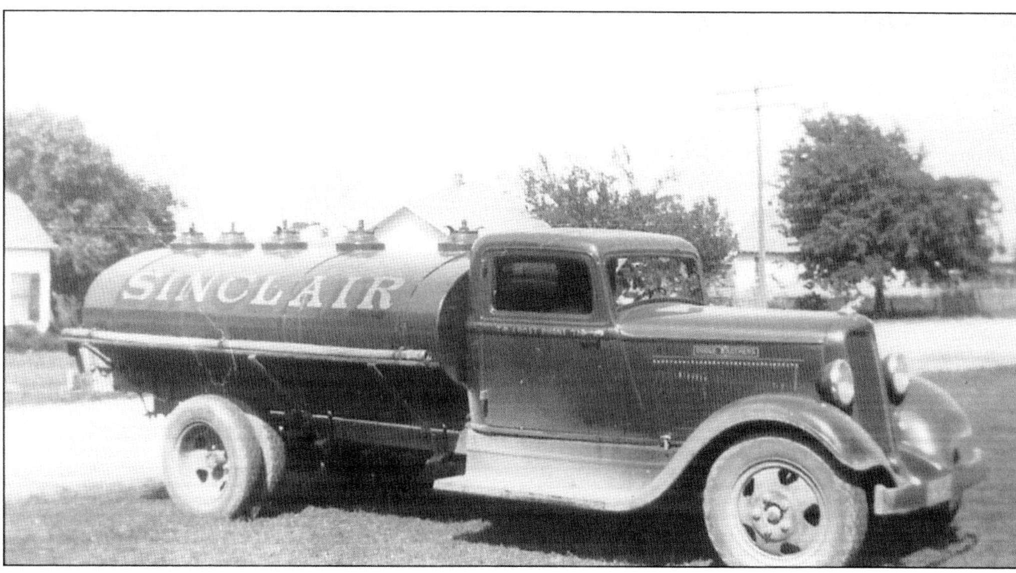

Ted R. Frost operated the wholesale fuel deliveries for Sinclair stations. In 1938, this was his Mack fuel truck. (Charles Frost.)

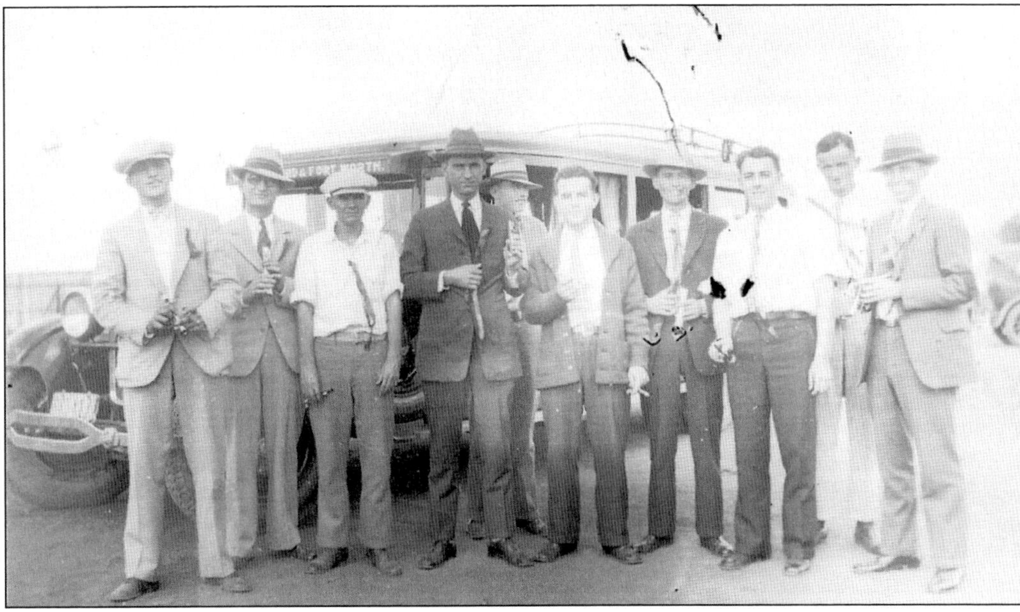

The Harvey Lines, formerly Harvey and Robinson "Stage," ran a special for Weatherford Junior College football fans to go to Cisco Junior College in 1924. (Bill Witherspoon.)

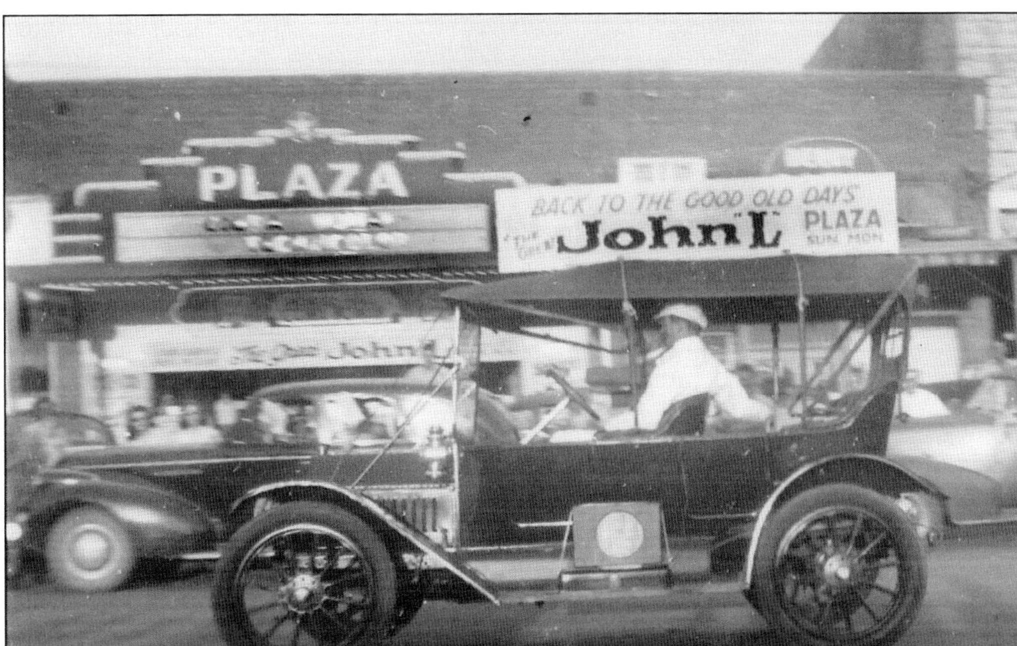

The Plaza Theatre, 109 College Avenue, opened in 1941. It uses an old car to advertise the "Great John L." in 1945. (Carla Hollingsworth.)

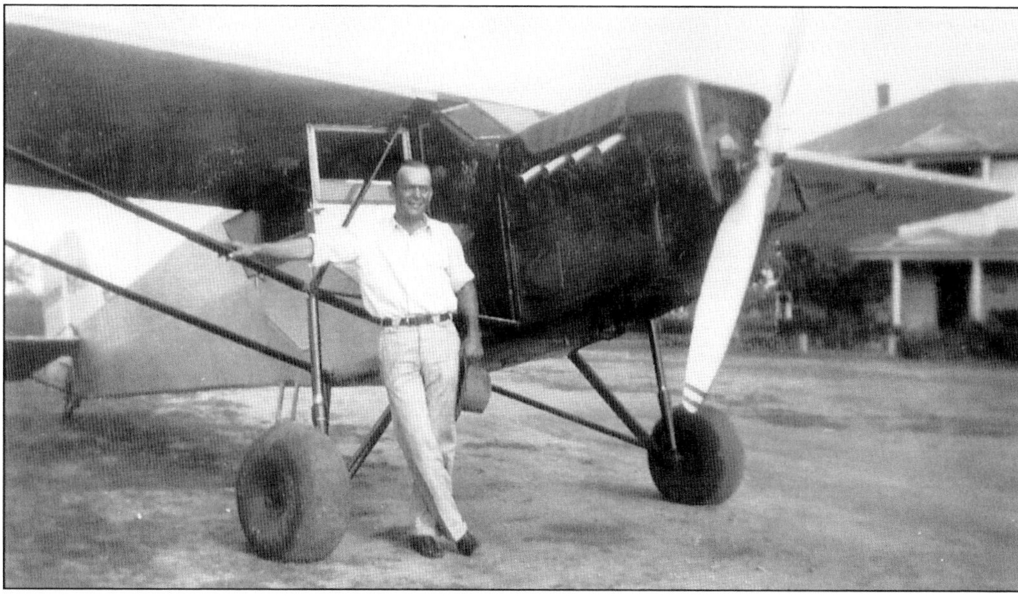

The Weatherford airport opened in October 1931. It was parallel to Bowie Drive. At that time, Ted Frost looks over a Curtiss "Robin" airplane parked at the 500 block of that dirt road. Attorney V.P. Craven's home is in the background. (Charles Frost.)

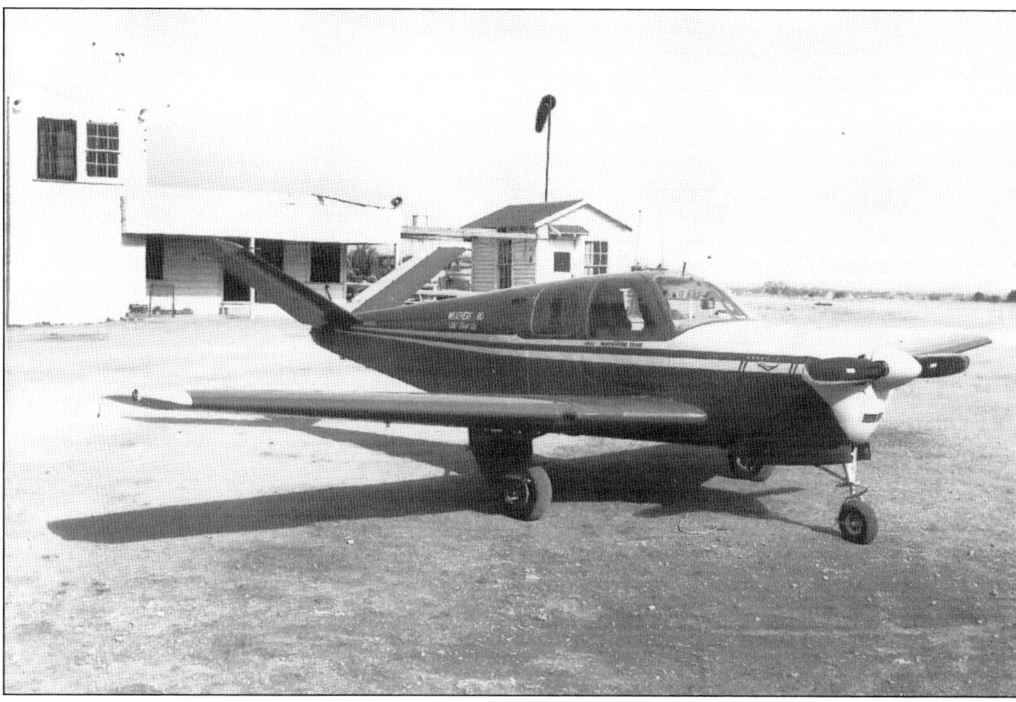

After World War II, the Weatherford Oil Tool Company purchased a fleet of Beechcraft "Bonanza" aircraft, the largest private aircraft fleet up to that time. In 1949–50, the company flew polio victims to distant hospitals for treatment. The Weatherford airport brought a lot of light aircraft to town. (Jess Hall Jr.)

Nine

Agriculture and Ranching

Ranching and farming are the backbone of Weatherford, just as the ranchers and farmers need the city. The Trade's Day, later called "First Monday," brings the county people into town. But many, like Oliver Loving, moved into town for protection during the Indian raids of the 1860s and 1870s. The drought of the 1880s also caused many to move into town.

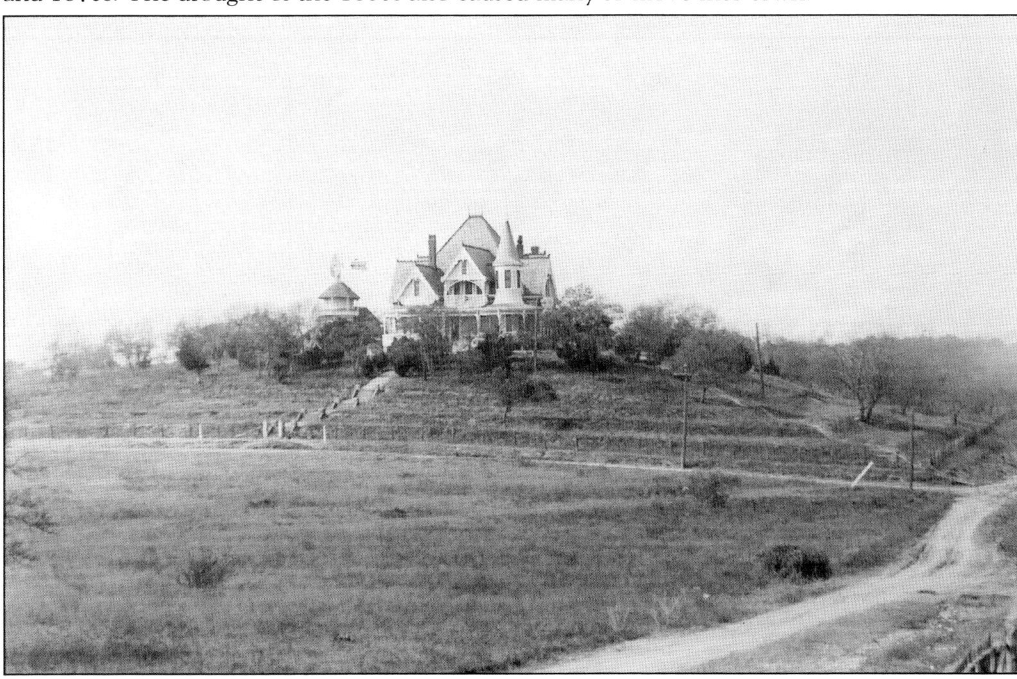

The property on South Lamar at Norton Drive, seen here in 1915, was the site of the city's first rodeo arena. In 1945, an informal roping group met here to work calves and ride horseback, and this friendship developed into the Parker County Sheriff Posse. (WL.)

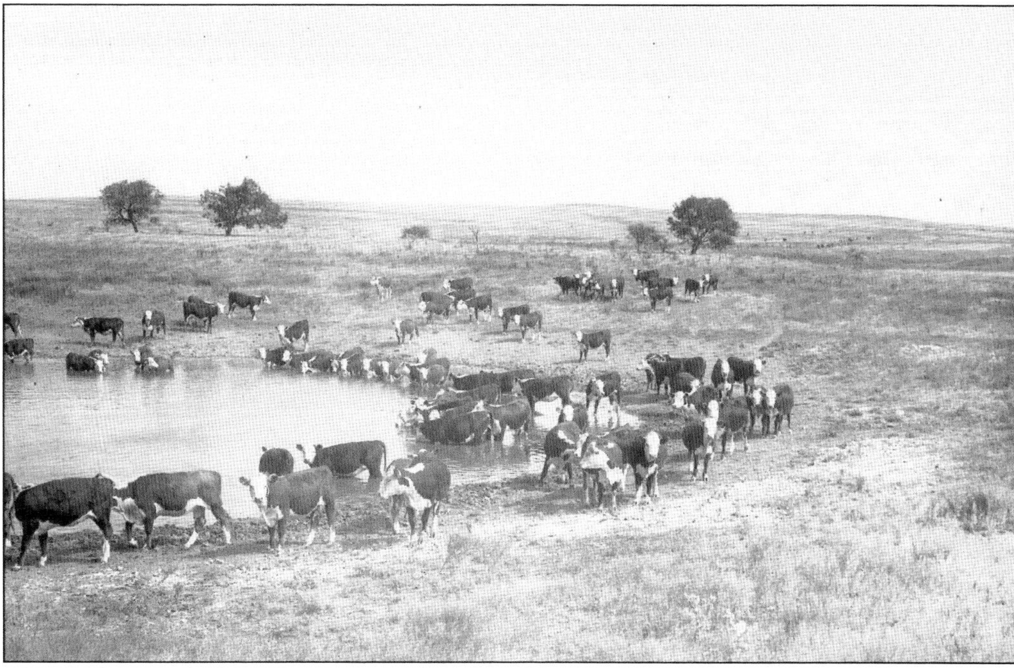

The cattle quench their thirst at a "tank" on the LS spread in the 1950s. Ranchers were better prepared for the drought of the early 1950s than the infamous drought of 1886. Clara Barton, president of the Red Cross, made a report to President Grover Cleveland on the poor conditions of North Texas in 1887. (Eloise Smyth.)

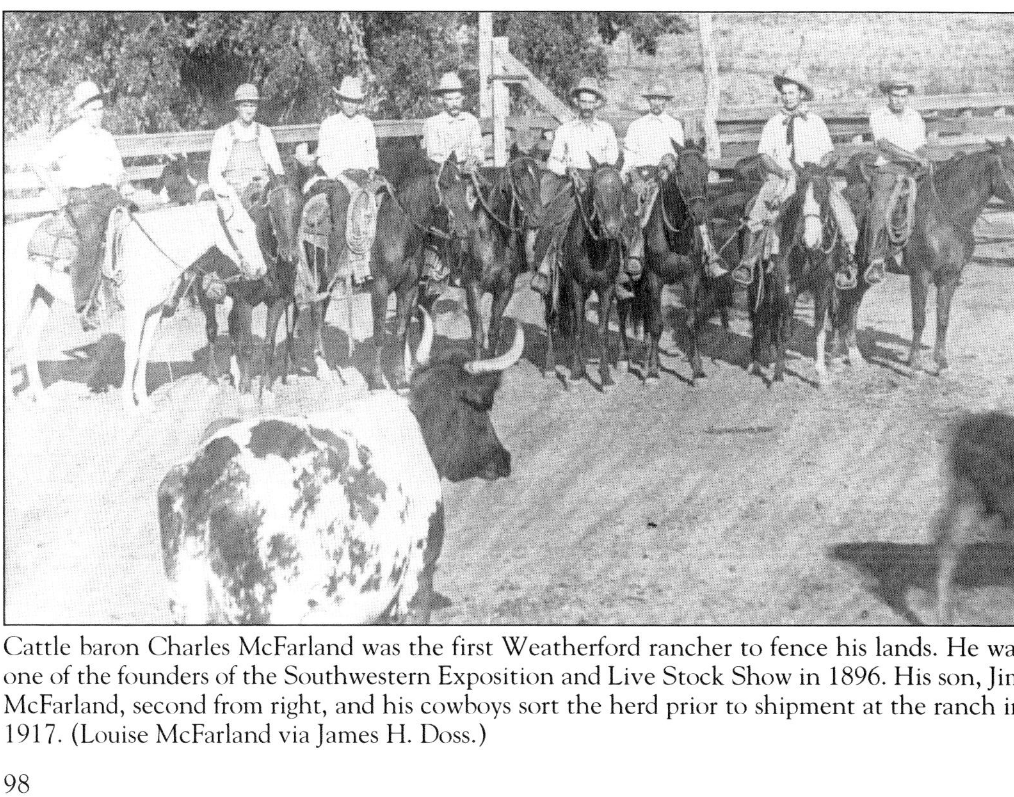

Cattle baron Charles McFarland was the first Weatherford rancher to fence his lands. He was one of the founders of the Southwestern Exposition and Live Stock Show in 1896. His son, Jim McFarland, second from right, and his cowboys sort the herd prior to shipment at the ranch in 1917. (Louise McFarland via James H. Doss.)

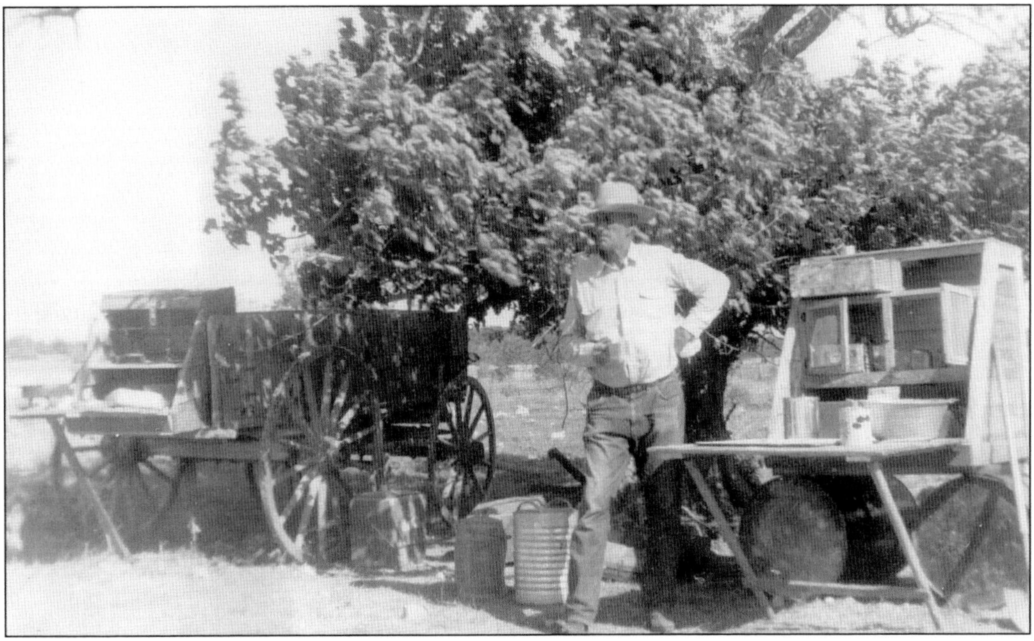

The chuckwagon was the lifeblood of the cowboy. The first one was designed by Charles "Chuck" Goodnight on the heavy-duty iron chassis of an ex-Civil War military wagon. Alfred Teneyck was the cook for the LS ranch in the late 1940s. (Eloise Smyth.)

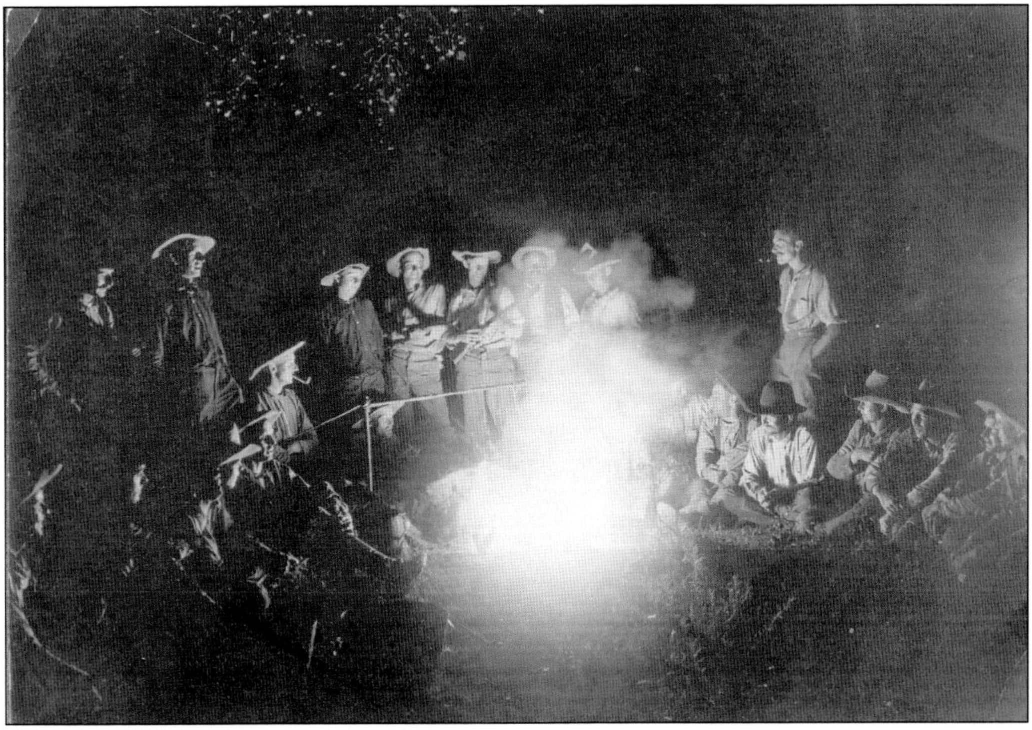

The lifestyle of the cowboy was difficult. With the cattle bedded down, life on the range demands some great yarns. Stories of Weatherford and outlaw Sam Bass, Spanish treasure, and even Belle Starr were stretched until the facts were ignored. (WL.)

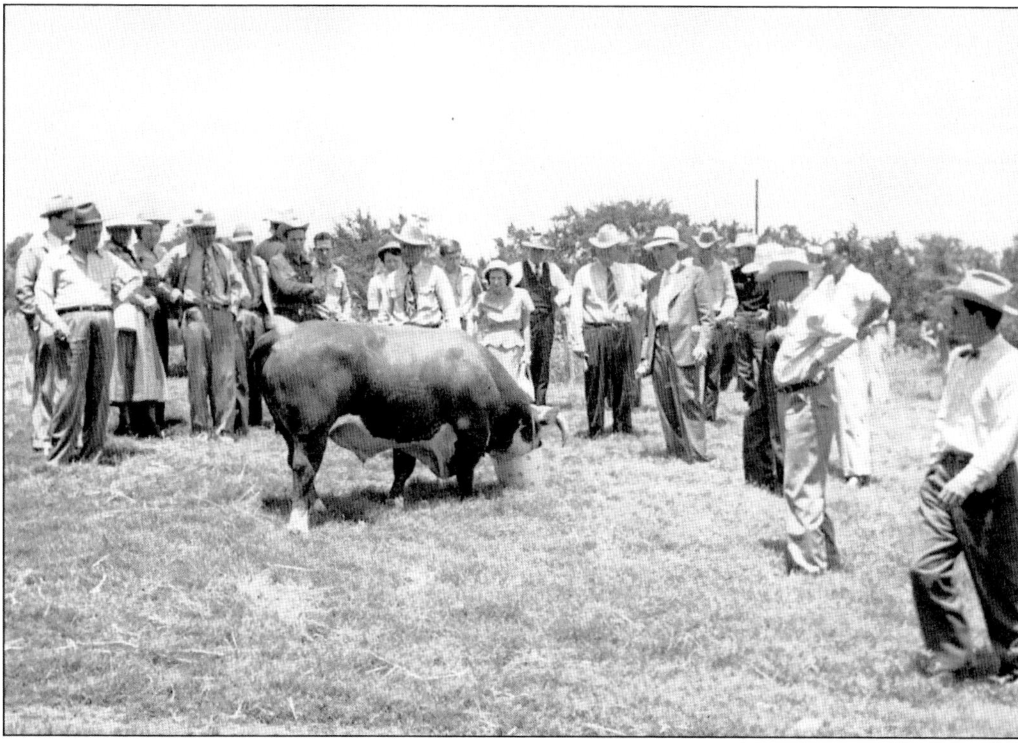

In 1946, the Mid-North Texas Hereford Association Tour came to Ted R. Frost's ranch west of town (seen here) and Tom Saunders's Twin Valley Ranch. (Charles Frost.)

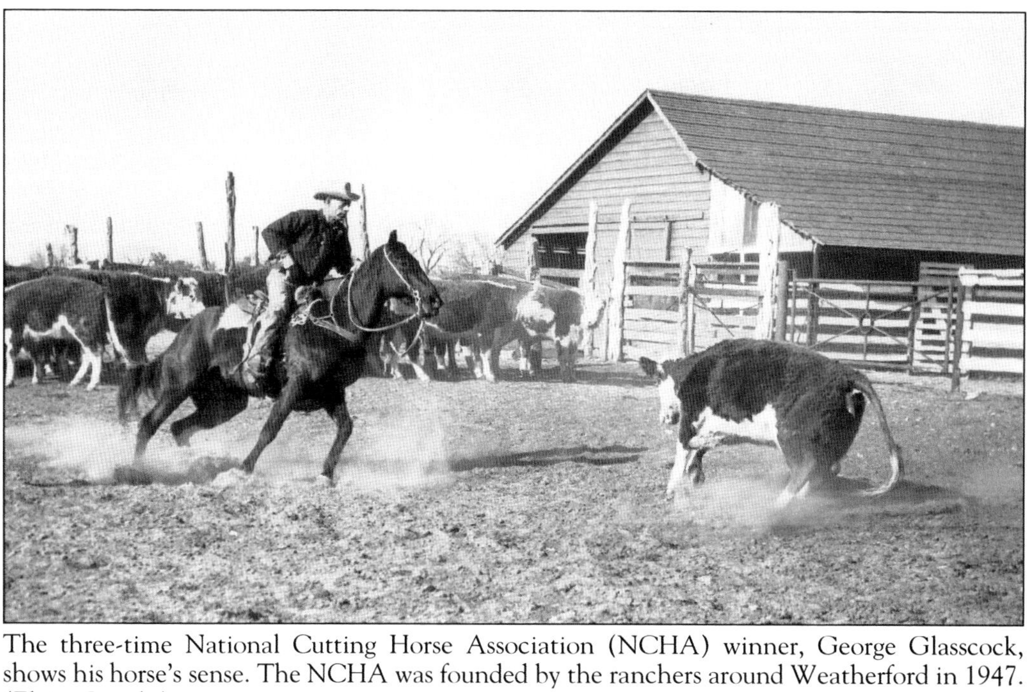

The three-time National Cutting Horse Association (NCHA) winner, George Glasscock, shows his horse's sense. The NCHA was founded by the ranchers around Weatherford in 1947. (Eloise Smyth.)

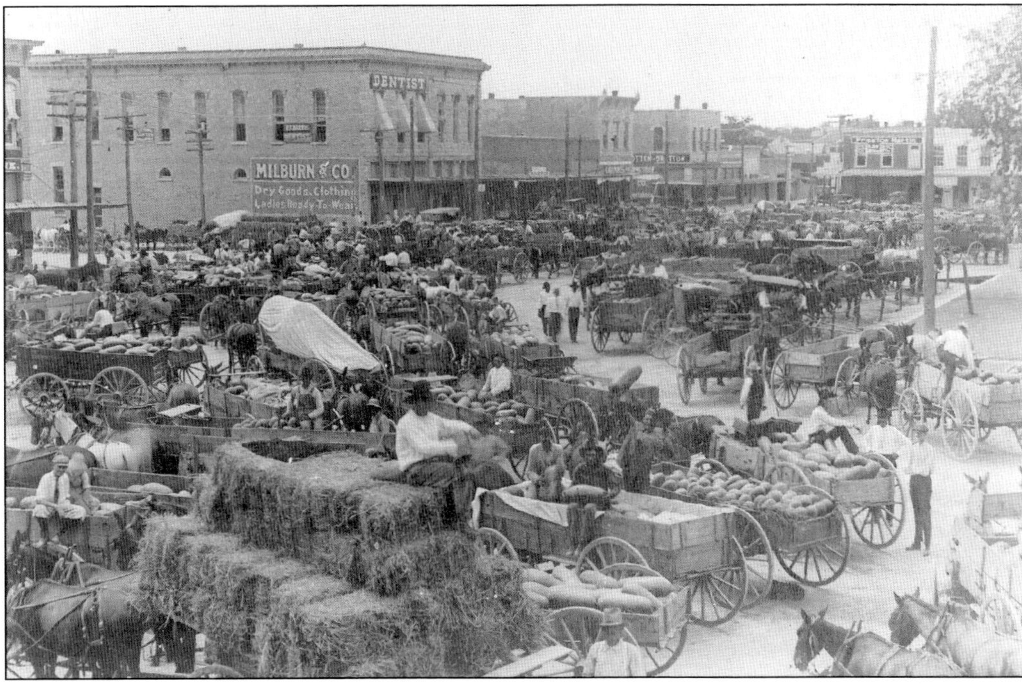

Trade's Day on the square became known as "First Monday" in 1909. This view is from 1924. "First Monday" weekend is quite a tourist attraction. (Maurine McCoy.)

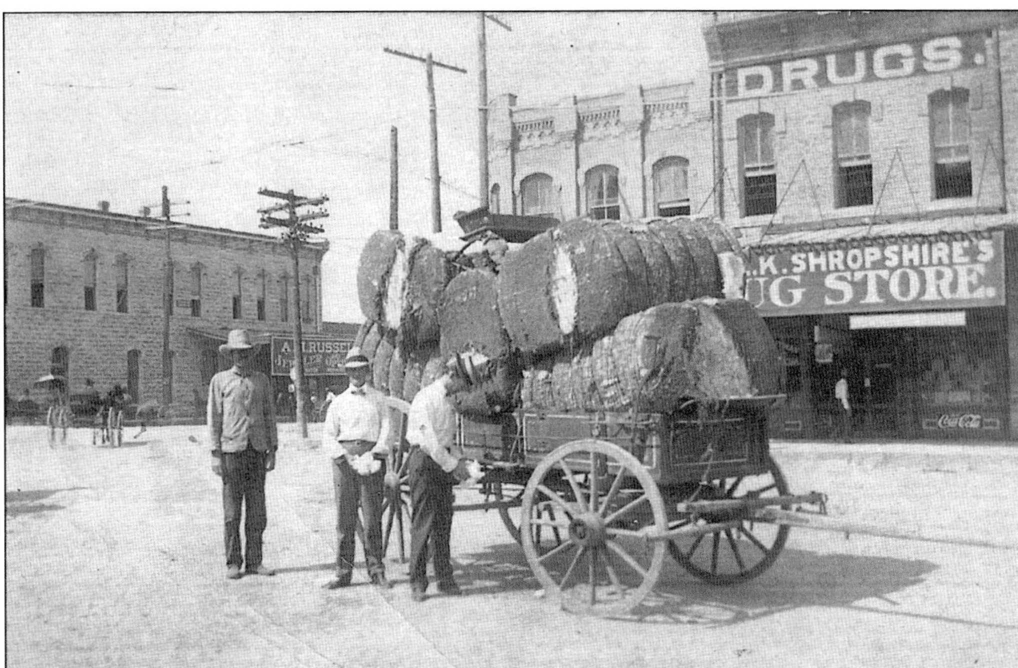

When Cotton was King! In 1900, Joe Neal delivered his five bales from neighboring Peaster, Texas. In 1914, Weatherford produced 46,000 bales. At one point Parker County had almost 40 cotton gins. (Marie Grigsby Schaub.)

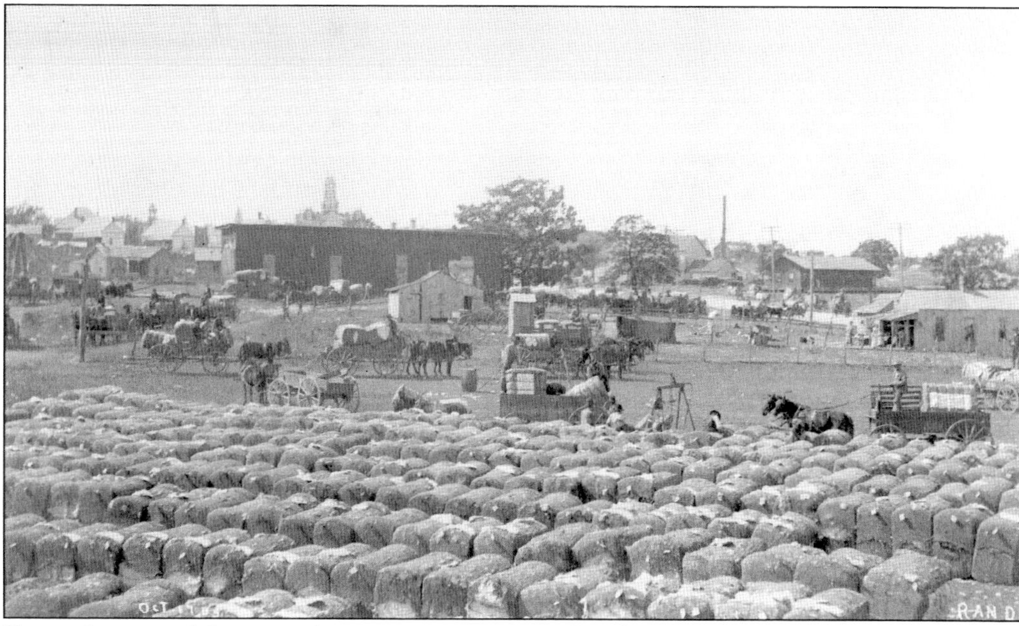

Shown here is a delivery to the cotton compress in October 1903. The Santa Fe freight depot on the far right was replaced in 1910 by the passenger depot. The viaduct across the railroad was built in 1935 long after this view. (Maurine McCoy.)

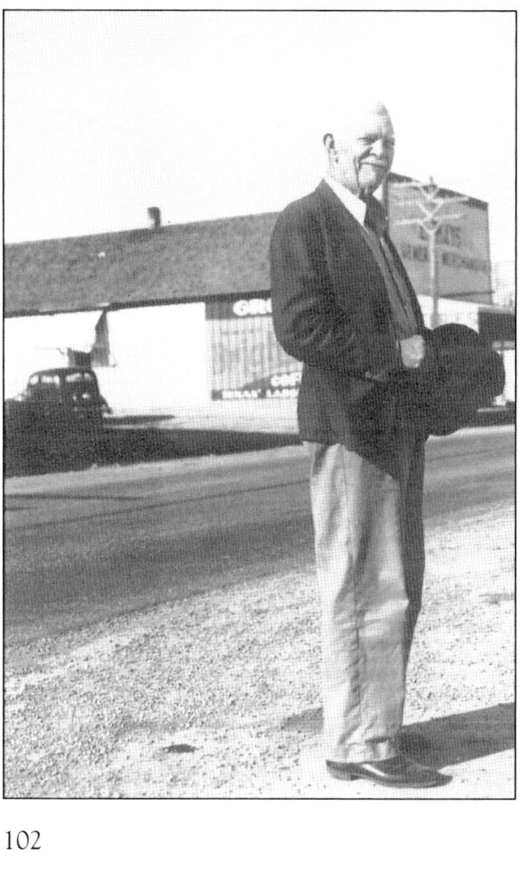

W.C. "Bill" Ragsdale, a cowboy for Charles Goodnight in the 1880s, became an inventor and worked at the cotton compress. He designed a banding buckle that helped to revolutionize the industry. (Bill Fant.)

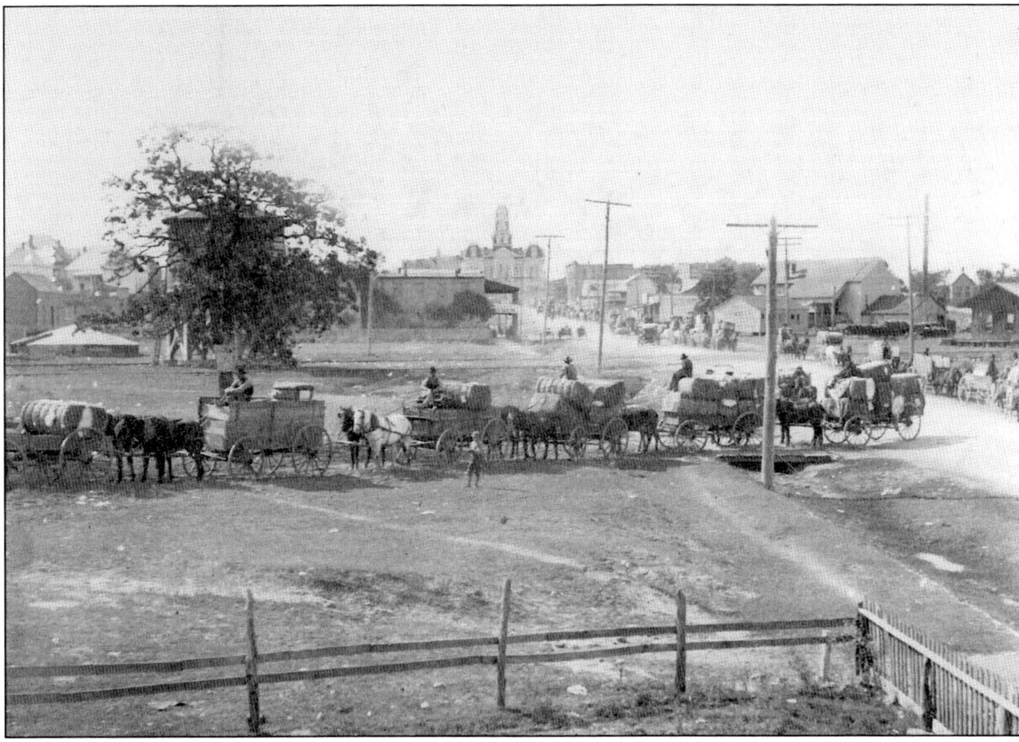

Farmers' wagons loaded with huge bales jammed Fort Worth Street in route to the T & P railroad shipping point next to the cotton compress. The Santa Fe Railroad water tower is behind the trees. (Maurine McCoy.)

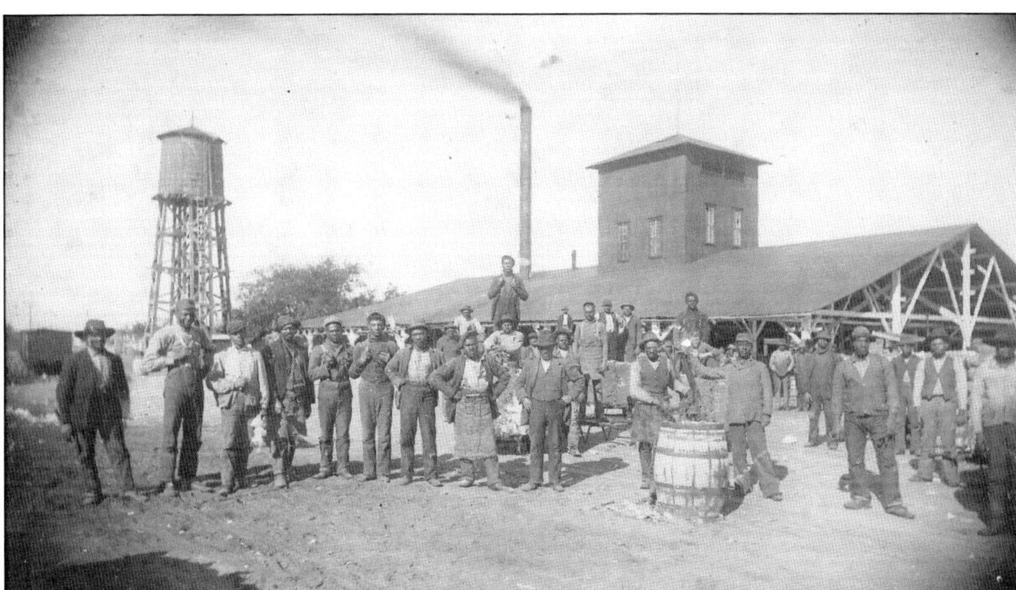

Cotton compress employees take a break to pose for this photograph. The boll weevil dropped the bottom out of the cotton market in 1915 and stopped this Weatherford industry. (WL.)

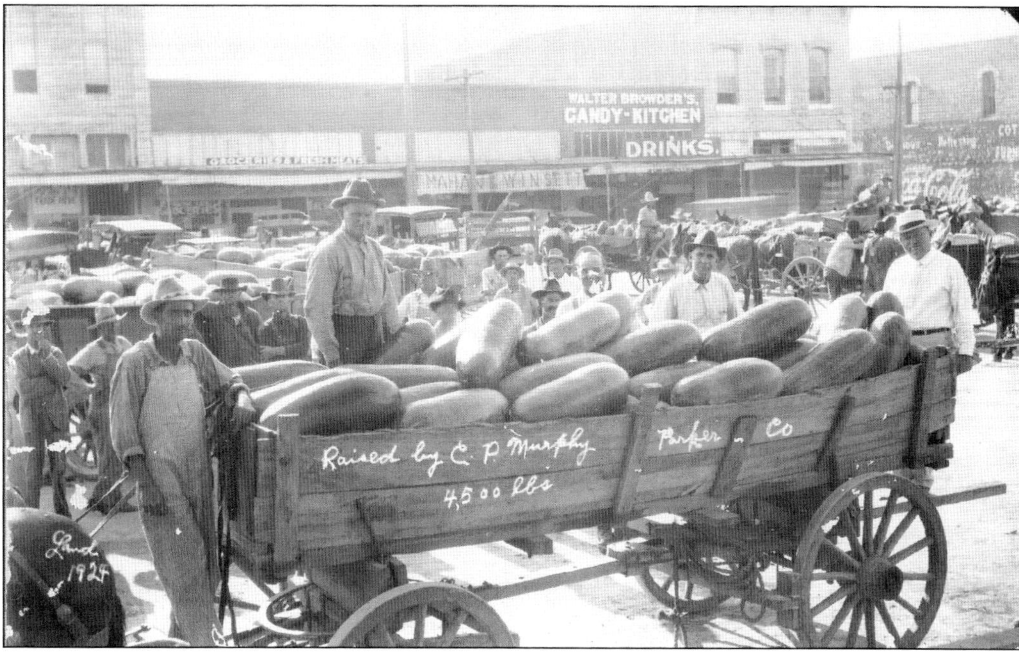

Watermelons helped keep agriculture alive in Weatherford. The huge watermelons developed were the hit of the St. Louis World's Fair in 1903. Here is a load on the east side of the square. Walter Browder's Candy Kitchen is at 109 College Avenue. (Vernell Hutcheson.)

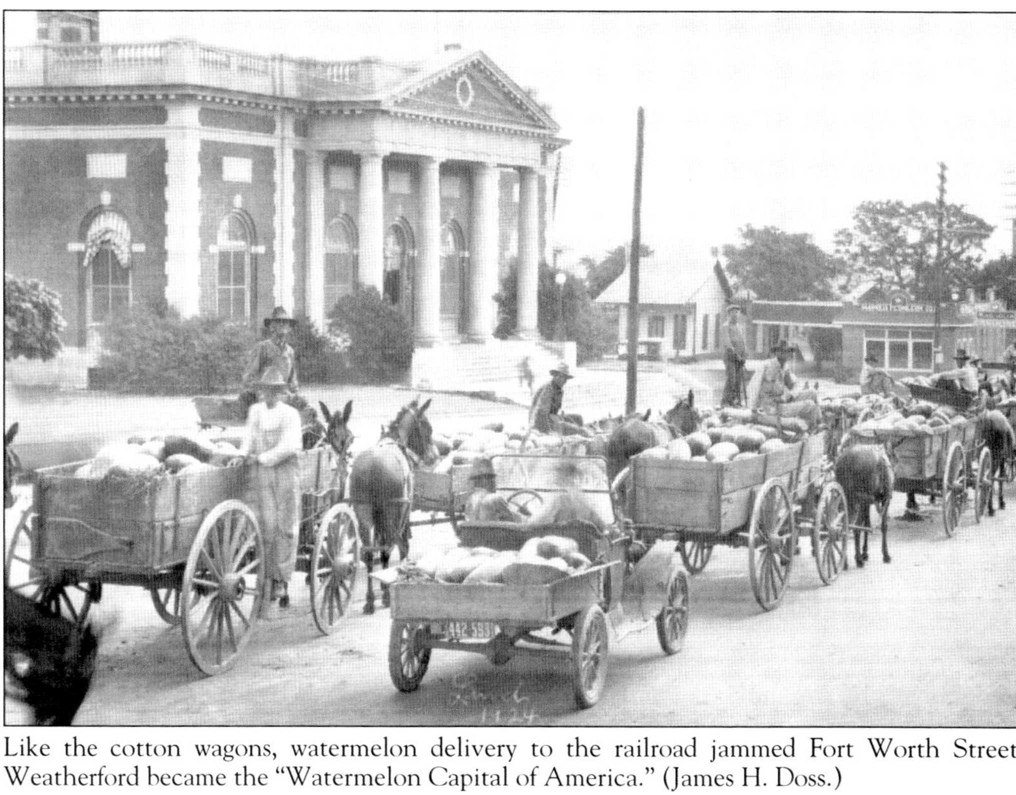

Like the cotton wagons, watermelon delivery to the railroad jammed Fort Worth Street. Weatherford became the "Watermelon Capital of America." (James H. Doss.)

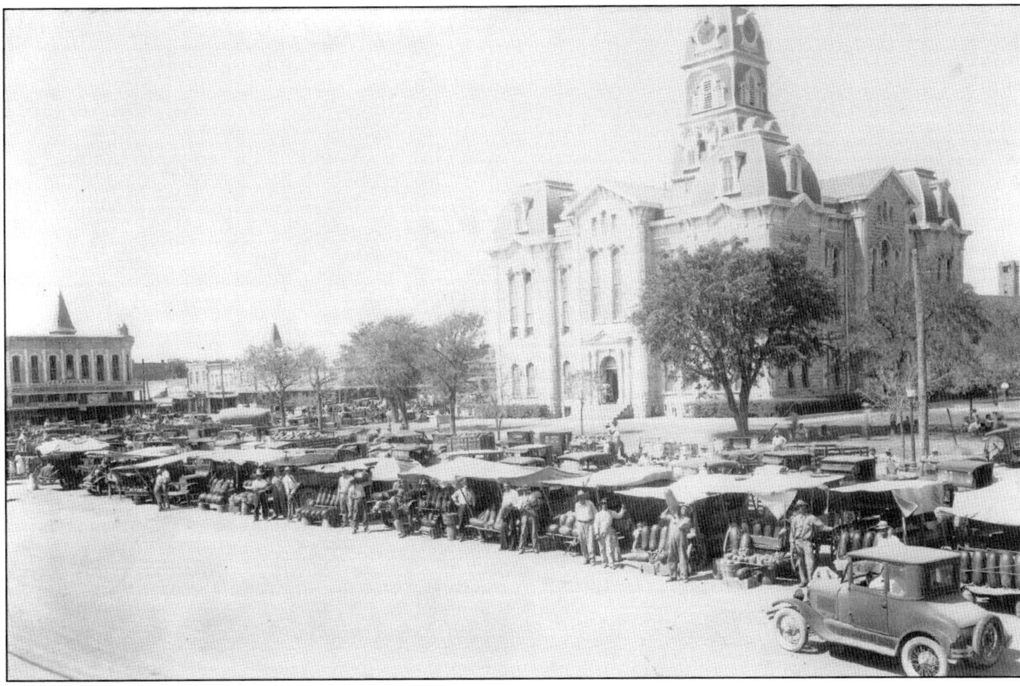

The morning sun reveals "First Monday" on the square and the famous tin watermelon on the southeast side of the courthouse lawn. Jim Pond, fifth from right, sold watermelons out of his truck (*c.* 1928–9). The size of these watermelons caused sales to weaken as the public needed a smaller size product. (Michael's Studio.)

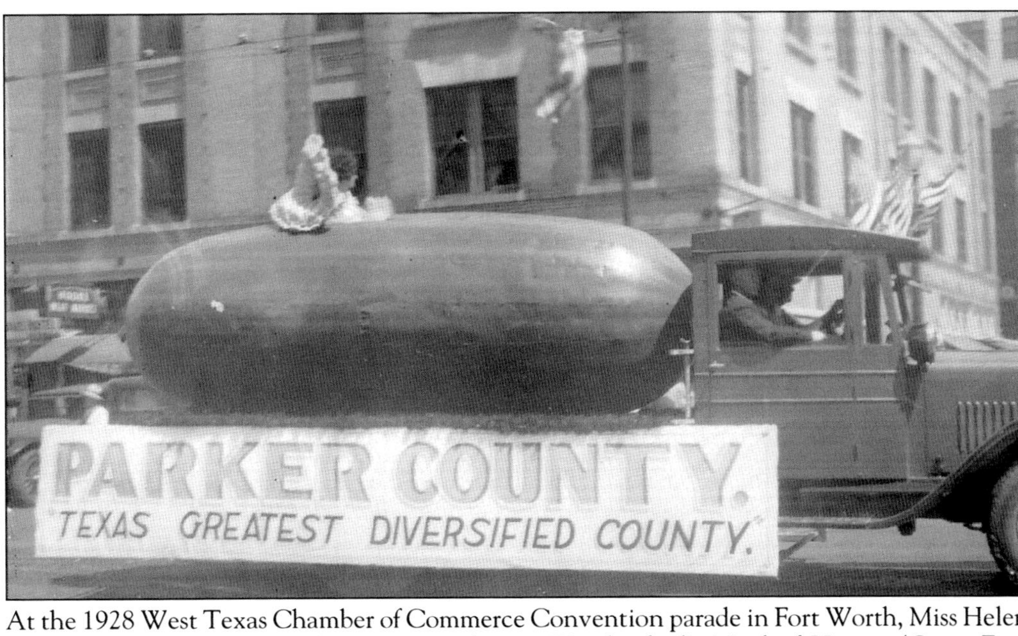

At the 1928 West Texas Chamber of Commerce Convention parade in Fort Worth, Miss Helen Massey rode in the 20-foot-long watermelon as Weatherford's Maid of Honor. (Grace-First Presbyterian Church archive.)

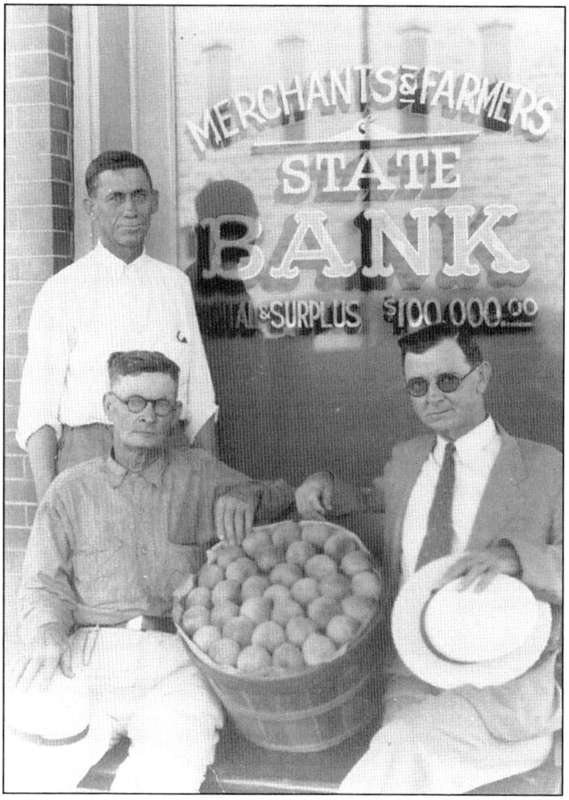

The Merchants and Farmers State Bank hosted a huge exhibit of peaches from the Ames Orchard in 1934. From left to right are Charlie Woodridge (standing) and Charlie Ames with bank Vice President W.V. Shadle. (James H. Doss.)

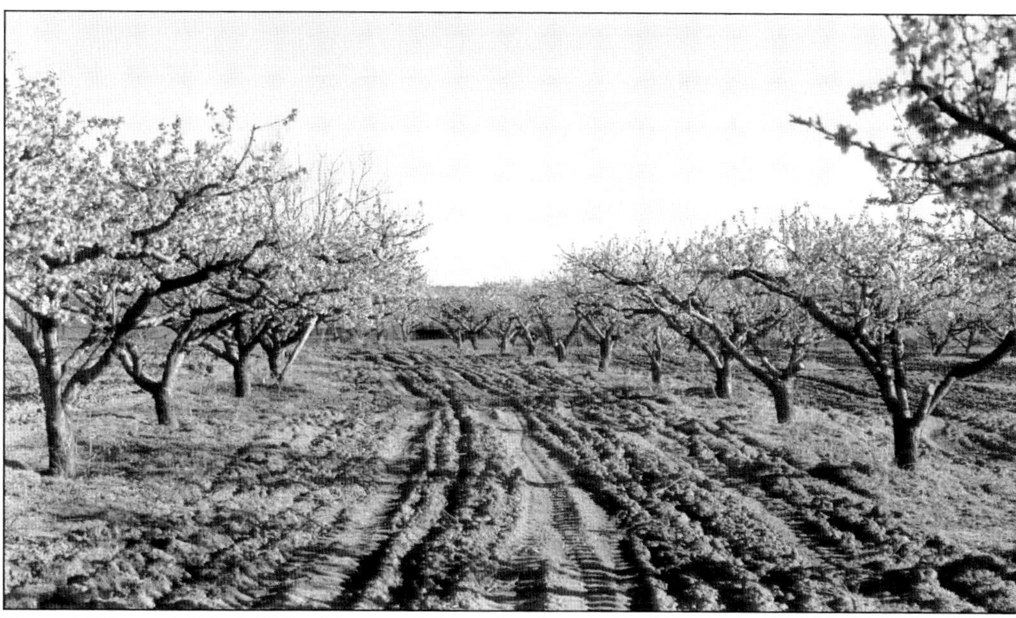

From 1939 until World War II started, Weatherford hosted the "Peach Blossom Pilgrimage." At one count, over 5,000 cars were tallied driving the 19 miles through the peach orchards of Parker County. The peach blossoms are still beautiful. (Lafrieta Hutton.)

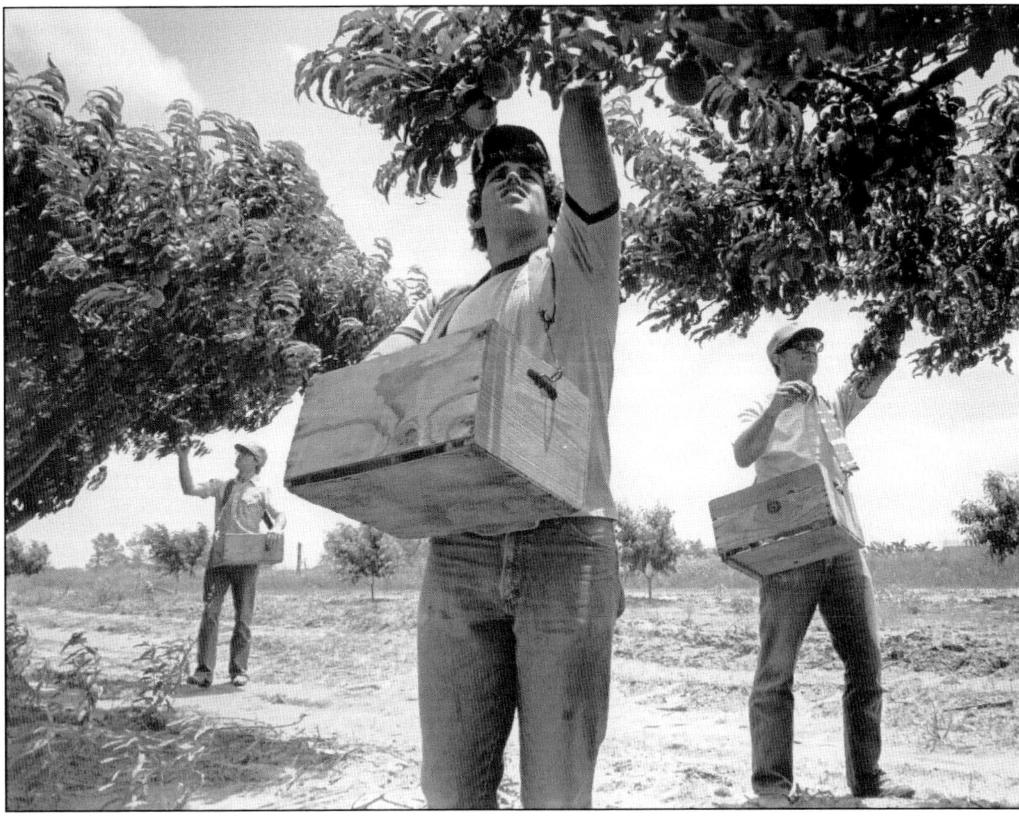

Weatherford can still boast to be the "Peach Capital of Texas." The Hutton family—Gary, Jimmy, and Charles—are seen here picking peaches for the Weatherford Peach Festival in the early 1980s. (Lafrieta Hutton.)

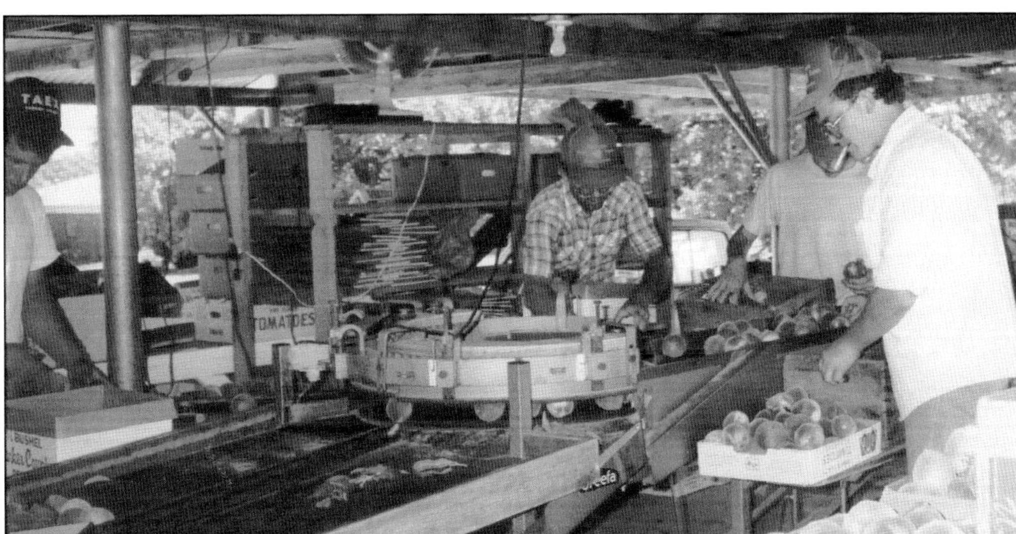

Jimmy and Gary Hutton are joined by John Stanford (right), with modern equipment to pack peaches for shipment. (Lafrieta Hutton.)

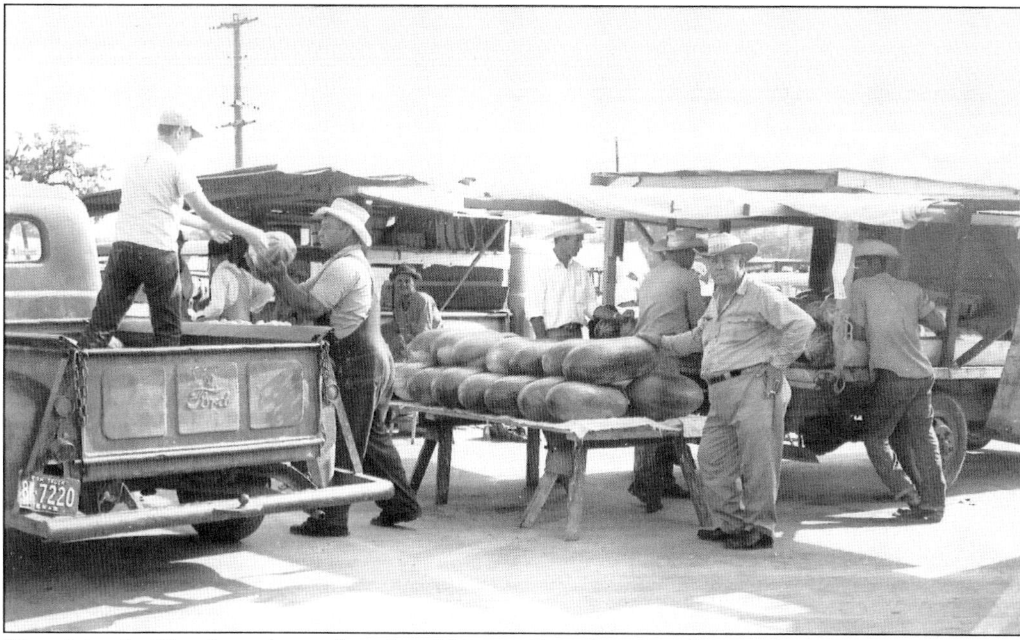

"First Monday" has been located in the old Santa Fe railroad yard since the 1970s. Watermelons are still a major product sold. (Chamber of Commerce.)

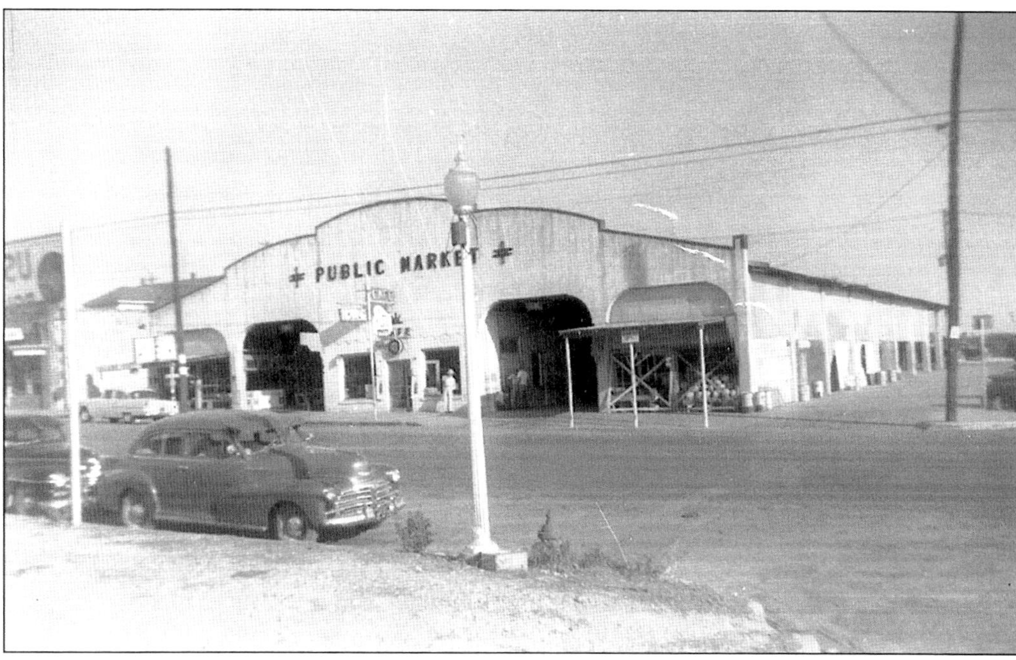

The Public Market opened in 1940 and still sells the freshest produce from the county. (WL.)

Ten

Fun and Entertainment

Lives, old and young, learn how to work and have fun. Work and parties, barn raising, and quilting bees, mumbly peg, riding horses, dancing, or just cruising down South Main have kept generations of kids busy and out of trouble. In 1887, two boys in neighboring Garner, Texas, got caught playing cards, so they invented a domino game similar to "bridge" and called it "forty-two."

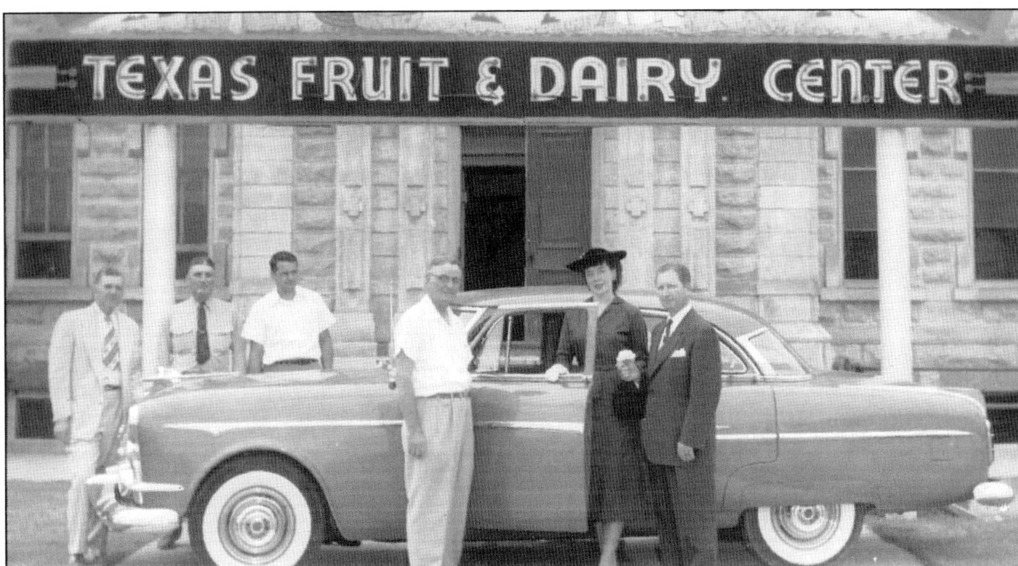

In a national writing contest, Mrs. Sammye Robbins won a brand-new 1953 Packard "Clipper." Chamber of Commerce officials that helped are Arval Allen, Burette Hobson, Bob Bergman, Bryan Patrick with Packard representative Alfred Meeks. The neon signs announcing Weatherford were placed on the square in May 1937 and replaced the famed tin watermelon. (Chamber of Commerce.)

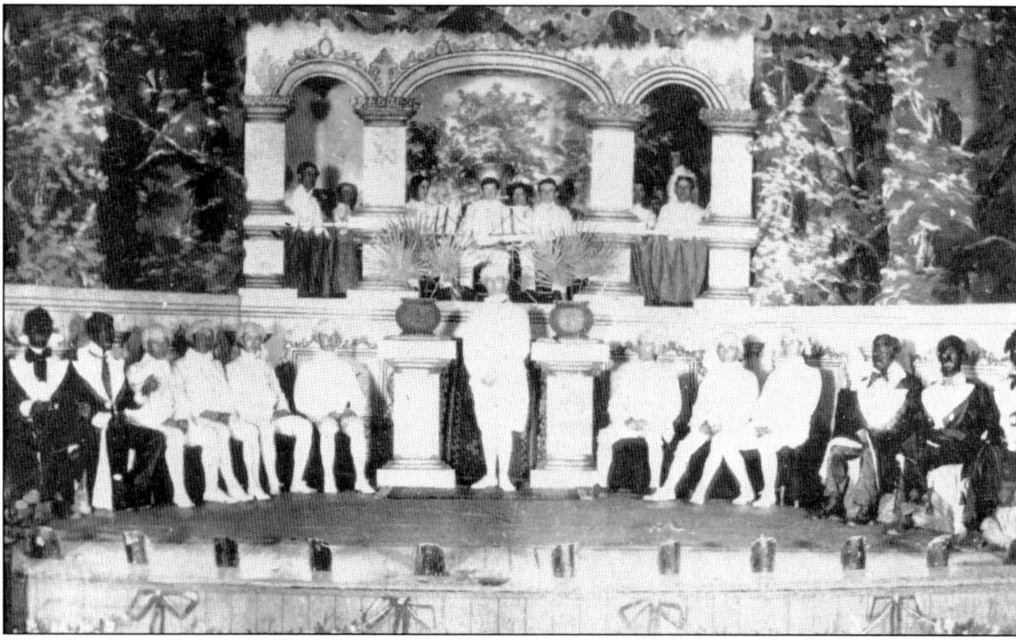

In the 1880s, the entertainment center was the Haynes Opera House on the northwest side of the square. This 1909 production included a black-faced satire. The outlaw Cole Younger was sighted at the opera house in March 1910. The opera house burned in 1914. (WL.)

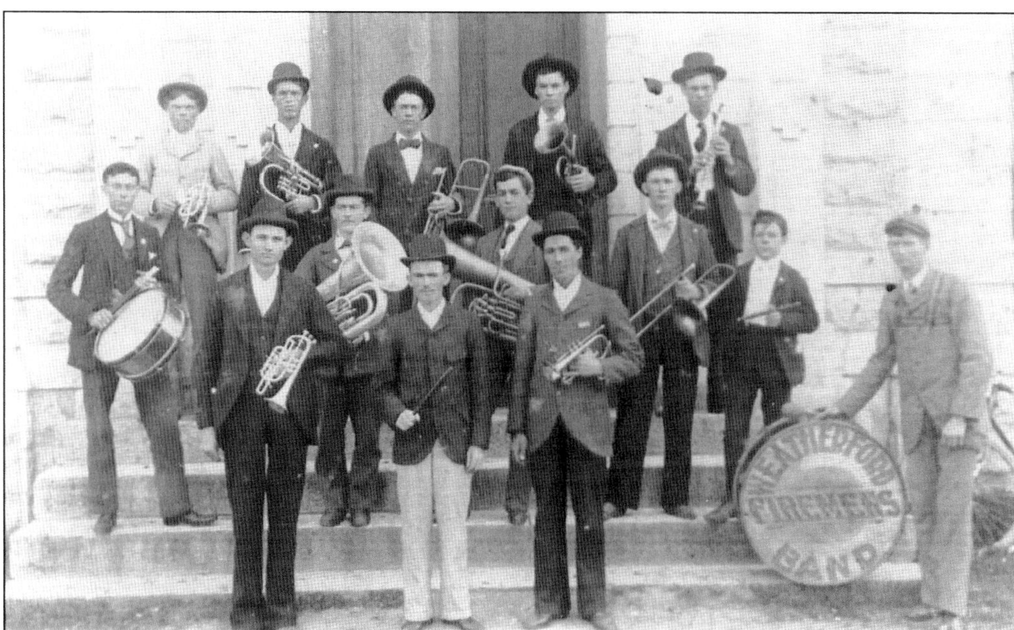

At the 1918 Fireman's Ball, the band played "When Apples Grow on the Lilac Trees" for five-year-old Mary Martin's singing debut. (WL.)

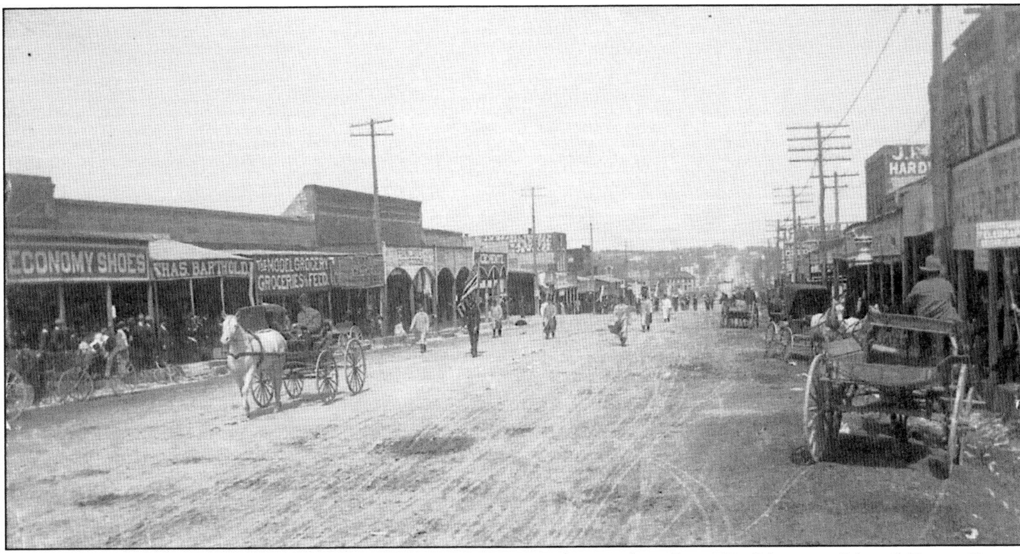

The Fourth Regimental Band played in the minstrel parade of 1907. Cherry-Akard Drug Store, 114 North Main, has a huge mortar and pestle advertisement. The parade route was from the Texas and Pacific Depot around the courthouse and back. L.F. Wright Groceries has recently moved from 115 North Main to 101 College Avenue. (WL.)

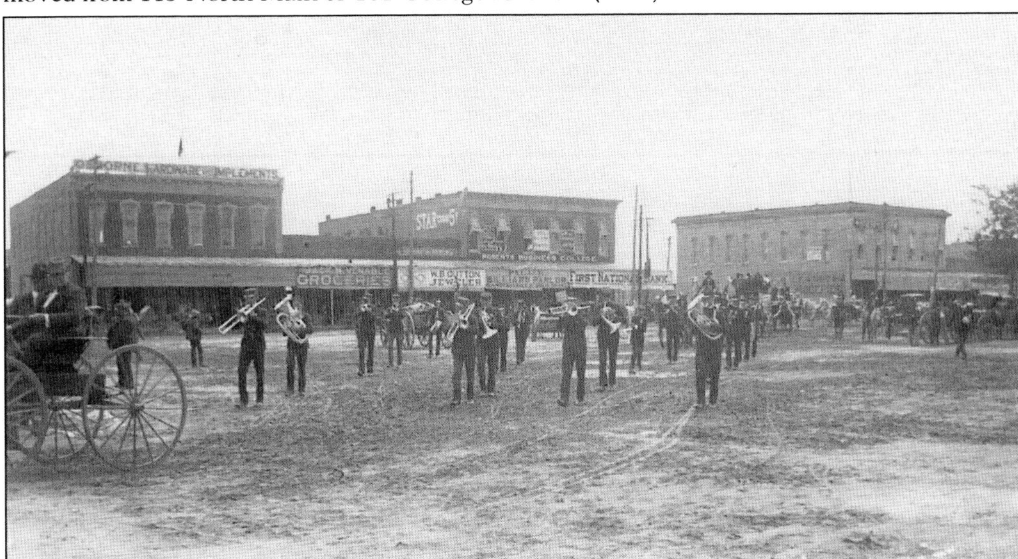

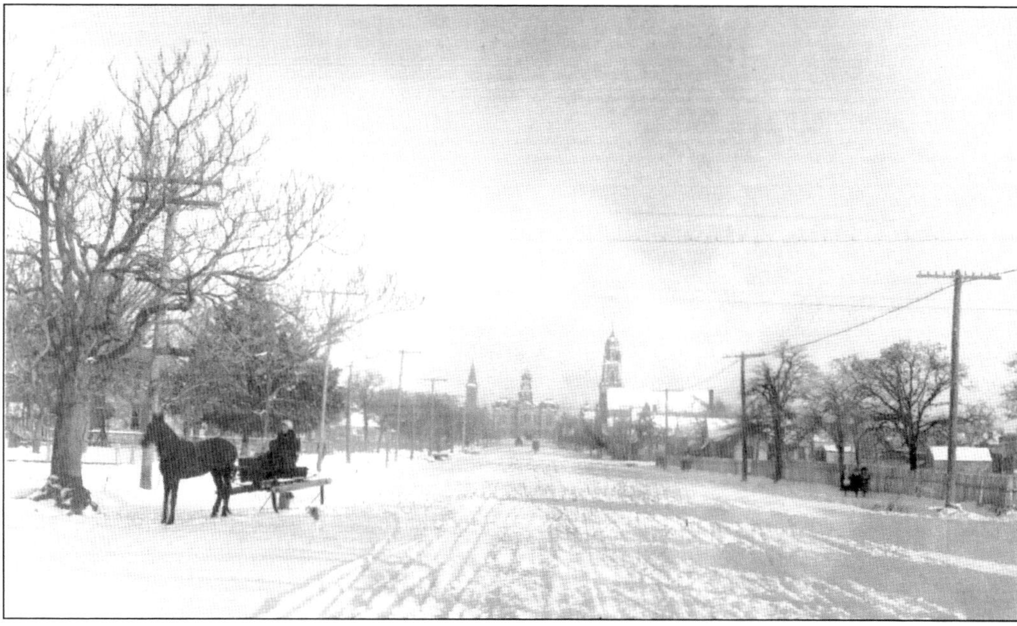

In February 1899, it was 15 below zero, the coldest temperature on record. Perry M. Baker rigged up his buggy with runners and offered his girl a ride, but her dad refused. The photograph shows another girl on Perry's sleigh. His girl often talked of this after their wedding! (Randy Carter via James H. Doss.)

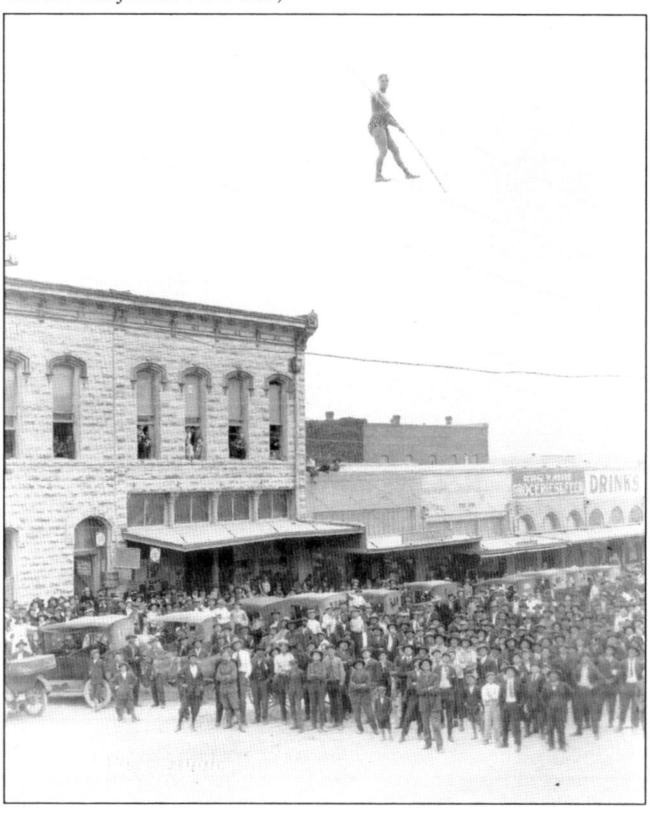

The circus came to Weatherford in a big way in 1909 and covered the square. An aerial act was on North Main. Note the Chamber of Commerce was located at the first awning in the Citizen's Bank building. The "Midway" and Ferris wheel were on South Main. (WL.)

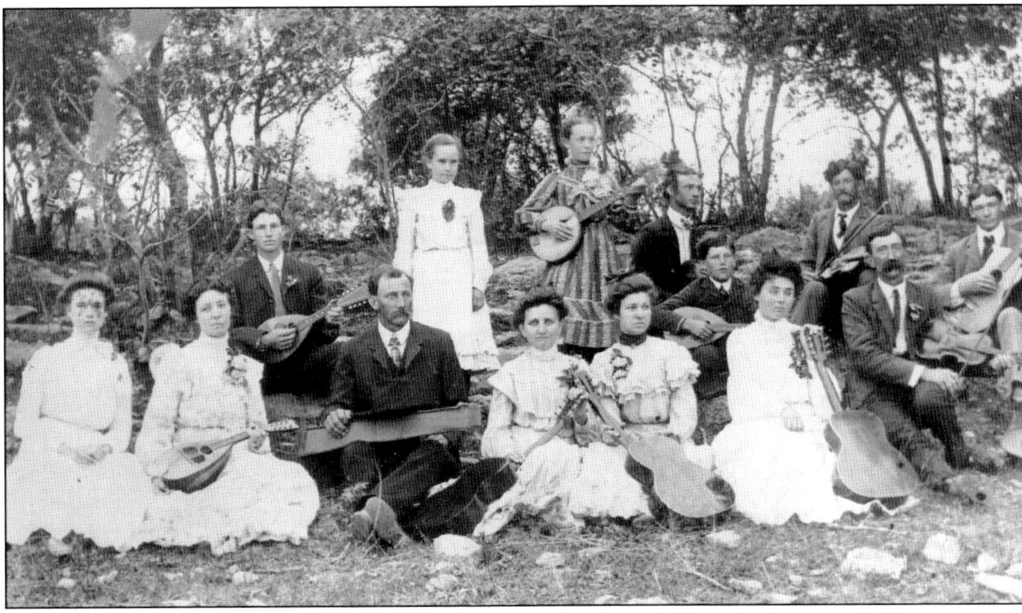

The is first string band organized in Weatherford, which was a predecessor of the city municipal band. The lady on the right is Laura Meniza Prichard (see page 60). (Zan Statham.)

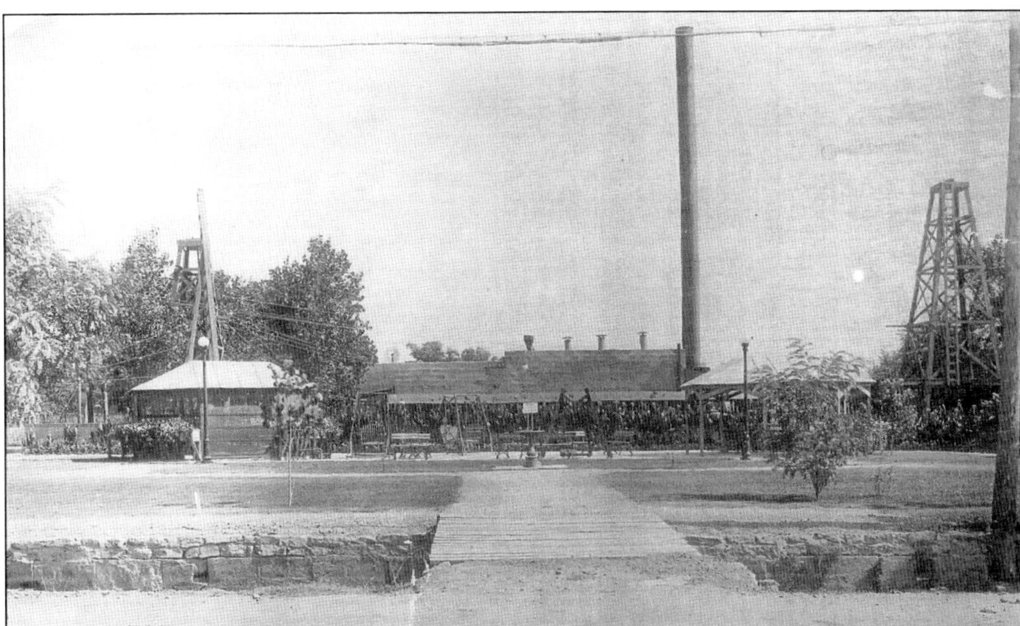

The small park (*c.* 1911) on the corner of Lee and Davis Street on the Weatherford Water and Light property was enlarged to its present size, in 1924. It was named for Frank Cherry, utility manager. Four thousand people attended the opening. Six tons of watermelon were sliced! (Heritage Gallery via Robert P. Henry.)

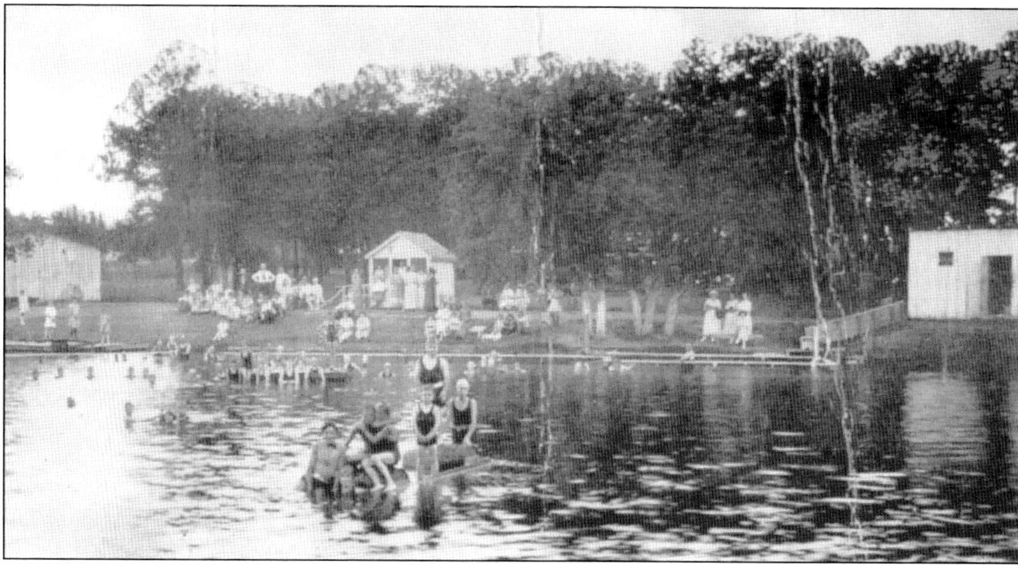

Holland's Lake, a 45-acre site, was a great attraction with picnic tables and bathhouses. It was the best public swimming area until the City built a pool at Cherry Park after World War II. (WL.)

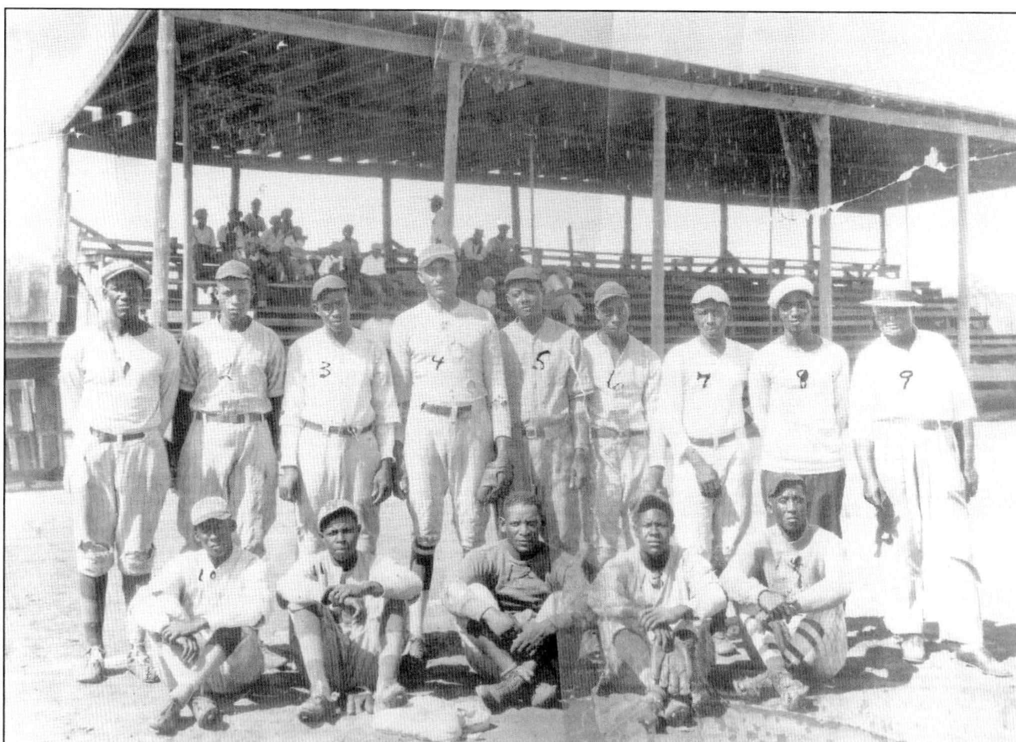

The grandstand and public ball field at 200 East Russell is seen here in the 1920s. It was replaced by Kangaroo Stadium. Weatherford's farm team for the Negro League played there. Cub Young (1) later played in the majors. Hugh "Dink" Ikard (7) was a cousin of the famous cowboy. (Melvin George via Donald George.)

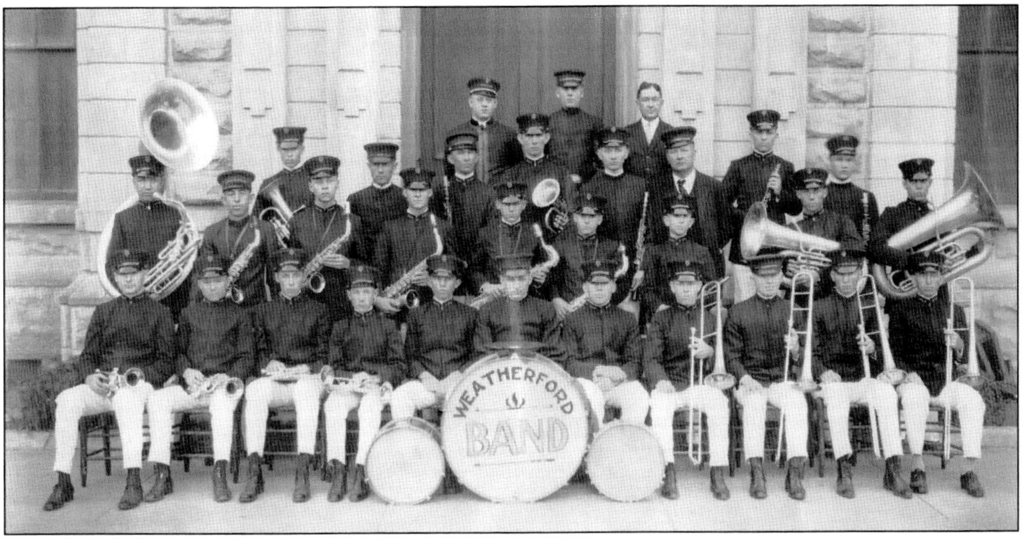

This photograph depicts the Weatherford Municipal Band in the fall of 1922. The next spring a nice watermelon was painted on the bass drum. They won a gold medal in the West Texas Chamber of Commerce championship competition in 1923. (Bill Witherspoon.)

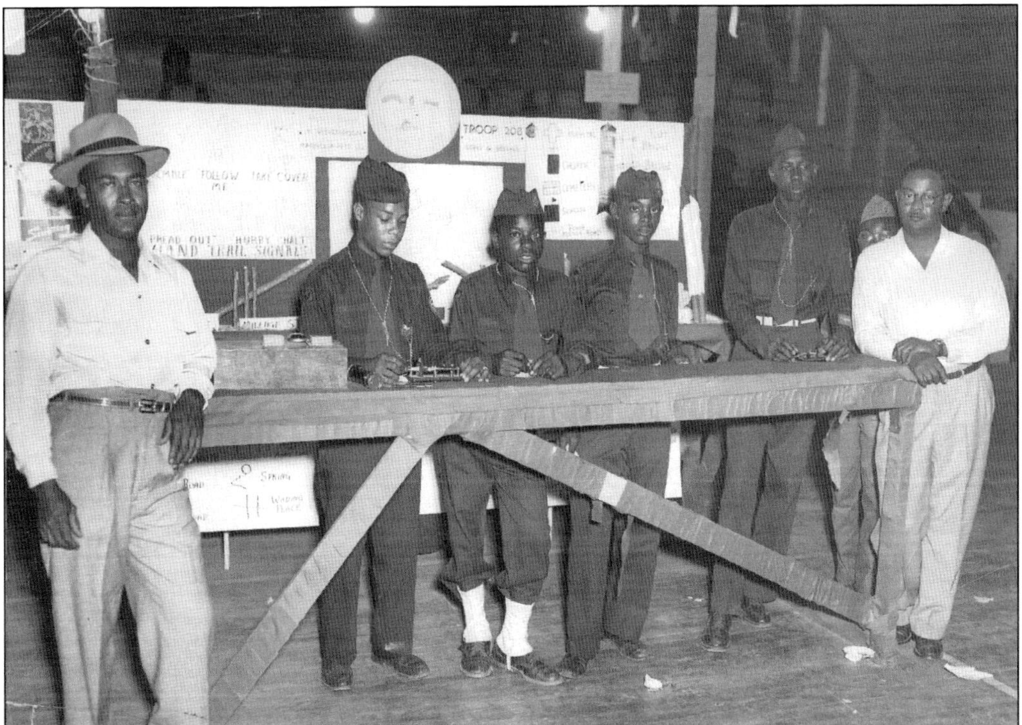

Weatherford has several Boy Scout troops. At the 1951 Jamboree, Troop 208 set up in the Weatherford College gym to show their Morse code skill. From left to right are William Robinson, assistant scoutmaster; Don George; Clem Smith, retired as deputy police chief in 1999; Roy James Gratts; Raymond George; Weldon Woodfolk Jr.; and Scoutmaster Melvin George. (Melvin George via Donald George.)

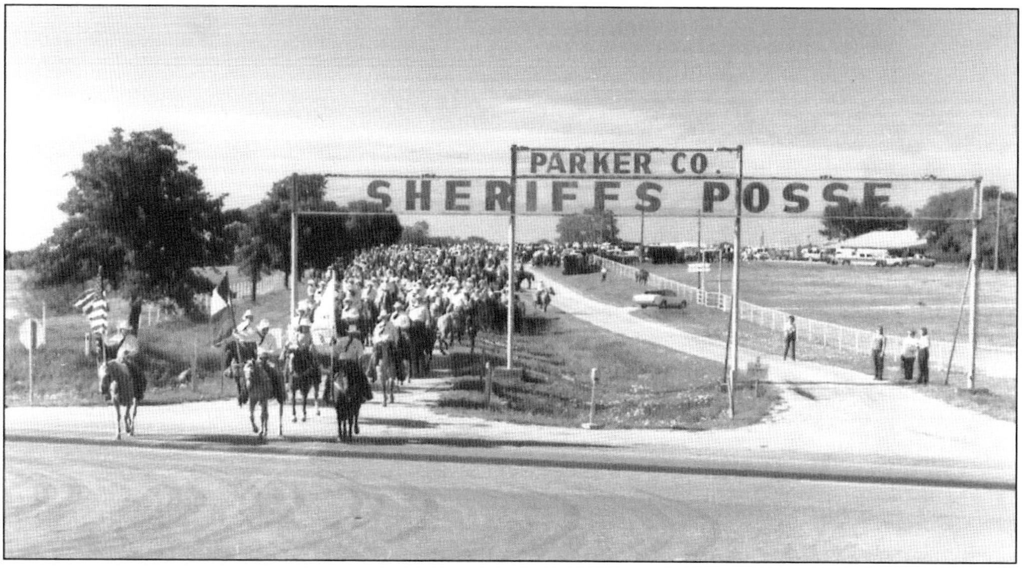

The Parker County Sheriff Posse, organized in 1947, has a yearly trail ride for fun. The Posse assists the sheriff in the more traditional manhunts and other duties. (Eugene Polser.)

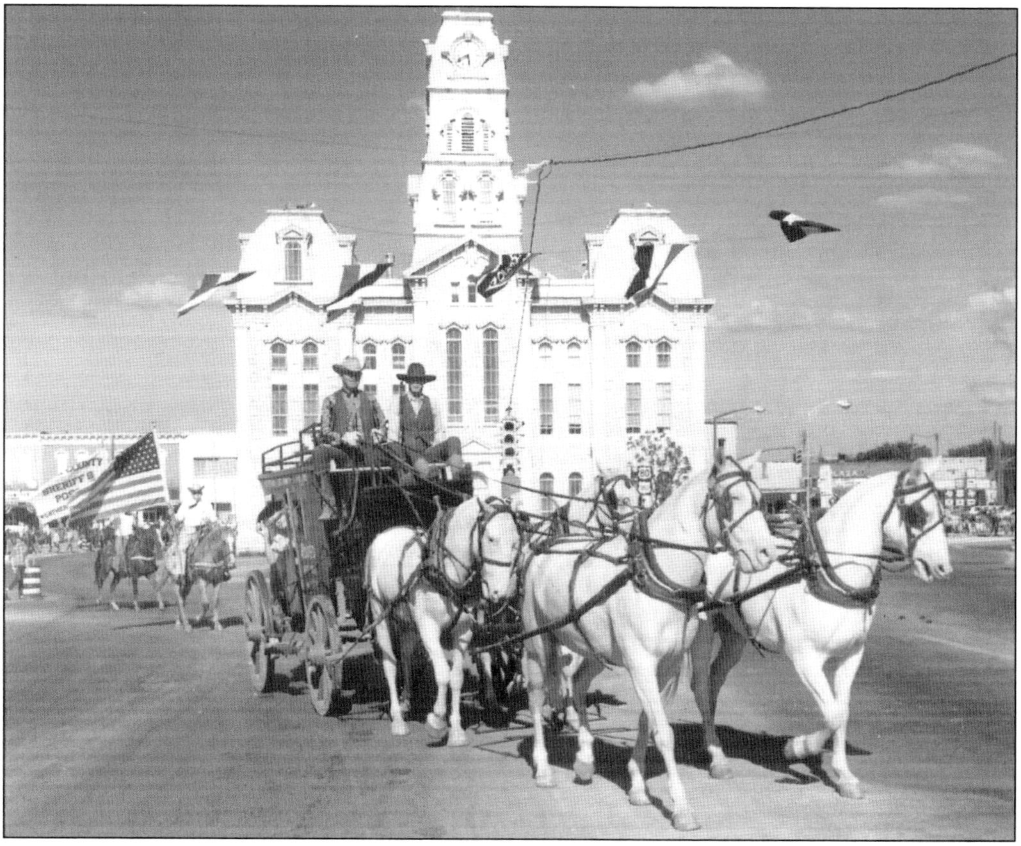

The Weatherford Centennial in 1956 brought out this stagecoach reined by Bob Rothel, a champion cowboy from the city. (Sheriff Posse via Wayne Bryant.)

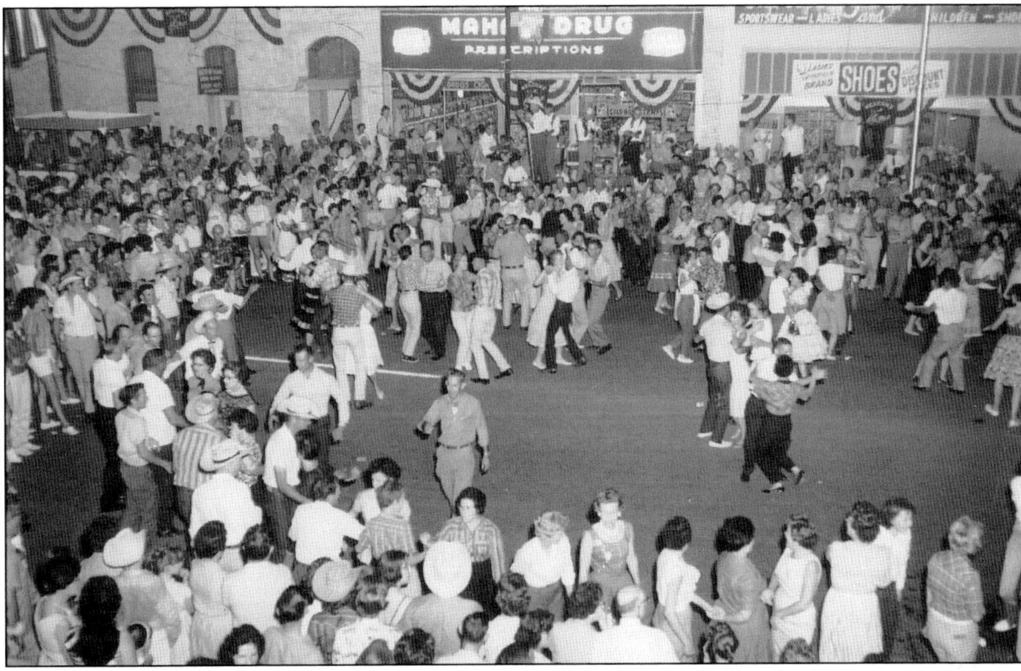

The yearly Sheriff Posse Rodeo has a street dance. This one was during the centennial. Once on the square, it has moved to the Posse grounds. (Sheriff Posse via Wayne Bryant.)

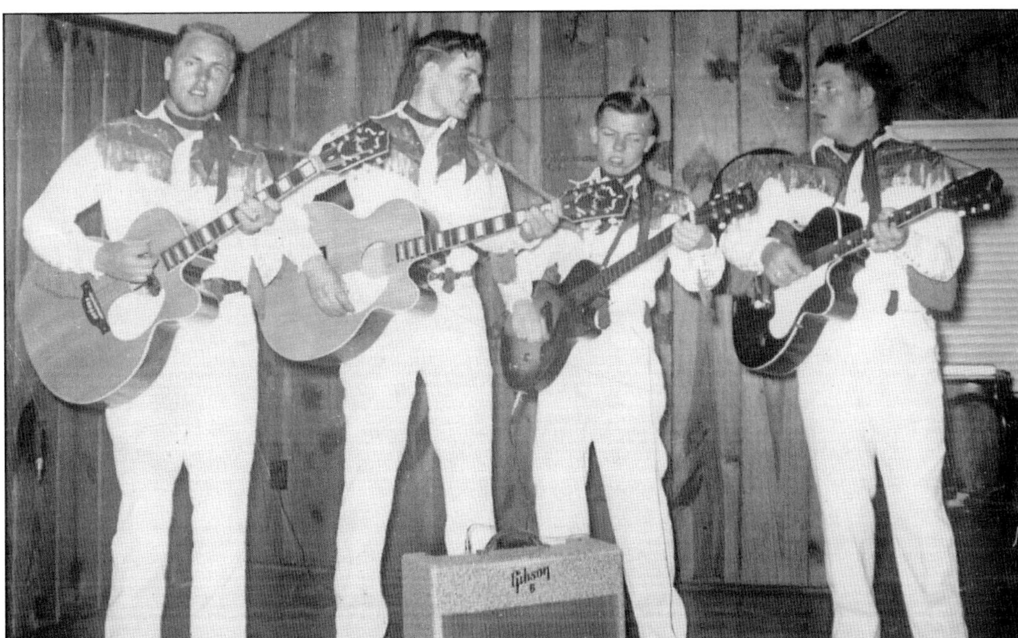

In 1955–56, the rising music sensations from Weatherford were Ralph Clark, David Stone, Royce Gilbert, and James Mathison as the "Rollin' Stones." David was killed in a car accident in route from a Fort Worth "gig" in 1956, and another music group used the name. (James Mathison.)

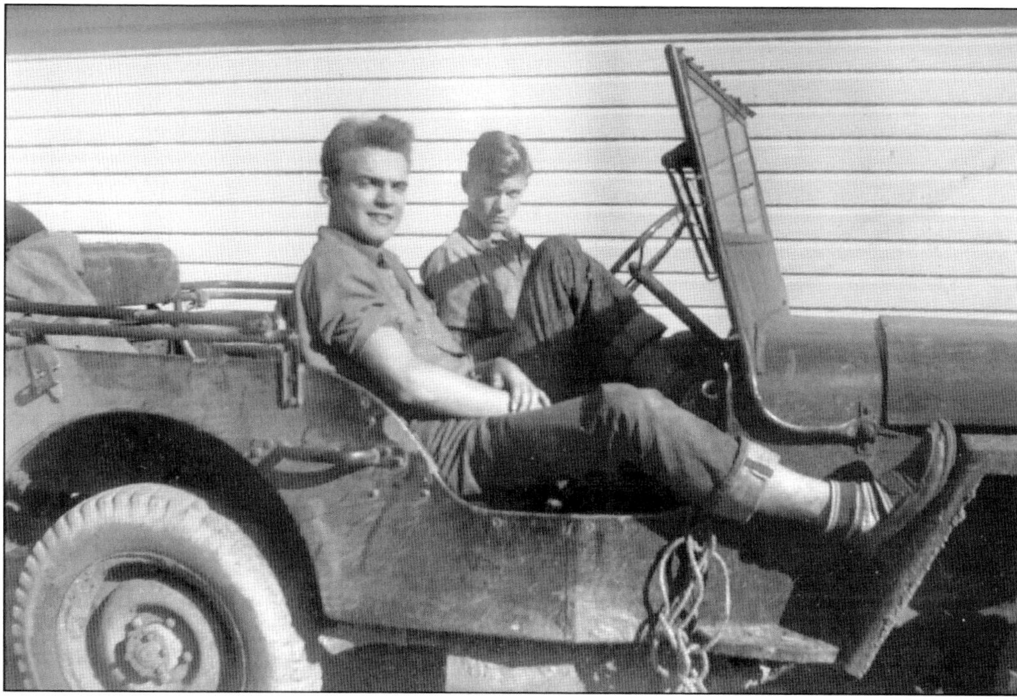

Bob Hamilton rides with Larry Hagman, both 17, as they cruise Weatherford in Ben Hagman's ex-military jeep in the spring of 1951. Two years before, Larry had starred in *This Girl Business* at Weatherford High School. (Charles Frost.)

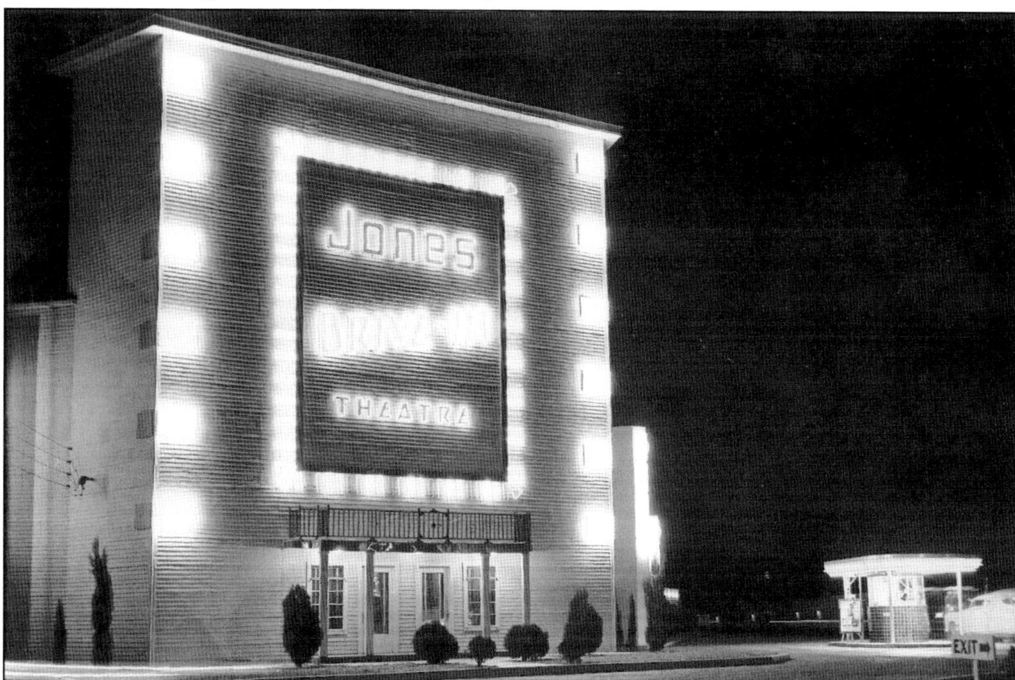

Carlos H. Jones, owner of the Plaza Theatre, made night life better with the opening of his Jones Drive-in Theatre in May 1948. (Carla Hollingsworth.)

Eleven

Duty, Honor, Country

The price the veteran has paid brings tears, pride, and patriotism. Weatherford's men and women have answered the call to arms from defending their homes from Indian raids, especially in the Civil War when men folk had gone, to battles on foreign soil. Our honored cemeteries grow weary with proof.

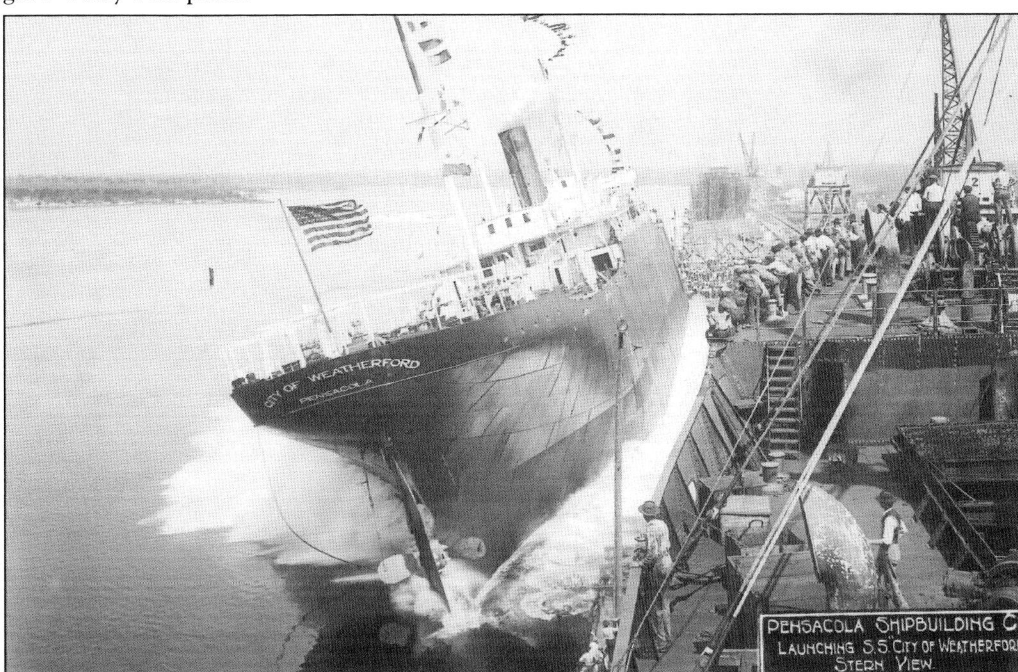

Weatherford citizens purchased the Merchant Marine liberty ship, S.S. *City of Weatherford* in a World War I war bond drive, led by Mr. W.C. Shropshire. It was christened on May 22, 1920, by Mrs. Oscar Barthold, in Pensacola, Florida. (WC.)

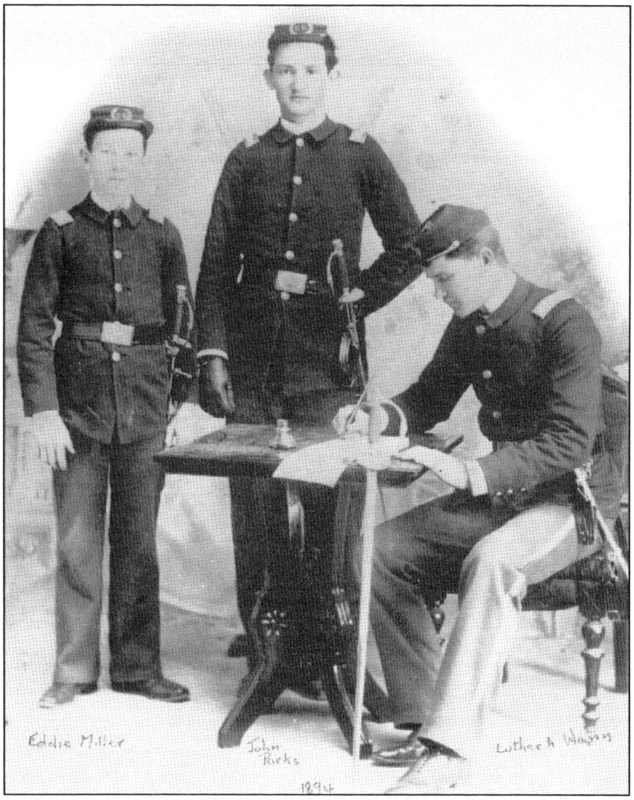

Officers from the Weatherford College military drill company in 1894 were John Paris (center) and Luther Wann (right). At left was Eddie Miller, still the drummer. These classes in military drill, ceremonies, and tactics helped prepare Weatherford men for service to the nation. (WC.)

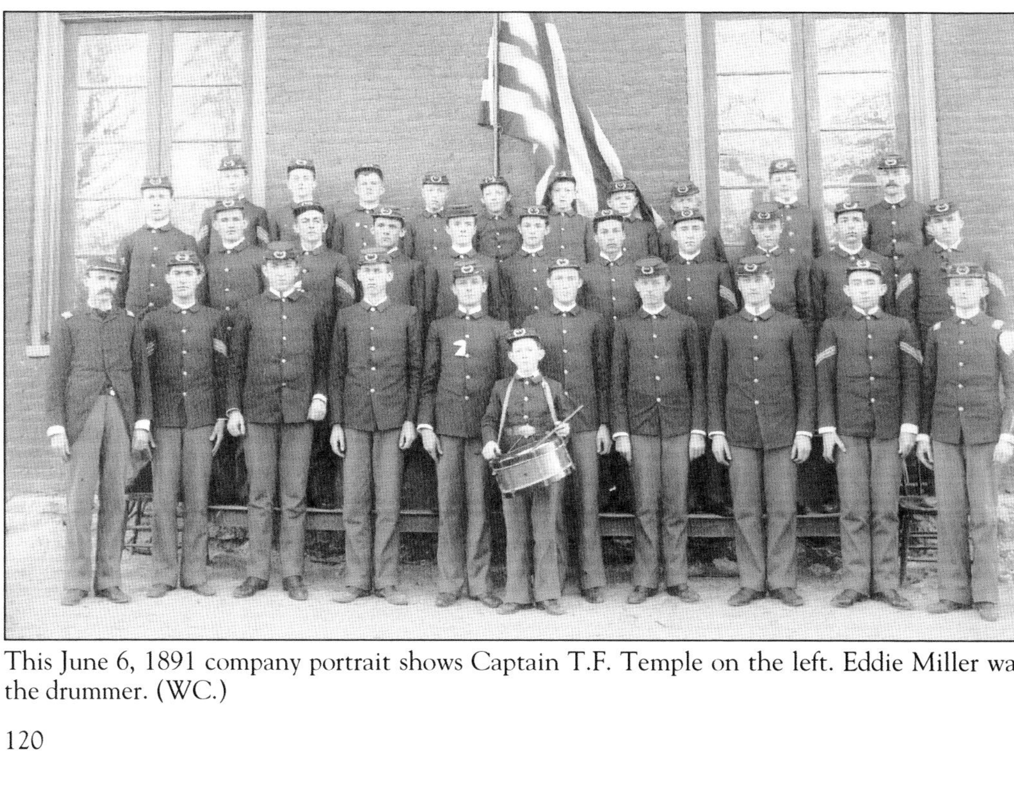

This June 6, 1891 company portrait shows Captain T.F. Temple on the left. Eddie Miller was the drummer. (WC.)

Captain Hiram Baker, first publisher of the *Democrat* newspaper, quit to command Weatherford's Company E, 39th U.S. Volunteer Infantry, in their Philippine combat actions from December 7, 1899. (WL.)

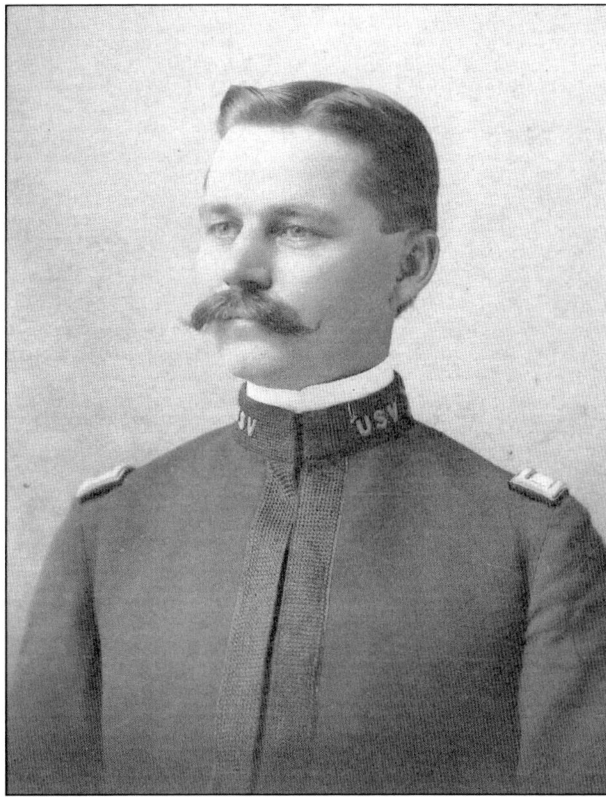

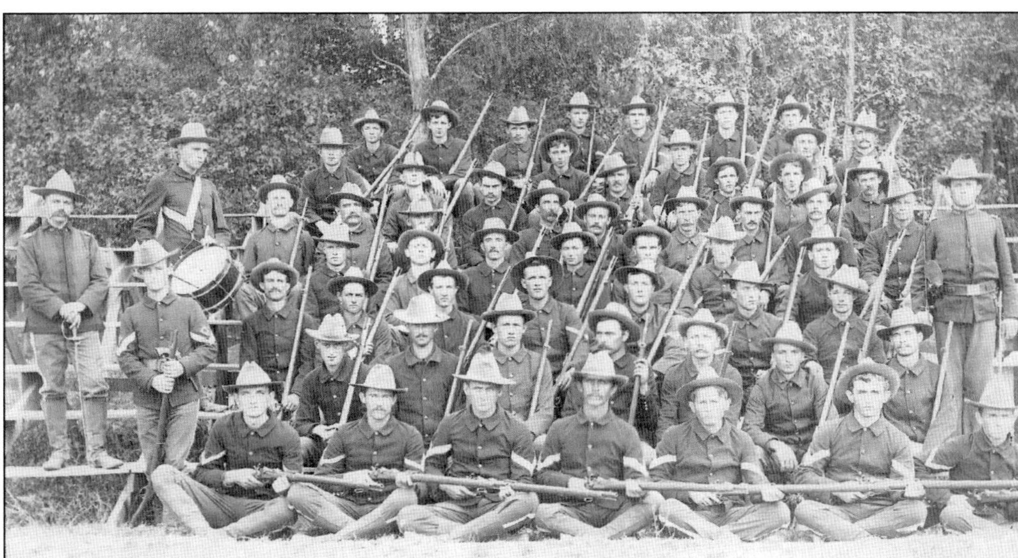

Company E posed upon their return to muster out on May 6, 1901. Two were killed in combat, and three died of disease. Captain Baker is on the far left. (WL.)

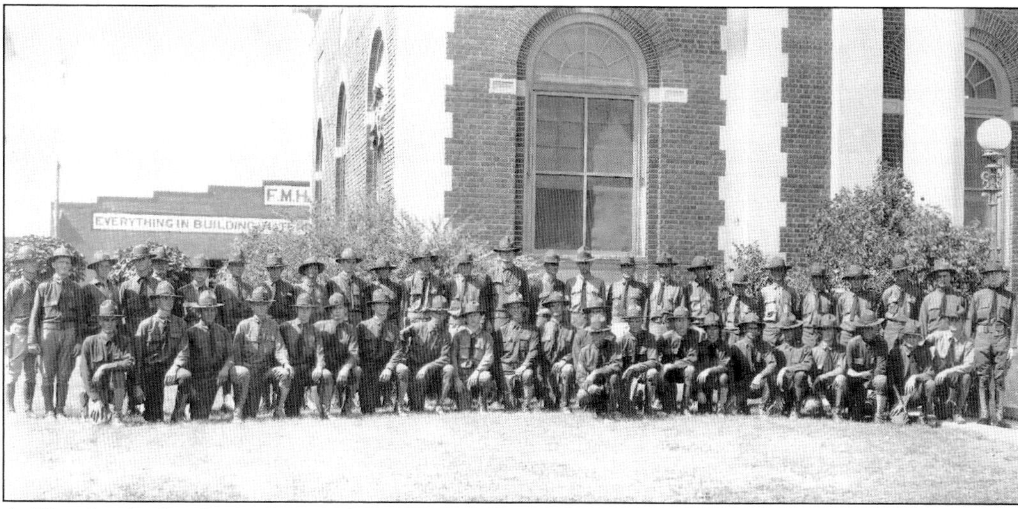

A Weatherford military unit at the U.S. Post Office, 109 Fort Worth Street, is ready to ship out for WWI duty. (WL.)

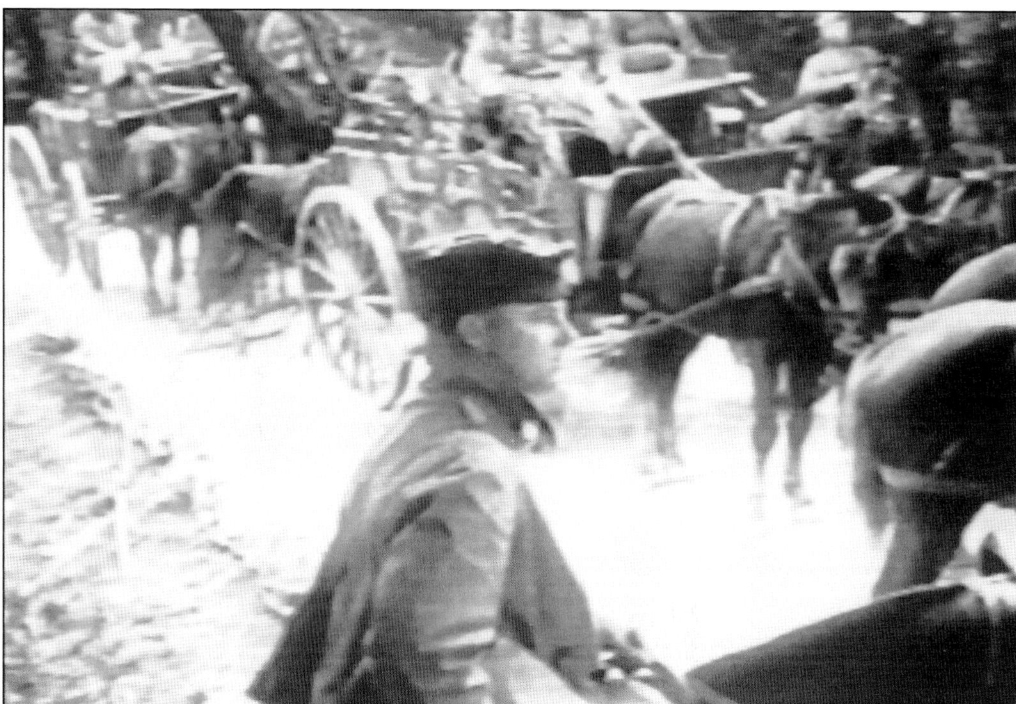

Somewhere in France, Marine Captain Walter S. Fant Jr., on horseback, watches his troops head for the Battle of Argonne Forest. He was wounded in actions for which he was cited for bravery. His senior commanding officer nominated him for the Medal of Honor; however, that officer was killed before the paperwork was processed. (Bill Fant.)

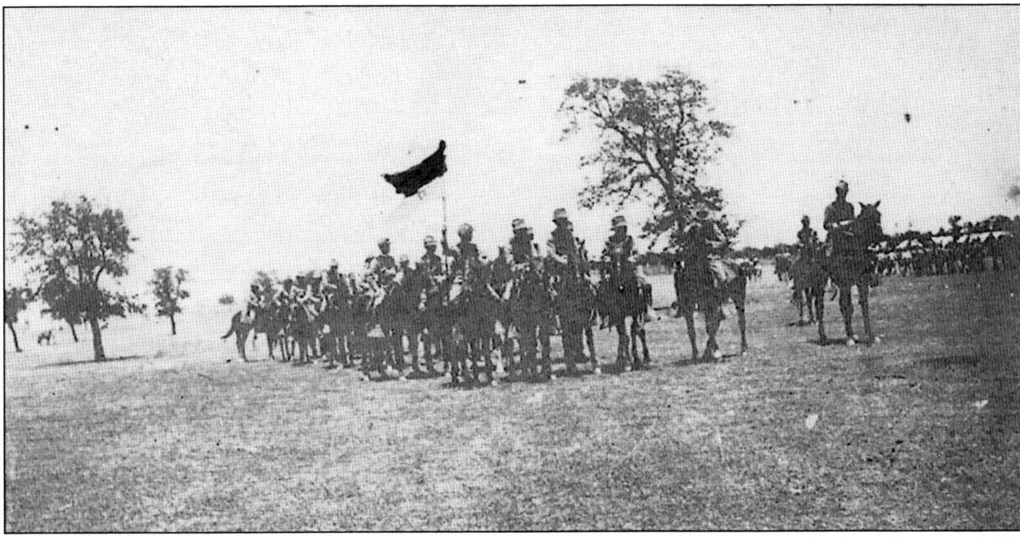

In 1918, a Weatherford calvary unit was organized, but the war was over before they could be sent overseas. (WL.)

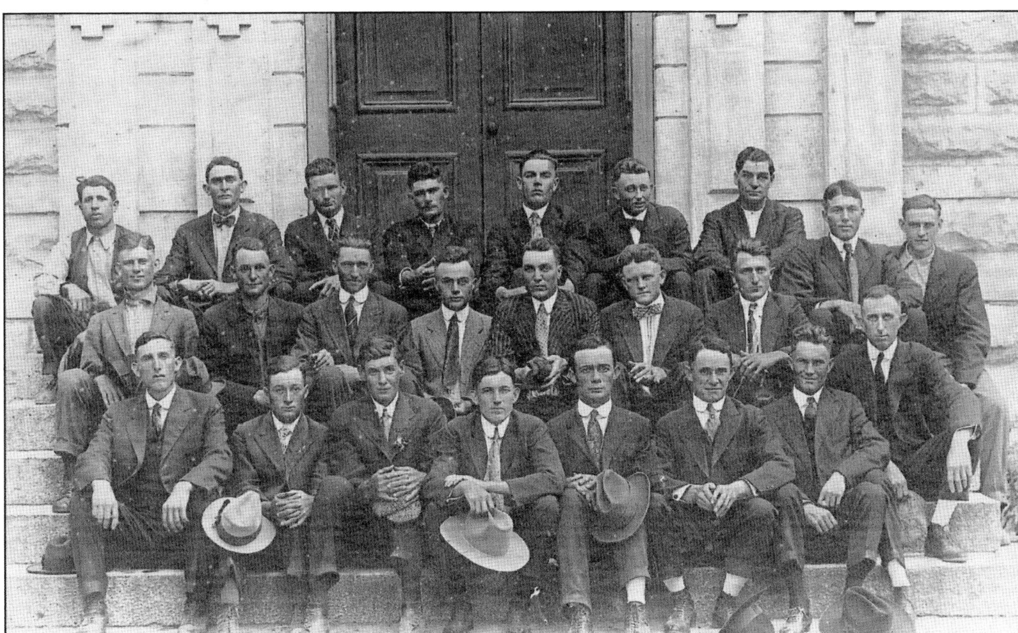

The Weatherford volunteers for World War I were sent in batches to the military. As the war's death toll rose, the volunteers were called "cannon fodder." (WL.)

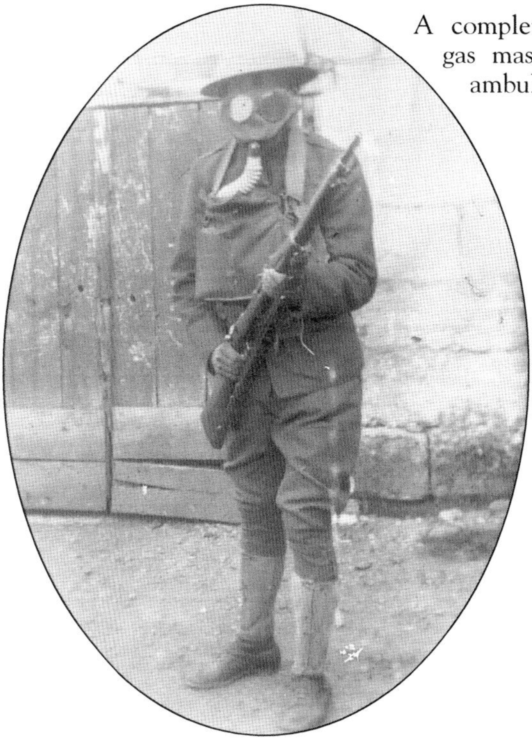

A complete WWI army field uniform, including a gas mask, disguises Charles Ragsdale. He was an ambulance driver in France. (Bill Fant.)

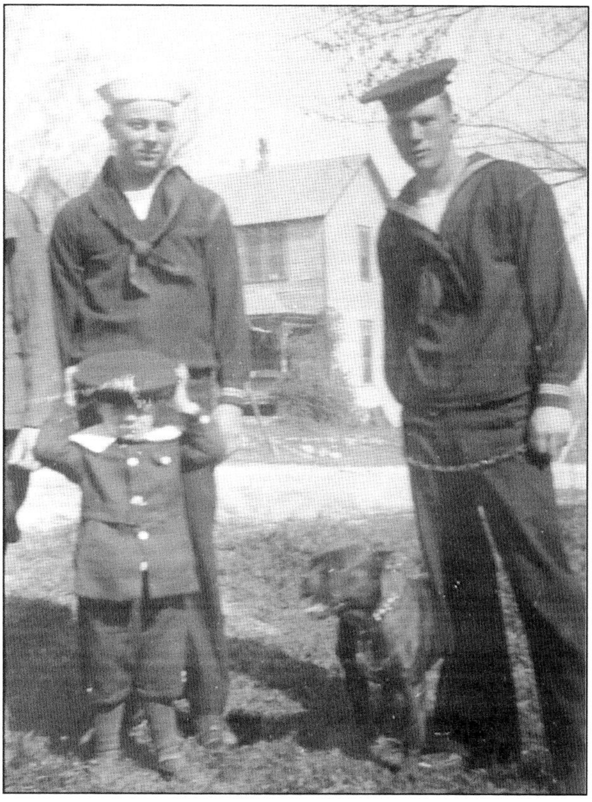

Gilbert Ragsdale, a Merchant Marine, swapped hats with his brother, Paul, a U.S. Navy sailor. Little Bill Ragsdale seems involved, too. (Bill Fant.)

In World War II, again Weatherford heard the call to arms. Lieutenant Knox McFall Fant was killed in an airplane-training crash shortly after he posed with his father, George Fant, president of First National Bank. (Bill Fant.)

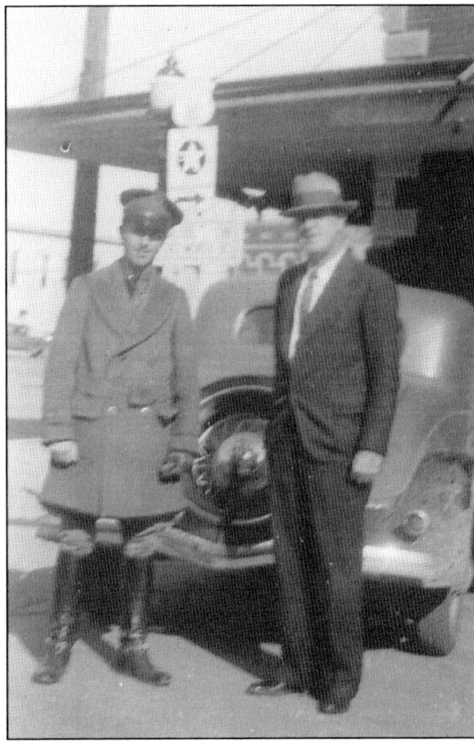

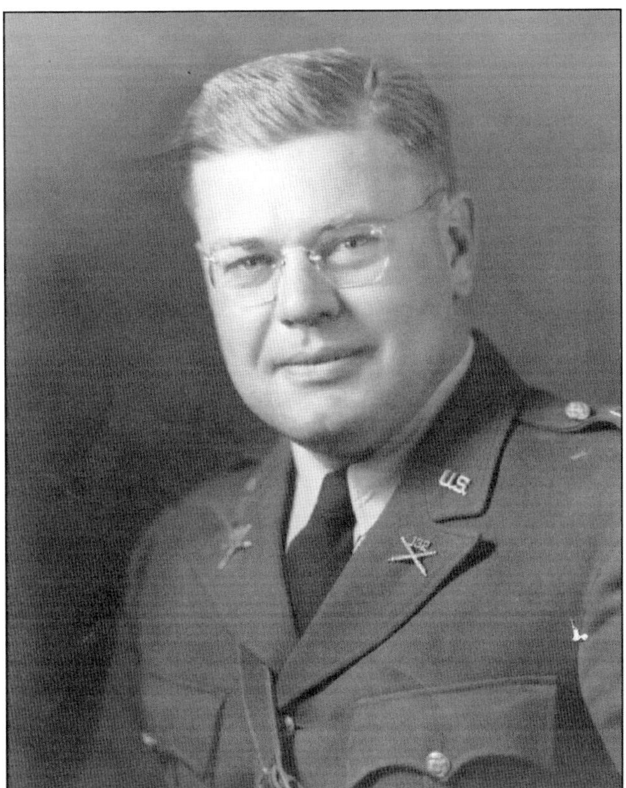

Colonel Ben Hagman was wounded in the Belgian Battle of the Bulge in 1944. He was presented a Bronze Star for his actions, but did not report his wounds to receive the Purple Heart. (Gary and Linda Hagman.)

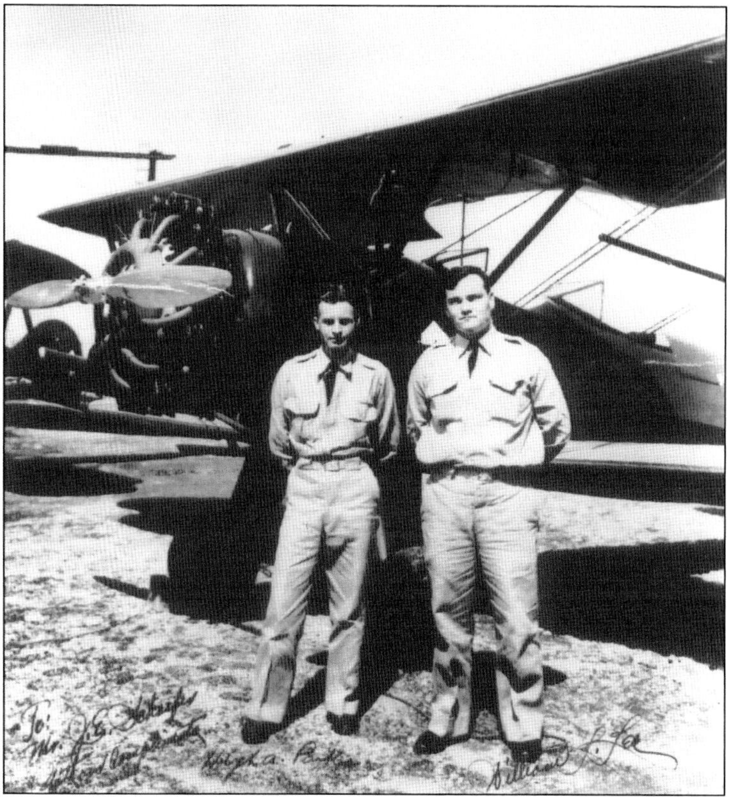

Photographed in the Philippines in the late 1930s, Lieutenant William L. Lee (right), of Weatherford, taught the Philippine cadets how to fly as well as General Douglas McArthur's aide, Major Dwight Eisenhower. Called the "Father of the Philippine Air Force," Lee became Ike's aide through WWII and a brigadier general. (Dwight D. Eisenhower Presidential Library.)

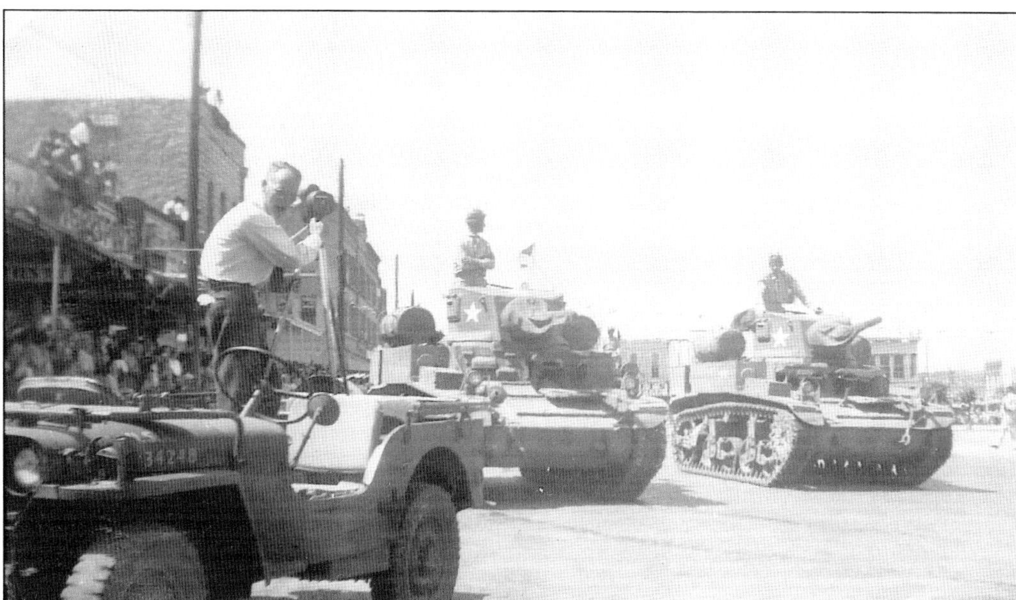

The 1945 "Welcome Home" parade for Hood Simpson had "Stewart" tanks. He had commanded the U.S. Ninth Army in Europe. (Charles Frost.)

General William Hood Simpson graduated from Weatherford College in 1909 and fought in the Philippines, as well as in Mexico against Pancho Villa, WWI, and in WWII. (WC.)

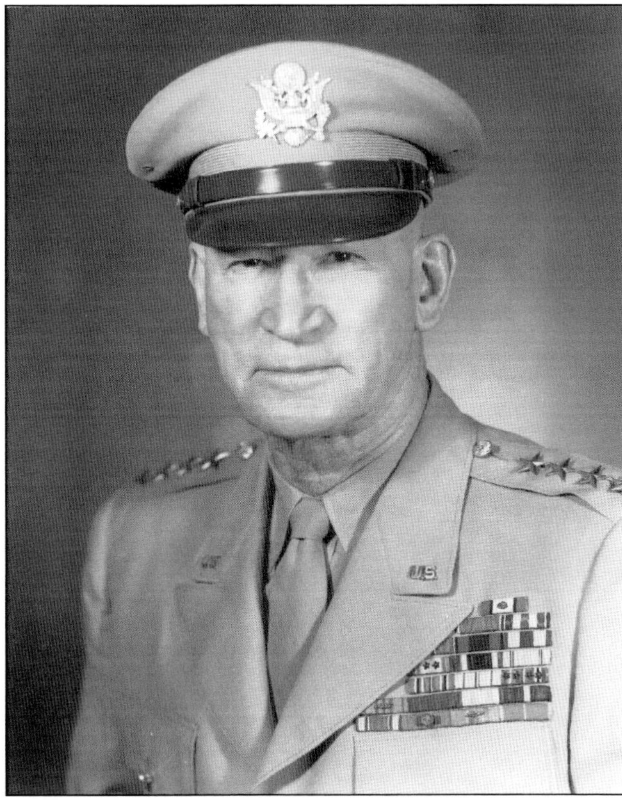

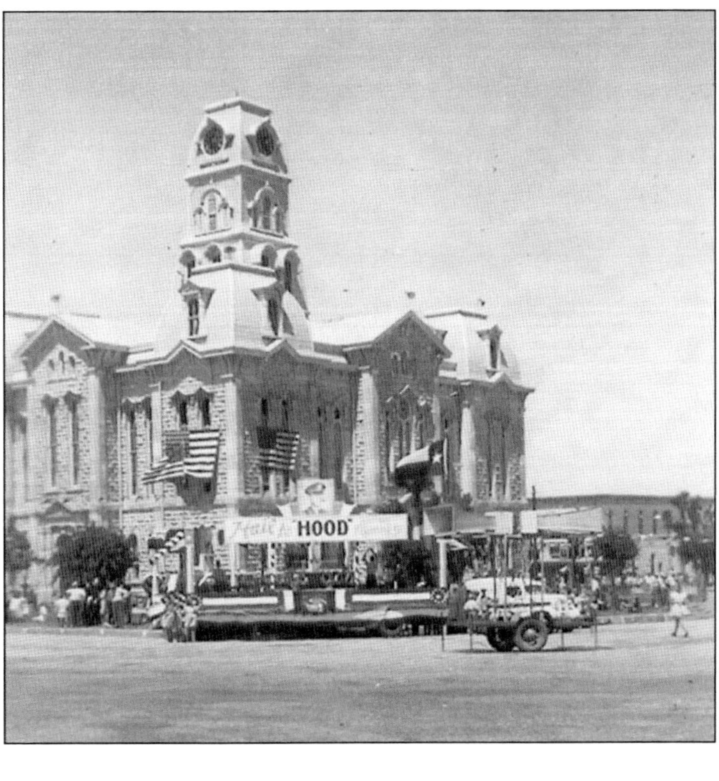

This is the review stand for General Simpson on the southeast side of the courthouse. The photograph reveals the immense space on the square for parades. (Charles Frost.)

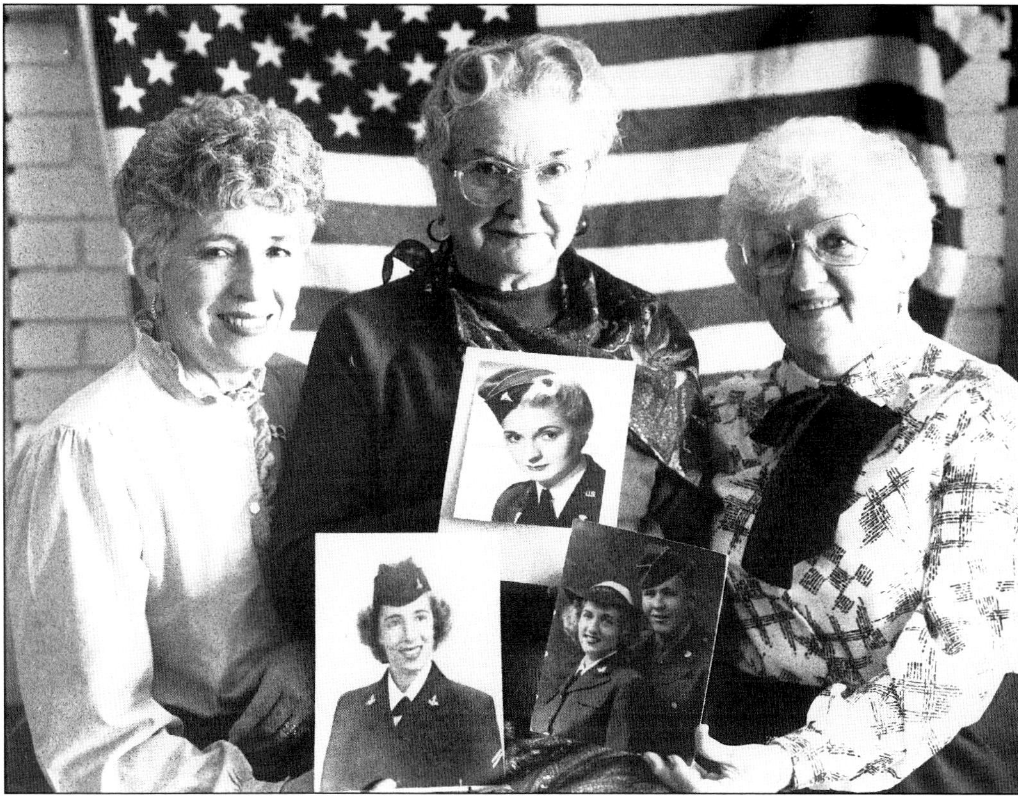

World War II women veterans from Weatherford include these three American Legion members, Mary Ellen Guay, Virginia Alexander (head nurse at Campbell Hospital), and Margaret Howle. (*Weatherford Democrat* via American Legion Post 163.)

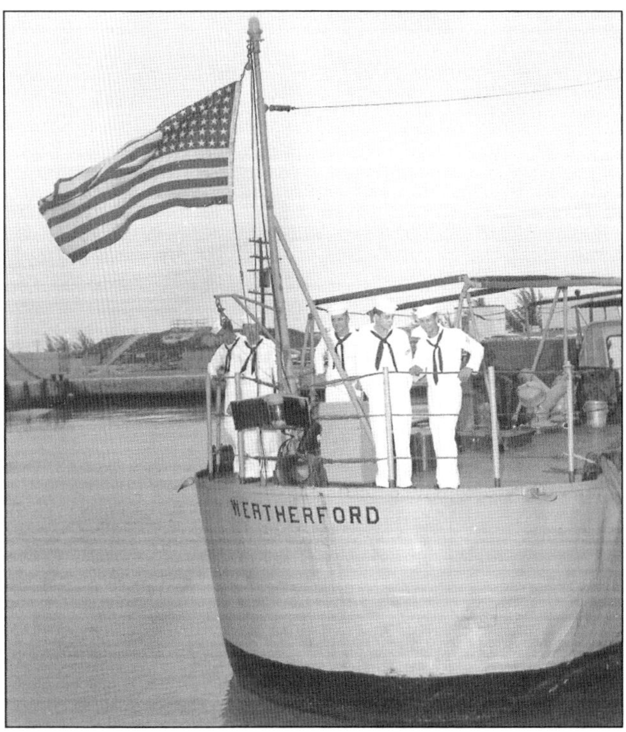

A World War II anti-submarine patrol ship was renamed USS *Weatherford* on February 15, 1956. It made one probable submarine kill claim off the Miami coast and was damaged by a German shore battery on D-Day, June 6, 1944. (Chamber of Commerce.)